ENGAGED LEARNING FOR PROGRAMMING IN C++

A Laboratory Course

Second Edition

James Robergé
Matthew Bauer
George K. Smith

JONES AND BARTLETT PUBLISHERS
Sudbury, Massachusetts
BOSTON   TORONTO   LONDON   SINGAPORE

World Headquarters
Jones and Bartlett Publishers
40 Tall Pine Drive
Sudbury, MA 01776
978-443-5000
info@jbpub.com
www.jbpub.com

Jones and Bartlett Publishers
Canada
2406 Nikanna Road
Mississauga, ON L5C 2W6
CANADA

Jones and Bartlett Publishers
International
Barb House, Barb Mews
London W6 7PA
UK

Senior Aquisitions Editor: Michael Stranz
Development and Product Manager: Amy Rose
Director of Manufacturing and Inventory Control: Therese Bräuer
Cover Design: kō Design Studio
Composition: Northeast Compositors, Inc.
Printing and Binding: Courier Stoughton
Cover printing: John Pow Co.

Cover image © Masao Mukai/Photonica

Library of Congress Cataloging-in-Publication Data
Robergé, Jim.
    Engaged learning for programming in C++ / Jim Robergé, George Smith, Matthew
Bauer.--2nd ed.
        p. cm.
    ISBN 0-7637-1423-2 (pbk.)
    1. C++ (Computer program language)   I. Smith, George, 1959 Dec. 28.   II. Bauer,
Matthew.   III. Title.

QA76.73.C153 R57 2000
005.13'3--dc21   00-055823

This book was typeset in FrameMaker 5.5 on a Macintosh G4. The font families used were Caslon, Frutiger, and Courier. The first printing was printed on 50 lb. Decision 94 opaque.

Printed in the United States of America
04 03 02 01 00   10 9 8 7 6 5 4 3 2 1

To my sons, Michael and Edward, for sharing their amazingly bright and exciting world.

—JR

To my parents, for everything they have done to make me what I am, and to my wife, Jackie, for filling my life with joy.

—MJB

To my cousin Seal, for his courage in coping with adversity and for teaching me to appreciate whatever life has to offer.

—GKS

Preface

OVERVIEW

Engaged Learning For Programming In C++ takes an interactive, learn-by-doing approach to programming. It is written in a straightforward, informal style that appeals to students of all ages. We feel strongly that in order to learn a subject, you need to immerse yourself in the subject—learning by doing rather than by simply observing. We also feel strongly that computer science is more than simply programming—it is using programming as a tool to create solutions to challenging problems. This emphasis on "hands on" learning is used throughout our *Engaged Learning For Programming in C++* manual. In each laboratory exercise, students create programs that apply a particular language feature and problem solving technique. As they create these programs, they learn how C++ works and how it can be applied. The resulting programs are working pieces of software that they can use in later laboratories and programming projects.

The exercises in this book use the laboratory to involve students as active, creative partners in the learning process. By making the laboratories the focal point of the course, students become immersed in the course material. This approach challenges students and yet provides them with structure, feedback, and support that they needed to meet the challenge. The exercises are well defined, yet open-ended enough to allow the better students to do some exploring. Program testing and debugging are emphasized throughout the book.

Our most important goal in developing this material over the years was to create programming exercises that are practical, pedagogically sound, and focus on novel applications—rather than simply reconstituting exercises that have survived since the "Dawn of the Computer Age." In many application exercises students write programs that use HTML to create interesting web pages that they can view using any standard web browser. Note that only a small subset of HTML is used and that all of the required HTML syntax is explained in the exercises. Our students love these problems. We think they are fun too! Let us know what you think.

We believe that it is important for students to learn to use classes early in an introductory C++ programming class. The *AP classes* are a subset of the Standard Template Library provided by the College Board for Advanced Placement Computer Science. We take advantage of these classes in several of our labs and believe that they enable students to learn to create objects and to use member functions early in their programming careers. By using objects early, we have found students are better equipped to create and implement their own classes.

Laboratory Structure and Organization

When we first began using laboratories, we attempted to shoehorn the creative process into a series of closed laboratory sessions. The result was a pressure cooker that challenged everyone, but helped no one. In experimenting with solutions to this problem, we developed a laboratory framework that retains the creative element, but shifts the time-intensive aspects outside of the laboratory period proper. Within this structure, each laboratory consists of three parts: Core, Reinforcement, and Analysis.

Core

The **Core** exercises cover the fundamental topics and concepts for a CS1 course. In these exercises, students explore and create on their own, and at their own pace. Their goal is to synthesize the information that they learn during lecture, along with material from their textbook and online resources, to produce a set of programs. The Core exercises can be used in a variety of ways to support different pedagogical styles and available laboratory resources. In the so-called "closed lab" model, students begin each Core exercise as a homework problem and complete it during a lab session (or sessions) where they can get focused constructive feedback on their work—and thus get their programs to run! In an "open lab" model, the students do the exercises as homework, with support and feedback provided in a less-structured—but equally valuable—manner during "open" lab hours, class, and instructor office hours.

Each Core exercise includes a Background section that introduces a programming technique and the associated C++ language constructs, a Warmup exercise in which the students complete a "fill-in-the-blank" problem to practice the syntactic details of the language construct, and an Application exercise in which the students apply the programming technique to solve an interesting real-world problem. The entire Core assignment—including a review of the relevant lecture and resource materials—typically takes about four to six hours to complete.

Note that due to time constraints, you may choose to cover only the Background and Warmup exercises for some Core exercises. This will not be a problem. Although the labs build on one another in terms of the concepts used, the reuse of code from one lab to another is limited to selected, well-identified cases.

We believe it is important for students to test and debug their programs right from the "get-go." For each Core Application the students develop a test plan that they then use to evaluate their code. This exercise provides an opportunity for students to become independent learners by evaluating their Core programs and resolving any difficulties they might have encountered.

Reinforcement

In the **Reinforcement** section, students get a chance to extend or apply the concepts introduced in the Core. The Reinforcement exercises are generally more open-ended than the core application exercises and provide the top students with challenging problems to solve. Reinforcement exercises generally take from one to two hours to complete.

Analysis

The last phase of each laboratory is a homework assignment that is done following the laboratory session. In the **Analysis** exercise, students are asked to prepare a written analysis of a program, programming technique, or language construct. Each Analysis exercise should take roughly thirty minutes to complete.

Topic Coverage

Laboratories 1 through 16 cover the essentials of C++ programming. These laboratories build on each other in terms of content and applications. In each lab, there are a variety of creative and interesting exercises from which to choose. You may choose to use parts of these labs or all of them. In addition, the online links enable instructors to augment the existing application exercises and use them as "jumping off" points for class discussions.

Object-based programming is briefly introduced in Laboratory 2 with the introduction of the College Board `apstring` class. More in-depth object-based programming is used in Laboratories 9, 10, and 11 using the `apvector`, `apstring`, and `apmatrix` classes provided by the College Board. For instructors who want to utilize objects throughout their course, Laboratory 19 contains a set of object-oriented online exercises related to the *APCS Marine Biology Case Study* that can be introduced starting in Laboratory 6.

Object-Oriented Programming Project

Laboratory 16 is a multi-week object-oriented programming project in which students solve a more open-ended problem than in earlier laboratories. During the first week, they analyze a problem in terms of objects and develop a design for the problem. During the second week, they create and test an implementation based on their design.

Laboratory 16 begins by walking the students through the design and implementation of a simple children's calculator program. The software development framework used in this example stresses object-oriented design and programming, iterative code development, and systematic testing. The students then apply this framework to the solution of a more challenging—and more interesting—problem where they reuse the class that they implemented in Laboratories 14 and 15 and create several new classes. For instructors who choose to have their students implement the project in teams, suggestions for structuring team software development are included with the Instructor's Resources.

Grading

We do not view quantifying student performance to be the primary goal of the laboratory assignments. Students who work hard and master the material covered in the laboratories are better prepared for exams and, as a result, tend to perform better on exams. Once students realize that the laboratories are the most important part of the course—(yes, even more important than our lectures)—and that they learn a great deal from the laboratory assignments, we have little trouble getting our students to complete their lab assignments. Grades do seem to provide needed motivation for some students, however, and for this reason we grade the laboratory exercises. Our grading standards for the laboratories are designed to reflect effort as much as results.

One approach to grading is to view the Core Warmup exercises as preparatory work and not to formally grade these problems. During the lab, the lab instructor executes each Core Application exercise using selected test cases from a student's test plan. If problems are discovered, the instructor reviews them with the student, and the student is given an opportunity to make corrections based on this feedback. The same is true if the Reinforcement exercise is assigned. Analysis exercises are graded outside of lab.

Student Support Materials

Challenging students is easy; helping them to meet a challenge is not. The student CD-ROM included with this manual contains a set of tools that makes it easier for students to create programs. These tools include the following: the programs included in the Background sections, program shells for the Warmup exercises, test programs, and data files. A series of content-specific links are also available online, including debugging tutorials, C++ language support, HTML tutorials, and background information on the applications discussed in each laboratory.

Instructor Support Materials

Instructor's Resources, including solutions to all exercises, sample course syllabi, lecture outlines, instructor notes for each laboratory, quizzes/exams, an interactive FAQ, and additional laboratory exercises, are available upon request from Jones and Bartlett.

Comments and Suggestions

We are very interested in receiving feedback on this manual. Send your comments and suggestions to any of the following email addresses:

roberge@cs.iit.edu
matthew.bauer@iit.edu
gks@charlie.iit.edu

Acknowledgements

We would like to thank our editors at Jones and Bartlett, Michael Stranz, Amy Rose, Jennifer Jacobson, Brooke Albright, and Amanda Green, for their support and encourage. They saw the potential in this project, and their vision and support helped guide it to completion. We would also like to thank Jeanine Ingber, University of New Mexico; Christian Day, Phillips Exeter Acadamy; Roseann Krane, Monte Vista High School; Janice Gintzler, Morgan Park High School; Dennis Ray, Old Dominion University; and Katharine Paine, Southern Arkansas University for reviewing the manuscript.

We are also grateful to the students at the Illinois Institute of Technology and Morgan Park High School where the laboratory exercises have been class tested over the last four years. Many of their comments and suggestions have been incorporated in the final versions of the laboratories.

Contents

CONTENTS

Getting Your Feet Wet

OVERVIEW

Before starting any project, you need to become familiar with the tools and resources that you have at your disposal and with the process that you will use to complete the project. In the context of writing computer programs, these tools and resources often are referred to as the **program development environment** and the process as the **program development process**.

The steps in the program development process (and the appropriate tools in the program development environment) for structured programming covered in the first half of this lab book are as follows.

1. Carefully read and understand the problem description.

2. Write **pseudocode**, which are English sentences or instructions (like a recipe) describing how to solve the problem. Pseudocode may include a description of the inputs to the problem, the outputs expected, and how to get from the inputs to the outputs that you want. This step is usually a good time to write down some example input and output sets so that you can check the accuracy of the program (called creating **test data and expected results**).

3. Open a file in the program development environment. This step may include opening a new or existing file (usually on your computer's hard drive, C:, and not the floppy drive, A:).

4. Write C++ code, using the program development editor. Editing may include typing, copying, pasting, and deleting text (C++ code).

5. **Compile** your program, using the program development compiler. Programs don't always work the first time; sometimes the compiler reports warnings and syntax errors and may help you correct them.

6. **Link** your program using the program development linker (sometimes called creating the executable, or .exe, file).

7. **Run** your program and check your test data and expected results that you created previously.

8. If you did not get correct results, **debug** your program using your program development environment debugger. The debugger enables you to step through the code to ensure that it is doing what you expect; you can trace a bug (e.g., logic error, divide by zero, or incorrect calculations) in the program.

In this laboratory you explore the commonly used editing, compiling, and debugging tools and resources available in your programming development environment.

 See the "Engaged Learning for Programming in C++" link on **http://www.jbpub.com/cs** for "how to" demonstrations for editing, compiling, running, and debugging programs in various popular program development environments.

You begin a hands-on tour of your program development environment in Core Exercise 1 by compiling, linking, and running (executing) a sample C++ program. This program calculates the growth in principal (a sum of money) invested at a certain interest rate. You then explore several features of the editor by modifying the program to do additional investment calculations.

The tour continues in Core Exercise 2 as you use some of the more common checkpoint tools for source-level debugging. You examine how the computer can guess your age by using breakpoints and variable watches to track changes in the value of a variable as a program executes. Your tour concludes in Core Exercise 3 with an introduction to the common types of errors you will encounter as a programmer. You use the debugging tools that you have studied to help you fix a program containing a syntax error and a logic error.

In Core Exercise 4 you create a Quick Reference Survival Guide—a list of frequently performed activities and functions in your environment. You complete the Survival Guide by writing the steps—commands, keystrokes, and mouse actions—needed to perform each function.

LABORATORY 1: Cover Sheet

Name

Hour/Period/Section

Date

Place a check mark (✔) in the Assigned column next to the exercises that your instructor has assigned to you. Have this sheet ready when your lab instructor checks your work. If your exercises are being checked outside the laboratory session, attach this sheet to the front of the packet of materials that you submit.

Exercise		Assigned	Completed
Core 1	Editing and Executing C++ Programs *The Rule of 72 (ruleof72.cpp)*		
Core 2	Debugging Your Programs *Step by Step, Inch by Inch (guessage.cpp)*		
Core 3	Syntactic and Logic Errors *Slippery Slope (slope.cpp)*		
Core 4	Touring Your C++ Environment *Quick Reference Survival Guide*		
Analysis	Error Analysis		
Total			

LABORATORY 1: Core Exercise 1—Editing and Executing C++ Programs

A program written in a high-level programming language such as Pascal, Java, or C/C++ must be translated into a form that your computer can process. This form often is referred to as **machine language**. The C++ compiler uses a two-stage process to translate your C++ program into machine code. First, the **compiler** translates the program into machine language instructions that are stored as an object file on disk. The second stage, called **linking**, combines the object file with other object files and produces an executable file. For your first several C++ programs, these other object files consist primarily of the library routines used to perform input and output. In later labs, you divide your programs into several source files that are independently compiled and then linked into a single executable file. Once a program is in executable form, you can **run** it and check whether the program produces the desired results.

In this exercise, you use your program development environment to compile, link, and run the program in the file *ruleof72.cpp*. Then you make changes to the program and run it again.

 Don't forget to reference the "Engaged Learning for Programming in C++" link on **http://www.jbpub.com/cs** for "how to" demonstrations for editing, compiling, running, and debugging programs in various popular program development environments.

APPLICATION EXERCISE: The Rule of 72

You often hear someone on TV (especially between midnight and 4 A.M.) make the claim that by using his or her system you can double your investment in a few months or years. The "Rule of 72" provides an easy way to compute how long it takes to double your money. The formula for this rule is

$$\text{years to double investment} = \frac{72.0}{\text{interest rate}},$$

where *interest rate* (as a % of 100) is the interest you earn annually on the investment. The rule is based on the assumption that interest is compounded annually and is not taxed.

Step 1: Compile, link, and run the following program from the file *ruleof72.cpp*.

```
// Determines years to double an investment using the "rule of 72".

#include <iostream.h>

int main ()
{
    double interestRate,      // Annual interest rate input by user
           yearsToDouble;     // Years to double investment computed

    // Prompt the user for the annual interest rate (as a % of 100)
    // and read the number from the keyboard.
    cout << "Enter the annual interest rate (as a % of 100): ";
    cin >> interestRate;

    // Compute the number of years it takes for an investment to double.
    yearsToDouble = 72.0 / interestRate;

    // Output the number of years it takes for an investment to double.
    cout << "Years to double investment: "  << yearsToDouble << endl;

    return 0;
}
```

Step 2: Complete the following test plan and run your program multiple times to check your results.

Test Plan for *ruleof72*

Test case	Sample data	Expected result	Checked
High interest rate (12.5%)	12.5	5.76 years	
Medium interest rate (8%)	8.0	9 years	
Low interest rate (4%)	4.0	18 years	

Step 3: Close *ruleof72.cpp* and any project workspace that your program development environment created. Reopen *ruleof72.cpp* and add the following code to calculate the first year's interest earned on a user input principle investment. **Add these lines of C++ code immediately before the** return 0; **statement**. Note: Pay particular attention to punctuation and spacing when typing in the C++ code.

```
double principle,         // Initial investment principle input by user
       firstYearInterest; // Interest earned during first year

// Prompt the user for the initial investment principle
// and read the number from the keyboard.
cout << "Enter the initial investment principle: ";
cin >> principle;

// Compute the interest earned the first year.
firstYearInterest = principle * interestRate / 100.0;

// Output the interest earned during first year.
cout << "First year interest earned: " << firstYearInterest << endl;
```

Step 4: Save the modified program under the new name *myrule72.cpp*.

Step 5: Compile, link, and run the modified program.

Step 6: Swap the two parts of the program by moving the 'first year interest' part of the code that you just typed in at the beginning of the program—after the following output and input statements:

```
// Prompt the user for the annual interest rate (as a % of 100)
// and read the number from the keyboard.
cout << "Enter the annual interest rate (as a % of 100): ";
cin >> interestRate;
```

Step 7: Save the modified program as *myrule72.cpp*.

Step 8: Compile, link, and run the modified program.

LABORATORY 1: Core Exercise 2—Debugging Your Programs

To find the mistakes (or bugs) in your programs, you will frequently need to execute the program line by line. Many program development environments include **debugging** features that allow you to step through a program and watch the values of variables change as the program executes. Tracing through a long program in this way can become very tedious. Often you are only interested in what is occurring beginning at a certain point in the program. You can signal the debugger to stop execution at a particular line by setting a **breakpoint** at the line. When you run the program, execution stops at the breakpoint. You can then set **watches** on selected variables and step through the rest of the program, examining any changes in the contents of the variables as the program executes. If your program development environment doesn't have a debugger, you can check out how a program is functioning by outputting intermediate results throughout the program.

In this exercise you begin to learn debugging techniques and how to use debugging tools. Doing so is easier on a program that you know already works, so you can use the debugging tools to see the flow of the program and how input is used to calculate the desired output. Core Exercise 3 shows how to use debugging tools when a program doesn't work.

 Don't forget to access the "Engaged Learning for Programming in C++" link on **http://www.jbpub.com/cs** for "how to" demonstrations for editing, compiling, running, and debugging programs in various popular program development environments.

APPLICATION EXERCISE: Step by Step, Inch by Inch

In this exercise, you examine the execution of the following program from the file *guessage.cpp*.

```cpp
// Determines a person's age based on a "magic" number.

#include <iostream.h>

int main ()
{
    int num;

    // Explain how to compute a "magic" number.
    cout << endl;
    cout << "I can guess your age from a magic number that "
         << "you compute as follows:" << endl;
    cout << "  1. Add 21 to your age." << endl;
    cout << "  2. Double the result of step 1." << endl;
    cout << "  3. Add your age to the result of step 2." << endl;
    cout << "  4. Subtract 18 from the result of step 3." << endl;
```

```
    // Prompt the user for the magic number and read the number from
    // the keyboard.
    cout << "Enter your magic number: ";
    cin >> num;

    // Compute the user's age.
    num = num / 3;
    num = num - 8;

    // Output the user's age.
    cout << "You are " << num << "."<< endl;

    return 0;
}
```

Version A: Use if a debugger is available.

Step 1:   Set a breakpoint at the following line.

```
cin >> num;
```

Step 2:   Run *guessage.cpp*. Note that execution stops where the breakpoint was set.

Step 3:   Set a watch on the variable num.

Step 4:   Step to the next line and enter your magic number.

Step 5:   What value is now stored in num?

num: _____

Step 6:   Step to the next line. What value is now stored in num?

num: _____

Step 7:   Step to the next line. What value is now stored in num?

num: _____

Step 8:   Step through the remainder of the program.

Step 9:   Remove the breakpoint.

Step 10:   You can combine the pair of calculations that compute the user's age into one calculation. Replace these statements with the single statement

```
num = num / 3 - 8;
```

Step 11:   Save the modified program as *guessage.cpp*.

Step 12:   Compile, link, and run the modified program.

Version B: Use if no debugger is available.

Step 1:   Insert the statement

```
cout << "Before division" << num;
```

after the statement

```
cin >> num;
```

Step 2:   Insert the statement

```
cout << "After division" << num;
```

after the statement

```
num = num / 3;
```

Step 3:   Run *guessage.cpp*.

Step 4:   How does the value of num change?

```
Input value of num:  _____
After division:      _____
After subtraction:   _____
```

Step 5:   You can combine the pair of calculations that compute the user's age into one calculation. Replace these statements with the single statement

```
num = num / 3 - 8;
```

Step 6:   Save the modified program as *guessage.cpp*.

Step 7:   Compile, link, and run the modified program.

LABORATORY 1: Core Exercise 3—Finding and Fixing Errors

Natural languages such as English, Spanish, and Chinese have standard rules of usage for syntax and grammar. For example, the sentence

> *no money i got*

violates several rules for standard English. Similarly, programming languages such as C++ also have standard sets of syntax rules describing how to write statements. If your code violates a C++ grammar rule, a message noting your **syntax error** is displayed when you attempt to compile your program. These types of mistakes are usually fairly easy to figure out when you're using a compiler that displays meaningful error messages.

A more subtle kind of error is a semantic error or error in meaning. A statement with a semantic error is syntactically correct (legal) but functionally wrong. For example, imagine that while on vacation in Australia you unexpectedly run into a friend from Spain that you haven't seen in more than 10 years. Upon seeing you, your Spanish friend says, "The world is a handkerchief!" At first, this response puzzles you, but then you realize that your friend has literally translated the expression "El mundo es un pañuelo" from Spanish. The sentence is syntactically correct, but the expression has no meaning in English. In programming, these semantic errors are called **logic errors**. A logic error occurs in your program when your code compiles without syntax errors, but produces results that are not what you intended.

The third type of programming errors is **runtime errors**. A runtime error occurs in your program when your code compiles without syntax errors and produces results that are what you intended, but on a certain input value(s) the program cannot compute something and the program ends without completing the run. An example of this is if a formula in your program produces a "divide by zero" error on a certain input value(s).

 Don't forget to refer to the "Engaged Learning for Programming in C++" link on **http://www.jbpub.com/cs** for "how to" demonstrations for editing, compiling, running, and debugging programs in various popular program development environments.

APPLICATION EXERCISE: Slippery Slope

The user enters the coordinates for two points on a line—(x_1, y_1) and (x_2, y_2)—and the slope is computed with the formula

$$\text{slope} = \frac{y_2 - y_1}{x_2 - x_1}.$$

The program in the file *slope.cpp* contains a syntax error, a logic error, and (on a certain set of input values) a runtime error. You must first correct the syntax error so that the program compiles. Then execute the "corrected" program and find the error in program logic and the runtime error.

Step 1: Attempt to compile the following program from the file *slope.cpp*.

```
// Finds the slope of a line between two points (x1, y1), (x2, y2).

#include <iostream.h>

int main()
{
    double x1,        // First point x coordinate
           y1,        // First point y coordinate
           x2,        // Second point x coordinate
           y2,        // Second point y coordinate
           slope;     // Slope of line

    // Prompt the user for x and y coordinates for the
    // first point and read them in.
    cout << endl       // What's missing?
    cout << "Enter the first point x1 and y1: ";
    cin >> x1 >> y1;

    // Prompt the user for x and y coordinates for the
    // first point and read them in.
    cout << "Enter the second point x2 and y2: ";
    cin >> x2 >> y2;

    // Calculate and display the slope of the line.
    slope = ( x2 - x1 ) / ( y2 - y1 );
    cout << "The slope of the line is " << slope << endl;

    return 0;
}
```

Step 2: Write the error message(s) that your compiler displays.

Step 3: Correct the syntax error in the program.

Step 4: Save the revised program as *slope.cpp*.

Step 5: Compile, link, and run *slope.cpp*.

Step 6: Enter values of 0 and 0 (separated by a space) for the coordinates of the first point and 1 and 3 (separated by a space) for the coordinates of the second point.

Step 7: Write the output value the program displays in the space provided.

```
The slope of the line is _____
```

Step 8: Determine whether the result is reasonable. (*Hint:* Should the slope of the line through the user input coordinates be greater than 1 or less than 1?)

Step 9: If you believe that the results aren't reasonable, check the slope formula and make any necessary adjustments.

Step 10: Save the revised program as *slope.cpp*.

Step 11: Compile, link, and run *slope.cpp*.

Step 12: Write the new output value your program produces for the same input as before.

```
The slope of the line is _____
```

Step 13: If the output still isn't correct, make any necessary changes and repeat Steps 9 through 12.

So far we have provided you with test cases, sample data, and expected results in the test plans for the programs that you have created. Most programs that you develop from this point on—both in this lab book and in the real world—require that you develop your own test plans.

Create a test plan for the slope program. Your test plan should include cases in which the slope is positive, negative, 0, and undefined (this test case will reveal the runtime error).

Test Plan for *slope*

Test case	Sample data	Expected result	Checked

LABORATORY 1: Core Exercise 4—Touring Your C++ Environment

Many software packages include a keyboard template or reference card that lists frequently used commands and functions and the necessary steps to execute each command or function. You can use this card for quick reference instead of looking up a command in a manual or accessing online help. In this exercise, you create your own Quick Reference Survival Guide—a list of commonly used commands and functions in your C++ program development environment.

APPLICATION EXERCISE: Quick Reference Survival Guide

The following two pages contain an outline of various tasks that you need to perform when creating a program. For each task, list the commands, keystrokes, or mouse actions needed to perform the task. Space is provided after each section to insert additional tasks that you find useful. Use any available resources that describe the operating system, editor, compiler, and debugger (if available) you are using to complete the exercise. Possible resources include user's manuals, online help, and a system tutorial.

Quick Reference Survival Guide

SYSTEM-LEVEL FILE USE

Open a file for editing
Display the contents of a file
Copy a file to a different disk or directory
Rename a file
List the names of the files stored on a disk or in a directory
Print the contents of a file

EDITING A FILE

Go left one character
Go right one character
Go up one line

Go down one line
Go to the beginning of the file
Go to the end of the file
Go to the beginning of the current line
Go to the end of the current line
Insert a character
Delete a character
Insert a line
Delete a line
Delete multiple lines
Move multiple lines to a new location in the file
Save the file
Save the file with a new name

PROGRAM EXECUTION

Compile a program*
Link object files*
Run a program
View program output
*On some systems compiling, linking, and/or running are performed as a single step.

DEBUGGING DURING PROGRAM EXECUTION (IF AVAILABLE)

Trace program execution line by line (stepping through a program)
Set a breakpoint at a specific line
Remove a breakpoint
Set a watch on a variable
Remove a watch

LABORATORY 1: Analysis Exercise

Error Analysis

Name _____

Hour/Period/Section _____

Date _____

Part A

Imagine that you write a C++ program that generates several syntax errors when you try to compile it. In your program development environment, how would you determine at what lines in the program the errors occurred and what the errors are?

Part B

Imagine that you write a C++ program that compiles correctly—it doesn't contain any syntax errors—but that does not generate the expected results for certain test data. In your program development environment, how would you determine where the errors in logic occurred in the program and what the errors are?

C++ Program Elements I

OVERVIEW

Laboratory 1 introduced you to the environment that you are using to create C++ programs. Now that you are familiar with your program development environment, you can examine more closely the language elements and program structure of C++ and construct your first C++ programs from scratch.

In Core Exercise 1 you create a program that prompts the user for a single input value, performs some simple calculations, and displays the results on the screen. The program that you develop in Core Exercise 2 requires multiple inputs and multiple outputs. You examine how to write meaningful prompts so that the user knows exactly what kind of input the program expects. The code that you create in Core Exercise 3 requires a nonnumeric data type, the `apstring` class, to define variables (objects) that hold character strings (words in this case). You learn how to assign character strings to variables (objects) and you get more practice writing clear input prompts as part of a program that interactively creates a story. In Core Exercise 4 you examine the order in which C++ evaluates arithmetic operators. You experiment with changing the order in which operators are evaluated, using parentheses.

LABORATORY 2: Cover Sheet

Name _____

Hour/Period/Section _____

Date _____

Place a check mark (✔) in the Assigned column next to the exercises that your instructor has assigned to you. Have this sheet ready when your lab instructor checks your work. If your exercises are being checked outside the laboratory session, attach this sheet to the front of the packet of materials that you submit.

Exercise	Assigned	Completed
Core 1 Basic Program Structure *Baby, It's Cold Outside (chilly.cpp)*		
Core 2 Interactive Input and Output *Any Way You Slice It (pizzapi.cpp)*		
Core 3 Characters and Strings *The Rest of the Story (mystory.cpp)*		
Core 4 Arithmetic Expressions *Take It to Heart (training.cpp)*		
Reinforcement Translating Arithmetic Calculations *House Rules (mortgage.cpp)*		
Analysis Problem Solving and Programming Style		
Total		

LABORATORY 2: Core Exercise 1—Basic Program Structure

Background

What are the elements of a C++ program? Let's analyze the following program from the file *acreage.cpp*.

```cpp
// Converts from square feet to acres.

#include <iostream.h>

int main()
{
    const double SQFEET_PER_ACRE = 43560.0;

    double sqFeet,    // Area in square feet
           acres;     // Area in acres

    // Prompt for square feet and read it in.
    cout << "Enter the area in square feet: ";
    cin >> sqFeet;

    // Calculate the acreage.
    acres = sqFeet / SQFEET_PER_ACRE;

    // Output the acreage.
    cout << "The acreage is " << acres << endl;

    return 0;
}
```

Any text on a line following a `//` is a comment and is ignored by the C++ compiler. For example, the line

```cpp
// Converts from square feet to acres.
```

describes the purpose of *acreage.cpp*. Comments can appear on their own line or follow a C++ statement on the same line. The comment

```cpp
// Area in square feet
```

describes the purpose of the floating-point variable `sqFeet`. **Comments** such as these explain to others (or remind you) what a program does and how it works. Collectively, the comments are referred to as **program documentation**.

Almost all C++ programs contain at least one preprocessor directive. The line

```cpp
#include <iostream.h>
```

instructs the compiler to include the declarations for the standard input/output stream header file *iostream.h*. The angle brackets tell the compiler to look for the iostream header file in the standard include directory—this directory contains all the standard header files for C++.

Every C++ program requires a `main()` function. Write the reserved word `int` before `main()` because all the programs presented here end with a `return 0;` statement, which signifies to the operating system that the program has executed successfully. You learn much more about how functions work in Laboratory 8, but for now, use `int main()` to start each program and `return 0;` to end each program.

Braces, { and }, are used to group statements. The left brace, {, shows where a **block** of statements begins, and the right brace, }, shows where the block ends. The braces following `int main()` in *acreage.cpp* show where the body of the program begins and ends.

The statements in the body of `main()` demonstrate several fundamental programming operations that you use in nearly all the C++ programs you create. These operations include describing (defining) the data to be used, collecting and storing the data, processing the data, and displaying the results.

You use identifiers to name the **variables** and constants your program needs. The declaration

```
double sqFeet,    // Area in square feet
       acres;     // Area in acres
```

tells the compiler to set up locations in memory for two floating-point variables that can be referenced with the identifiers `sqFeet` and `acres` respectively. A standard way to name variables is to use lowercase for the first word in the variable name and capitalize the first letter of each following word (with no separating spaces or underscores). The semicolon, ;, signals the end of the declaration. The values assigned to these variables may change during execution of a program. You can use a **named constant** to represent a data value that will not be changed during execution of the program. For example, the keyword `const` in the declaration

```
const double SQFEET_PER_ACRE = 43560.0;
```

tells the compiler that the floating-point variable `SQFEET_PER_ACRE` will not change its value from `43560.0` (you must assign a value to a named constant when you declare it). A convention in C++ is to capitalize every letter in a named constant and to use underscores to separate the words in the identifier.

To handle standard input and output, use the input and output streams from the iostream library. The stream-insertion operator, `<<`, is used with the standard output stream object `cout` to display information to the screen. For example, the statement

```
cout << "Enter the area in square feet: ";
```

outputs the string of characters enclosed by the double quotation marks to the display screen.

You handle input by using the stream-extraction operator, `>>`, and the standard input stream object `cin` to get information from the keyboard. When the computer executes the statement

```
cin >> sqFeet;
```

it takes the number you enter from the keyboard and stores it in the variable `sqFeet`.

The assignment statement

```
acres = sqFeet / SQFEET_PER_ACRE;
```

evaluates the expression `sqFeet / SQFEET_PER_ACRE` and assigns the result to the variable `acres`. The value of `acres` then is displayed to the screen by the statement

```
cout << "The acreage is " << acres << endl;
```

Note that this statement uses the `<<` operator several times. The string in quotes is output first, followed by the value of `acres`. The iostream manipulator `endl` is used to signal the end of an output line. The computer responds to `endl` by moving the cursor to the beginning of the next line on the display screen.

Warmup Exercise

Complete the following program by filling in the missing comments and C++ code. A shell for this program is given in the file *cel2fahr.shl*. Here, `9.0` is a floating-point **literal constant** and `32` is an integer **literal constant**.

```
// Converts a Celsius temperature to its Fahrenheit equivalent.

#include _____    // Preprocessor directive for cin, cout, endl

int _____
{
    double celsius,      // Celsius temperature reading
           fahrenheit__  _____

    // Prompt for Celsius temperature and read it in.
    cout << endl << "Enter the Celsius temperature: ";
    cin >> celsius;

    // Calculate the equivalent fahrenheit temperature.
    fahrenheit = 9.0 / 5.0 * celsius + 32;

    // _____
    cout << "The Fahrenheit temperature is " << fahrenheit << endl;

    return 0;

_____
```

APPLICATION EXERCISE: Baby, It's Cold Outside

An important consideration when "bundling up" on a cold winter's day is the projected windchill factor. The windchill factor is the temperature without wind that has the same effect on exposed human skin as a given combination of wind and temperature—that is, the temperature you feel because of the wind. The windchill temperature gives an indication of the apparent temperature you feel based on the actual temperature and wind speed. Approximate windchill factor formulas can be derived for winds of various speeds. The windchill temperature in degrees Fahrenheit (°F) for various wind speeds in miles per hour (mph) are

> windchill factor for a 10 mph wind = (1.23) (actual temperature in °F) − 22;
>
> windchill factor for a 25 mph wind = (1.48) (actual temperature in °F) − 44;
>
> windchill factor for a 40 mph wind = (1.58) (actual temperature in °F) − 53.

These formulas are based on the assumption that the temperature is in the range −45°F to 45°F.

 See the "Engaged Learning for Programming in C++" link on **http://www.jbpub.com/cs** for more information on windchill.

Step 1: Create a program to compute the windchill factor for winds of 10, 25, and 40 mph, using the formulas shown. The user inputs the actual temperature in °F and the program outputs a table listing the windchill factors.

Input: Actual temperature (in °F)

Output: Windchill factors for winds of 10, 25, and 40 mph

Step 2: Save this program as *chilly.cpp*.

Step 3: Complete the following test plan.

Test Plan for *chilly*

Test case	Sample data	Expected result		Checked
		Wind	Windchill factor	
Actual temperature > 0	32	10	17.36	
		25	3.36	
		40	−2.44	
Actual temperature = 0	0	10	−22	
		25	−44	
		40	−53	
Actual temperature < 0	−10	10	−34.3	
		25	−58.8	
		40	−68.8	

Step 4: Execute your program in the file *chilly.cpp*.

Step 5: Check each case in your *chilly* test plan and verify the expected result. If you discover mistakes in your program, correct them and execute the test plan again. Your results may differ slightly in the number of decimal digits displayed. In Laboratory 5 you will learn how to format output to a specified number of digits.

LABORATORY 2: Core Exercise 2—Interactive Input and Output

Background

Most programs that you create require multiple input and output values. A common strategy for problems requiring multiple inputs is to prompt the user for each input value. For example, in a program requiring an employee's hours worked and hourly pay, you could write

```
cout << "Enter the hours worked: ";
cin >> hoursWorked;
cout << "Enter the pay rate: ";
cin >> payRate;
```

An alternative method is to request the inputs by using a single display prompt and a single `cin` statement. Multiple data items can be input by using a sequence of `>>` operators as in

```
cout << "Enter hours worked and pay rate (separated by a space): ";
cin >> hoursWorked >> payRate;
```

Warmup Exercise

Complete the following program by filling in the missing C++ code. A shell for this program is given in the file *rectangl.shl*.

```
// Finds the perimeter and area of a rectangular field given its
// length and width in yards.

#include <iostream.h>

int main()
{
    double length,      // Length of field in yards
           width,       // Width of field in yards
           perimeter,   // Perimeter of field in yards
           area;        // Area of field in square yards

    // Insert your code below to prompt the user for the length
    // and width of a field and read in these values.



    // Calculate the perimeter and area of the field.
    perimeter = 2 * (length + width);
    area = length * width;

    // Output the calculated perimeter and area.
    cout << "The perimeter is " << perimeter << " yards." << endl;
    cout << _____

    return 0;
}
```

APPLICATION EXERCISE: Any Way You Slice It

When ordering pizza, people often argue about which size buys you the most pizza per dollar. A round pizza's size is usually described by its diameter (10", 12", ...). You can compute its size in square inches by using the formula for the area of a circle

$$size = \frac{\pi \cdot diameter^2}{4}.$$

You can then calculate the pizza's price per square inch (in^2) by dividing the price of the pizza by its size.

Step 1: Create a program that computes the size of a pizza and then determines its price per square inch.

　Input:　Diameter of pizza in inches
　　　　　　Price of pizza in dollars and cents

　Output:　Size of pizza in square inches
　　　　　　Price per square inch in dollars and cents

Step 2: Save your program as *pizzapi.cpp*.

Step 3: Complete the following test plan.

Test Plan for *pizzapi*

Test case	Sample data	Expected result	Checked
Small pie 10-in. diameter Pizza price: $5.49	10 5.49	`Size of pizza: 78.54 square inches` `Price per square inch:$0.07`	
Medium pie 12-in. diameter $6.99		`Size of pizza: 113.10 square inches` `Price per square inch:$0.06`	
Extra large pie 16-in. diameter $10			

Step 4: Execute your program in the file *pizzapi.cpp*.

Step 5: Check each case in your *pizzapi* test plan and verify the expected result. If you discover mistakes in your program, correct them and execute the test plan again. Your results may differ slightly in the number of decimal digits displayed. In Laboratory 5 you will learn how to format output to a specified number of digits.

LABORATORY 2: Core Exercise 3—Characters and Strings

Background

C++ does *not* have a predefined data type to handle sequences of characters, or strings. However, programmers have developed their own C++ code to implement sequences of characters as a special data type. The Advanced Placement Board has developed a string class, called apstring, for dealing with sequences of alphanumeric characters or strings. This section focuses on operations that you can use with the Advanced Placement Board implementation of strings.

To use the apstring data type, you must include the following preprocessor directive at the beginning of your program, along with any other preprocessor directives.

```
#include <apstring.h>
#include <apstring.cpp>
```

The angle brackets tell the compiler to look in the standard include directory, which contains all the standard header files for C++.

 See the "Engaged Learning for Programming in C++" link on **http://www.jbpub.com/cs** for information on using apstring in different programming environments.

Since the Advanced Placement Board has developed its version of strings as a **class**, you declare **objects** (instead of variables) of type apstring. You will learn more about classes and objects in later labs, but for now just refer to apstring variables as objects. You declare objects of type apstring that store a string of any length by writing apstring followed by the object name. For example,

```
apstring firstName;
```

declares an object that you might use to store a person's first name.

You can assign a value to this object by using the assignment statement

```
firstName = "John";
```

You must enclose the string "John" within double quotation marks to distinguish it from other possible variables or objects named John. You can use the input stream object cin with the extraction operator >> to input strings. For example, you can write

```
cin >> firstName;
```

to read in a string from the keyboard and store it in the object firstName. You do not enclose a string in double quotes when typing it in from the keyboard.

You can read in three names in succession by using the statement

```
cin >> firstName >> middleName >> lastName;
```

If the user types in John F Kennedy, this statement stores "John" in firstName, "F" in middle-Name, and "Kennedy" in lastName.

Warmup Exercise

Complete the following program by filling in the missing C++ code. A shell for this program is given in the file *shady.shl*.

```
// Completes a story about some "shady characters" using the user's
// answers to a series of questions.

#include <iostream.h>
#include <apstring.h>
#include <apstring.cpp>

int main()
{
    _____    animal,           // An animal name
                preposition,      // A preposition
                cakeIngredient;   // A cake ingredient

    // Get an animal name, preposition, and cake ingredient.
    cout << endl;
    cout << "Enter an animal name: ";
    cin >> animal;
    cout << "Enter a preposition: ";
    cin >> _____;
    cout << "Enter a 5-letter ingredient in a cake: ";
    _____;

    // Output the completed story.
    cout << endl;
    cout << "            James 'Mad " << animal
         << "' Jones" << endl;
    cout << "Bank robber famous for shouting 'Stick 'em "
         << preposition << "!'" << endl;
    cout << "as he entered a bank. Claimed he robbed banks " << endl;
    cout << "because 'That's where they keep the "
         << cakeIngredient << ".'" << endl;

    return 0;
}
```

APPLICATION EXERCISE: The Rest of the Story

Now you get a chance to let the creative juices flow and write a story about your own set of "shady characters," or anything else that tickles your fancy.

Step 1: Write a program that creates a story. Your program should display a set of instructions and prompt the user to enter words. The words entered by the user should then be incorporated as part of your story. Use input prompts that are clear and descriptive so that the user knows the meaning of the data that you want entered.

    Input: A series of words

    Output: The completed story

Step 2:   Save your program as *mystory.cpp*.

Step 3:   Complete the following test plan.

Test Plan for *mystory*

Test case	Sample data	Expected result	Checked
Your data			
A friend's data			

Step 4:   Execute your program in the file *mystory.cpp*.

Step 5:   Check each case in your *mystory* plan and verify the expected result. If you discover mistakes in your program, correct them and execute the test plan again.

LABORATORY 2: Core Exercise 4—Arithmetic Expressions

Background

C++ uses the same rules of precedence for **arithmetic operators** that you learned in algebra. Operators of the same level of precedence are evaluated from left to right. For example, in the expression

```
10.0 / 2.5 * 2.0
```

10.0 is first divided by 2.5, giving 4.0. This result is then multiplied by 2.0 to yield a final result of 8.0.

When operations of different precedence are combined in a single expression, multiplication (*) and division (/) take priority over addition (+) and subtraction (-). For example,

```
9.0 - 4.0 * 2.0
```

yields a result of 1.0, as multiplication is performed before subtraction.

You can alter the normal order of operations in C++ with parentheses. In the algebraic expression

$$\frac{p+q}{r},$$

p and q are added and their sum is divided by r. If you translate the expression literally, you get

```
p + q / r
```

In this expression, q is first divided by r and the result added to p–not the order of operations you want. By placing parentheses around p and q, giving

```
(p + q) / r,
```

you indicate that the addition of p and q should be done before the division by r.

Warmup Exercise

The formula for the average velocity of a particle traveling on a line between points x_1 and x_2 in the time interval t_1 to t_2 is

$$\text{average velocity} = \frac{x_2 - x_1}{t_2 - t_1}$$

Complete the following program by expressing this formula in C++. A shell for this program is given in the file *avgvel.shl*.

```
// Finds the average velocity of a particle traveling between two points
// in a specified time interval.

#include <iostream.h>
```

```
int main()
{
    double x1,          // First point
           x2,          // Second point
           t1,          // Time reading at first point
           t2,          // Time reading at second point
           avgVel;      // Average velocity

    // Prompt the user for two points and read them in.
    cout << endl << "Enter points x1 and x2: ";
    cin >> x1 >> x2;

    // Prompt the user for the time readings and read them in.
    cout << "Enter times t1 and t2: ";
    cin >> t1 >> t2;

    // Calculate and display the average velocity.
    avgVel = _____
    cout << "The average velocity is " << avgVel << endl;

    return 0;
}
```

APPLICATION EXERCISE: Take It to Heart

Professional triathletes often use a heart monitor to check their heart rates during training and competition. The monitor beeps a warning tone if the heart rate is not within an acceptable pre-set range of values.

The weekend athlete can use a pair of simple formulas based solely on age to determine an acceptable heart rate when exercising aerobically. This heart rate is expressed as a range of values called the individual target heart rate zone (THRZ). To calculate your predicted maximal heart rate, subtract your age from 220. Then use the following formulas to determine the limits on your THRZ in beats per minute (bpm).

Lower limit (bpm) = 60% of the difference between 220 and your age

Upper limit (bpm) = 75% of the difference between 220 and your age

 See the "Engaged Learning for Programming in C++" link on **http://www.jbpub.com/cs** for more information on target heart rate zones.

Step 1:   Create a program to compute a person's THRZ, using the formulas shown.

Input: Age in years

Output: Lower and upper limits of the THRZ in beats per minute

Step 2:   Save your program as *training.cpp*.

Step 3: Complete the following test plan.

Test Plan for *training*

Test case	Sample data	Expected result	Checked
Eighteen-year-old teenybopper	18	THRZ: 121.2 – 151.5 BPM	
Thirtysomething	35	THRZ: 111 – 138.75 BPM	
Venerable 90-year-old		THRZ: 78 – 97.5 BPM	
You			

Step 4: Execute your program in the file *training.cpp*.

Step 5: Check each case in your *training* test plan and verify the expected result. If you discover mistakes in your program, correct them and execute the test plan again. Your results may differ slightly in the number of decimal digits displayed. In Laboratory 5 you will learn how to format output to a specified number of digits.

LABORATORY 2: Reinforcement Exercise—Translating Arithmetic Calculations

House Rules

When you contact a lending institution about acquiring a mortgage, it often provides you with guidelines for computing your maximum monthly mortgage payment. Common "rules of thumb" are that your maximum monthly payment should not exceed

28% of your gross monthly income

or

36% of your gross monthly income, minus monthly debt payments (loans, credit card, etc.),

where the mortgage payment includes principal, interest, taxes, and insurance.

Step 1: Create a program to compute the maximum monthly mortgage payment a person can afford for the percentages given.

| *Input:* | Gross monthly income |
| | Monthly debt payments |

| *Output:* | Maximum payment based on gross monthly income alone |
| | Maximum payment based on gross monthly income minus monthly debt payments |

Step 2: Save your program as *mortgage.cpp*.

Step 3: Test your program by using the following test plan. If you discover mistakes in your program, correct them and execute the test plan again.

Test Plan for *mortgage*

Test case	Sample data	Expected result	Checked
Low debts	2000	Maximum payment without debt payments: $560	
	100	Maximum payment with debt payments: $620	
High debts	3000	Maximum payment without debt payments: $840	
	500	Maximum payment with debt payments: $580	

LABORATORY 2: Analysis Exercise

Problem Solving and Programming Style

Name _____

Hour/Period/Section _____

Date _____

Part A

When you have been given a problem to solve with a computer program, the first step is to try to understand what the problem is asking for and the steps involved to solve the problem. Then you can start to write C++ code to solve the problem. Most of the basic programs we cover in the first five labs can be classified as Input–Process–Output programs. That is, they can all be broken into three basic steps.

- What are the inputs?
  - What format are they in? (e.g., integer, floating-point, character, or string)
  - How do you get them? (e.g., prompt user or read from file)
- What are the outputs?
  - What format are they in?
  - How do you output them? (e.g., on screen or to a file)
- How do you get from inputs to the outputs you want?
  - What are the calculation steps?
  - To follow these steps, what else do you need?
    - Other variables? (besides input and output variables)
    - Libraries (e.g., for writing to screen or reading from keyboard)

For the following problem, answering the preceding questions should help you understand what you need to program in order to solve it.

Clothing stores sometimes have sales during the year to attract customers and clear inventory. The final sale price of an item is calculated by deducting the sale percentage from the original price and then adding the tax percentage to the price. Given an original price of an item, a sale percentage, and a tax percentage, write a program to calculate the final sale price.

Part B

You have been hired as a summer intern to perform program maintenance for Quick-n-Dirty Software, Inc. Your main task is to clean up the code written by I. M. A. Hacker, who recently was transferred to the Data Utility Division (DUD). The following is an example of Mr. Hacker's code. The program executes but has many faults.

```
// File: pay.cpp
// Tells ya' your pay
#include <iostream.h>
const double r=4.25;
int main()
{
double h,t,w;
cout << "Hours: "; cin >> h;
cout << "Tips: ";  cin >> t;
w = h*r+t; cout << w;  return 0;
}
```

Compare this program to some of the programs given in the Warmup Exercises in this lab. List four things that you would do to improve this program in terms of readability, style, and ease of use.

C++ Program Elements II

OVERVIEW

One of C++'s strong features is the number and utility of the operators it provides. In Laboratory 2, you used several of the arithmetic operators in formulas involving floating-point numbers. The formulas were simple and easily translated into C++, using the appropriate arithmetic operator (+, -, *, and /). You also examined the order in which C++ evaluates arithmetic operators. However, most programs that you create require careful consideration of the use of operators and how they work on different data types. Some programming tools and techniques introduced in this lab give you more explicit control of data type conversions and formatted output, and some advanced arithmetic functions that are usually available on any standard calculator.

In Core Exercise 1, you use the arithmetic operations with C++'s integer data type (int). In addition, you use the remainder operator, %, to perform modular arithmetic on integer values. In Core Exercise 2, you solve problems that require mixing floating-point and integer data types. You examine how and when the C++ compiler automatically converts an integer value to a floating-point value and combines these two data types into a single expression. You also learn a method for explicitly specifying when a data type conversion should be done. In Core Exercise 3, you experiment with a set of standard C++ library functions.

LABORATORY 3: Cover Sheet

Name _____

Hour/Period/Section _____

Date _____

Place a check mark (✔) in the Assigned column next to the exercises that your instructor has assigned to you. Have this sheet ready when your lab instructor checks your work. If your exercises are being checked outside the laboratory session, attach this sheet to the front of the packet of materials that you submit.

Exercise	Assigned	Completed
Core 1 Integer Arithmetic *Five and Dime (change.cpp)*		
Core 2 Type Conversion *Extra Bases (slugger.cpp)*		
Core 3 Library Functions *Skin You're In (surface.cpp)*		
Reinforcement Applying Type Conversion and Library Functions *Let's Get Physique-al (bmi.cpp)*		
Analysis Choosing a Data Type		
Total		

LABORATORY 3: Core Exercise 1—Integer Arithmetic

Background

So far, you have written programs by using two of C++'s predefined types, `double` and `char`. In this exercise, you work with a third type, `int`, which is used for integer values. Values of type `int` do not contain a fractional part and are useful for activities such as counting, indexing, and performing modular arithmetic.

You can use the same arithmetic operators with integers that you used with floating-point numbers. Integer division is subtlety different from floating-point division, however. The floating-point expression

```
5.0 / 2.0
```

produces a result of `2.5`. However, the expression

```
5 / 2
```

evaluates to `2`. In this case, because both the numerator and denominator are integer values, integer division is used. **Integer division** retains only the quotient; the fractional part is lost.

You can use the **modulus operator**, `%`, to get the remainder from an integer division. The expression

```
5 % 2
```

for example, yields `1`, the remainder produced when `5` is divided by `2`. The modulus operator works only with integer data and has the same precedence level as `/` and `*`.

You can also use parentheses to vary the order in which integer operators are evaluated. However, integer division and the modulus operator make evaluation of integer expressions a bit trickier. Consider the expression `21 - 11 % 4 * (5 + 11 / 4)`. This expression yields the value `0`. The order in which the operators are evaluated is

```
21 - 11 % 4 * (5 + 11 / 4)
21 - 11 % 4 * (5 +   2   )
21 - 11 % 4 *     7
21 -   3   *     7
21 -         21
    0
```

Warmup Exercise

Complete the following program by filling in the missing C++ code. A shell for this program is given in the file *convsecs.shl*.

```
// Converts a time interval measured in seconds to its
// hours:minutes:seconds form.

#include <iostream.h>

int main ()
{
    int seconds,
        minutes,
        hours;

    // Prompt for time interval and read it in.
    cout << endl << "Enter the time interval (in secs): ";
    cin >> seconds;

    // Convert to hours:minutes:seconds form.
    hours = seconds ___ 3600;       // Find number of hours
    seconds = seconds % _____;      // Find remaining seconds
    minutes = _____ / 60;        // Find number of minutes
    seconds = seconds __ 60;        // Find seconds left at end

    // Display in hours:minutes:seconds format.
    cout << hours << ":" << minutes << ":" << seconds << endl;

    return 0;
}
```

APPLICATION EXERCISE: Five and Dime

You can use integer arithmetic to compute the mix of coins returned by a vending machine. The key is to represent all monetary amounts in cents as int values, rather than as fractions of a dollar.

Step 1: Create a program that calculates the coins returned from a vending machine as change from a purchase. Assume that the cost of the purchase and the amount of money put in the machine are measured in cents and are stored in variables of type int. Furthermore, assume that these values are multiples of 5 cents (no pennies please).

    Input: Amount of money put in the machine (in cents)

                     Actual cost of the purchase (in cents)

    Output: Total change amount returned

                     Number of quarters, dimes, and nickels returned

Step 2: Save your program as *change.cpp*.

Step 3: Complete the following test plan.

Test Plan for *change*

Test case	Sample data	Expected result	Checked
No change	50 50	0 cents change 0 quarter(s) 0 dime(s) 0 nickel(s)	
Only quarters returned	100 25	75 cents change 3 quarter(s) 0 dime(s) 0 nickel(s)	
At least one of each coin returned		65 cents change 2 quarter(s) 1 dime(s) 1 nickel(s)	
Only a dime returned			

Step 4: Execute your program in the file *change.cpp*.

Step 5: Check each case in your *change* test plan and verify the expected result. If you discover mistakes in your program, correct them and execute the test plan again.

LABORATORY 3: Core Exercise 2—Type Conversion

Background

You will often need to combine integer and floating-point values in the same expression. Whenever an arithmetic operator combines an integer value with a floating-point value, the integer value is automatically converted to floating-point form. This same conversion happens whenever an integer value is assigned to a floating-point variable. These implicit type conversions are referred to as type coercions or type promotions.

A better and more explicit way to convert data types is **type casting**. In this context, being typecast doesn't refer to the limited types of roles available to the cast of *Gilligan's Island* after syndication. Rather, a C++ cast operation consists of a type name and an expression to be converted (within parentheses).

The following program from the file *typecast.cpp* uses a pair of casts to produce the floating-point result of dividing two integer variables. Note that these casts generate floating-point values that are used in evaluating the expression. They don't change the type of variables j and k from int to double.

```
// Sample program using type casting for explicit type conversion.

#include <iostream.h>

int main()
{
    int j,k;
    cout << endl << "Enter two integers: ";
    cin >> j >> k;
    cout << "Integer division " << j / k << endl;
    cout << "Typecast floating-point division " << double(j) / double(k);

    return 0;
}
```

Sample run:

```
Enter two integers: 2 5
Integer division 0
Typecast double division 0.4
```

Warmup Exercise

The formula to convert a Fahrenheit temperature to its Celsius equivalent is

$$celsius = \frac{5}{9}(fahrenheit - 32).$$

Complete the following program by expressing this formula in C++. A shell for this program is given in the file *fahr2cel.shl*.

```
// Converts a Fahrenheit temperature to its Celsius equivalent.

#include <iostream.h>

int main()
{
    double celsius,         // Celsius temperature reading
           fahrenheit;      // Fahrenheit temperature reading

    // Prompt for Fahrenheit temperature and read it in.
    cout << endl << "Enter a Fahrenheit temperature: ";
    cin >> fahrenheit;

    // Calculate the equivalent Celsius temperature.
    _____


    // Output the Celsius temperature.
    cout << "The equivalent Celsius temperature is " << celsius;

    return 0;
}
```

APPLICATION EXERCISE: Extra Bases

One of the more interesting statistics for comparing power hitters in baseball is slugging percentage. A hitter's slugging percentage is calculated as follows:

$$\text{slugging percentage} = \frac{\text{singles} + 2 \cdot \text{doubles} + 3 \cdot \text{triples} + 4 \cdot \text{home runs}}{\text{at bats}}.$$

Step 1: Create a program to determine a baseball player's slugging percentage, using the formula shown. Assume that all inputs are stored in variables of type `int`.

Input: Number of singles, doubles, triples, home runs, and at bats for a player

Output: The player's slugging percentage

Step 2: Save your program as *slugger.cpp*.

Step 3: Complete the following test plan.

Test Plan for *slugger*

Test case	Sample data	Expected result	Checked

Babe Ruth (1920)
   Singles:73
   Doubles:36
   Triples:9
   Home runs:54
   At bats:458
		`Slugging percentage:   .847`	

Ken Griffey, Jr. (1994)
   Singles:72
   Doubles:24
   Triples:4
   Home runs:40
   At bats:433
		`Slugging percentage:   .674`	

Mark McGuire (1998)
   Singles:61
   Doubles:21
   Triples:0
   Home runs:70
   At bats:509
		`Slugging percentage:   .752`	

Your favorite player
   Singles:
   Doubles:
   Triples:
   Home runs:
   At bats:			

Step 4: Execute your program in the file *slugger.cpp*.

Step 5: Check each case in your *slugger* test plan and verify the expected result. If you discover mistakes in your program, correct them and execute the test plan again. Your results may differ slightly in the number of decimal digits displayed. In Laboratory 5 you will learn how to format output to a specified number of digits.

LABORATORY 3: Core Exercise 3—Library Functions

Background

A **function** is a named piece of code that performs a well-defined task. As your experience with programming increases, you will begin to notice that you do certain tasks over and over. Some tasks are so common—finding a square root, testing whether an alphanumeric character is a letter, generating a random number, and getting the current time, to name a few—that standard functions have been developed to perform these tasks. Functions that relate in some thematic sense are collected into standard libraries.

C++'s mathematical library, for instance, contains an extensive collection of mathematical functions. The following program from the file *sqroot.cpp* uses one of these functions, sqrt(), to calculate the square root of a number.

```
// Calculates the square root of a number using the sqrt() function.
#include <iostream.h>
#include <math.h>    // Include prototype for sqrt()
int main()
{
    double num;    // Number whose square root is computed

    // Prompt the user for a number and read it in.
    cout << endl << "Enter a number: ";
    cin >> num;

    // Display the square root of the number.
    cout << "Square root is " << sqrt(num) << endl;

    return 0;
}
```

The expression sqrt(num) is referred to as a **call** to function sqrt(). This call consists of two parts: the name of the function, sqrt, and the **argument**, num, whose value is passed to the function. Note that the argument is placed inside parentheses following the function name—a notational style borrowed from mathematics. When called, the sqrt() function takes the value of argument num and returns its square root.

Whenever you use a library function, you must include the header file for the library in your program. For example, the preprocessor directive

```
#include <math.h>
```

includes the header file for the standard math library. The header file for a library contains the prototypes for the functions in the library. Each **prototype** specifies the name of a function, the type of data returned by the function, and a list of function **parameters** that includes the data type of each parameter. A prototype for the sqrt() function from *math.h* is

```
double sqrt( double x );
```

This prototype indicates that the `sqrt()` function returns a value of type `double` and has one parameter, which also is of type `double`. The parameter name x given in the prototype is for informational purposes only and doesn't necessarily match the name of the argument used in a call to the function—the argument `num` in the call `sqrt(num)`, for instance.

Warmup Exercise

The natural logarithm function computes the value of ln(x)—that is, the natural logarithm of x. The *math.h* header file includes the following prototype for the C++ natural logarithm function, `log()`.

```
double log( double x );
```

Carbon-14 is a naturally occurring radioactive carbon isotope. A living plant contains the same proportion of carbon-14 as the atmosphere in which the plant grows. When the plant dies, its carbon-14 gradually undergoes radioactive decay. The rate of decay is exponential, with half the carbon-14 decaying approximately every 5,700 years.

If you have an artifact containing plant material—wood or cloth, for instance—you can compute the approximate age of the artifact from the amount of carbon-14 remaining in a sample of the plant material by using the formula

$$\text{age} = -5700 \cdot \frac{\ln(\text{percentage of carbon}-14 \text{ remaining})}{\ln(2)},$$

where age is the approximate age of the artifact (in years), percentage of carbon-14 remaining is the percentage of carbon-14 remaining in the sample (as a fraction of 1.0) at any particular time, and ln is the natural (Napierian) logarithm.

 See the "Engaged Learning for Programming in C++" link on **http://www.jbpub.com/cs** for links to more information about carbon dating.

Complete this program by filling in the missing C++ code. A shell for this program is given in the file *carbon.shl*.

```
// Computes an artifact's age using carbon-14 dating.
#include <iostream.h>
_____    // Header file for log()
int main ()
{
   double sample,    // Carbon-14 remaining in a sample (% of 1.0)
          age;       // Age of the sample (in years)
```

```
    // Prompt the user and read in a sample.
    cout << endl
        << "Enter amount of carbon-14 remaining in the sample "
        << "(as a % of 1.0) : ";
    cin >> sample;

    // Insert code that computes the sample's age and displays the result.


    return 0;
}
```

APPLICATION EXERCISE: Skin You're In

The equation commonly used in medicine to compute your body surface area (BSA), or the "skin you're in" is

$$\text{body surface area} = \text{weight}^{0.425} \cdot \text{height}^{0.725} \cdot 0.007184,$$

which yields the body surface area in square meters (m²) where the weight is in kilograms (kg) and height is in centimeters (cm).

 See the "Engaged Learning for Programming in C++" link on **http://www.jbpub.com/cs** for links to more information about body surface area.

The power function computes the value of x^y—that is, x raised to the power y. The *math.h* header file includes the following prototype for the C++ power function, pow().

```
double pow( double x, double y );
```

Step 1: Create a program to determine a person's BSA using the formula shown. Assume that all inputs are stored in variables of type double.

    Input: Weight in kg and height in cm

    Output: The person's BSA

Step 2: Save your program as *surface.cpp*.

Step 3: Complete the following test plan.

Test Plan for *surface*

Test case	Sample data	Expected result	Checked
Weight: 70 Height: 180		`Body surface area: 1.88628`	
Weight: 45 Height: 150		`Body surface area:  1.36977`	
You			

Step 4: Execute your program in the file *surface.cpp*.

Step 5: Check each case in your *surface* test plan and verify the expected result. If you discover mistakes in your program, correct them and execute the test plan again. Your results may differ slightly in the number of decimal digits displayed. In Laboratory 5 you will learn how to format output to a specified number of digits.

LABORATORY 3: Reinforcement Exercise—Applying Type Conversion and Library Functions

Let's Get Physique-al

Studies have shown that the risk of developing heart disease increases when a person's body mass index (BMI) is greater than 30. You can compute your BMI from your weight (in pounds, lb) and height (in inches, in.) by using the formula

$$\text{body mass index} = \frac{704.5 \cdot \text{weight}}{\text{height}^2}$$

 See the "Engaged Learning for Programming in C++" link on **http://www.jbpub.com/cs** for links to more information about body mass index.

Step 1: Create a program to compute a person's BMI, a real number, using the formula shown. Assume that the height and weight are integer values and are stored in variables of type `int`. Remember: You can use the `pow(x,y)` library function to square the height.

    Input: Weight (lb)

                Height (in.)

    Output: The person's BMI

Step 2: Save your program as *bmi.cpp*.

Step 3: Use the following test plan to test your program. If you discover mistakes in your program, correct them and execute the test plan again.

Test Plan for *bmi*

Test case	Sample data	Expected result	Checked
Thick physique	210 70	BMI: 30.1929	
Thin physique	100 60	BMI: 19.5694	
You			

LABORATORY 3: Analysis Exercise

Choosing a Data Type

Name _____

Hour/Period/Section _____

Date _____

Part A

Thus far, you have used variables of type `int` to store integers and variables of type `double` to store double precision floating-point numbers. Other numeric data types exist, as well. You can use variables of type `long`, for example, to store integer values too large to be stored with `int`. Similarly, you can use single precision floating-point type `float` for floating-point numbers that require less precision or have a smaller possible range than variables of type `double`. However, a trade-off is involved when you use `long` or `double` because these types require more memory (than `int` or `float`, respectively). They can hinder the performance of your program in terms of memory utilization and execution speed.

When deciding what type to declare a variable, you need to examine the kind of data the variable will hold and the potential range of values that the variable will represent. Complete the following table by listing the numeric range that each type supports on your system. Give an example of a quantity for which you might use each type (distance in miles, time in seconds, etc.).

Type	Numerical range	Example
int		
long		
float		
double		

See the "Engaged Learning for Programming in C++" link on **http://www.jbpub.com/cs** to see how to find out the valid ranges for C++ data types in various popular program development environments.

Part B

For computer systems on which type `int` is restricted to values in the range from $-32,768$ to $32,767$, the output from the program

```
#include <iostream.h>

int main()
{
    const int num1 = 500,
              num2 = 100;
    int sum, prod;
    sum = num1 + num2;
    prod = num1 * num2;
    cout << endl << "The sum is " << sum << endl;
    cout << "The product is " << prod << endl;

    return 0;
}
```

is

```
The sum is 600
The product is -15536
```

1. Why is the value output for the product inaccurate?

2. What code would you change in this program to output a correct product?

Selection

OVERVIEW

Until now, your programs have executed their statements in strict, sequential order from beginning to end. Most of your programs, however, will require control structures that allow the flow of execution to vary, depending on the data values input by the user (or read from a file). In this lab, you use the `if` statement to specify alternative paths through your program.

In Core Exercise 1, you use relational operators to form conditional expressions—expressions that evaluate to either true or false. You then use these conditional expressions in conjunction with the `if-else` selection structure to choose a particular statement to execute from among a set of statements. In Core Exercise 2, you write a selection structure that executes a compound statement (a block of statements) if a particular condition is true. You use logical operators in Core Exercise 3 to test multiple conditions in a single conditional expression. In Core Exercise 4 you use a `switch()` statement as a special multiple alternative selection control structure.

LABORATORY 4: Cover Sheet

Name _____

Hour/Period/Section _____

Date _____

Place a check mark (✔) in the Assigned column next to the exercises that your instructor has assigned to you. Have this sheet ready when your lab instructor checks your work. If your exercises are being checked outside the laboratory session, attach this sheet to the front of the packet of materials that you submit.

Exercise		Assigned	Completed
Core 1	`if-else` Control Structure *Hold onto Your Hats (stormy.cpp)*		
Core 2	Compound Statements *Good for the Sol (sunshine.cpp)*		
Core 3	Logical Operators *Rollin', Rollin', Rollin' (rolling.cpp)*		
Core 4	`switch` statements *Gung Hay Fat Choy (animal.cpp)*		
Reinforcement	Logical Operator Practice *Open Sesame (opendoor.cpp)*		
Analysis	Analyzing Selection Structures		
Total			

LABORATORY 4: Core Exercise 1—if-else **Control Structure**

Background

Many times, you only want to perform a particular action when a condition is true. In C++, you use **relational operators** to express true/false relationships. C++'s relational operators and their meanings are as follows.

Operator	Meaning
>	Greater than
>=	Greater than or equal to
<	Less than
<=	Less than or equal to
==	Equal to
!=	Not equal to

You form a **conditional expression** by combining a relational operator with a pair of values and/or variables. The resulting expression is either true or false. For example, the conditional expression

```
20 > 10
```

is true, whereas the conditional expression

```
18 == 15
```

is false. In C++, when outputting the value of a conditional expression, a true expression outputs the value 1 and a false expression outputs the value 0.

The following program from the file *relops.cpp* performs three comparisons between the numeric value 20 and a number entered by the user.

```cpp
// Comparing values using relational operators.

#include <iostream.h>

int main ()
{
    int number;
    cout << endl << "Number: ";
    cin >> number;
    cout << number << " > 20 is " << (number > 20) << endl;
    cout << number << " < 20 is " << (number < 20) << endl;
    cout << number << " == 20 is " << (number == 20) << endl;
    return 0;
}
```

The output of this program for the input value `10` is

```
Number: 10
10 > 20 is 0
10 < 20 is 1
10 == 20 is 0
```

The **if statement** is the simplest of C++'s selection structures. It uses a conditional expression to determine whether a given statement should be executed. The `if` statement

```
if ( temp>90 )
    cout << "Too hot" << endl;
```

outputs `"Too hot"` if `temp` is greater than 90°—that is, if the conditional expression `temp>90` is true.

You can write a more general `if` statement by adding an else branch. In this case, one statement is executed if the conditional expression is true and another statement is executed if it isn't. An example of an **if-else statement** is

```
if ( temp>90 )
    cout << "Too hot" << endl;
else
    cout << "I feel good" << endl;
```

where `"Too hot"` is displayed if `temp` is greater than 90°, and `"I feel good"` is displayed if it isn't—that is, if `temp` is less than or equal to 90°.

By nesting `if-else` statements, you can select from a set of alternatives, as in

```
if ( temp>90 )
    cout << "Too hot" << endl;
else
    if ( temp>32 )
        cout << "I feel good" << endl;
    else
        cout << "Too cold" << endl;
```

Suppose that `temp` is 43°. In this case, the first conditional expression is false. Thus the first `else` statement is executed, and `temp` is compared with 32°. The second conditional expression is true and the string `"I feel good"` is output. If `temp` is 25°, however, both conditional expressions are false and the string `"Too cold"` is output.

You can write this nested `if-else` structure in a form that is easier to read and interpret.

```
if ( temp>90 )
    cout << "Too hot" << endl;
else if ( temp>32 )
    cout << "I feel good" << endl;
else
    cout << "Too cold" << endl;
```

Note that this change is cosmetic—both forms execute in exactly the same way.

Warmup Exercise

A pollution index for a given day is often computed by taking readings at the same time at several different locations. These readings are then averaged, and this average is compared to some cutoff value to determine whether a hazardous condition exists.

Complete the following program by filling in the missing C++ code. A shell for this program is given in the file *polindex.shl*.

```
// Averages input pollution level readings and compares to a cutoff
// value for possible hazardous condition.  Displays a warning message
// if the index is greater than or equal to the given cutoff value.

#include <iostream.h>

const double CUTOFF = 50.0;    // Cutoff for hazardous condition

int main()
{
    double level1,level2,level3,    // Pollution level readings
           index;                   // Average of readings

    cout << endl << "Enter the 3 pollution readings: ";
    cin >> level1 >> level2 >> level3;
    index = (level1 + level2 + level3) / 3;

    // Check for hazardous condition.
    if _____
        cout << "Hazardous condition" << endl;

    _____
        cout << "Non-hazardous condition" << endl;

    return 0;
}
```

APPLICATION EXERCISE: Hold on to Your Hats

A tropical storm is classified as a hurricane when it has sustained winds of at least 74 mph. Larger hurricanes are further categorized by wind speed and storm surge effects. The Saffir/Simpson scale for classifying hurricanes is as follows.

Category	Definition and Effects
1	Sustained winds of 74–95 mph
	Damage primarily to unanchored mobile homes, shrubbery, and trees
2	Sustained winds of 96–110 mph
	Damage to roofing material, windows, and doors of buildings
3	Sustained winds of 111–130 mph
	Structural damage, mobile homes destroyed, and flooding near coastline

4	Sustained winds of 131–155 mph
	Major erosion of beach areas and major damage to lower floors of structures near the shore
5	Sustained winds of above 155 mph
	Complete roof failure on many residences and industrial buildings; massive evacuation required

 See the "Engaged Learning for Programming in C++" link on **http://www.jbpub.com/cs** for links to more information on classifying hurricanes.

Step 1: Create a program that determines whether a tropical storm is a hurricane, based on its sustained wind speed. If the storm is a hurricane, display the category of the hurricane. Note that you don't need to display the effects of the storm.

> *Input:* Wind speed in mph
>
> *Output:* Storm classification (nonhurricane, Category 1 hurricane, Category 2 hurricane, etc.)

Step 2: Save your program as *stormy.cpp*.

Step 3: Complete the following test plan.

Test Plan for *stormy*

Test case	Sample data	Expected result	Checked
Hurricane—Category 1	90	`Category 1`	
Hurricane—Category 3			
Hurricane—Category 5			
Below minimum hurricane threshold			

Step 4: Execute your program in the file *stormy.cpp*.

Step 5: Check each case in your *stormy* test plan and verify the expected result. If you discover mistakes in your program, correct them and execute the test plan again.

LABORATORY 4: Core Exercise 2—Compound Statements

Background

In most cases, you will need to execute more than one statement when a condition is true. You can create a **compound statement** by enclosing a series of statements within a pair of braces. Suppose that you want to output not only the fact that temperatures above 90° are too hot, but also to compute how much the temperature needs to change in order for you to feel comfortable. The following compound `if` statement does the job.

```
if ( temp>90 )
{
    cout << "Too hot" << endl;
    changeTemp = temp - 90;
}
```

For any `temp` value greater than 90°, both statements inside the braces are executed.

In most multiple alternative selection structures, you need to execute a compound statement for some or all the conditions. In the following code fragment, for example, the value of `temp` is used to select one of three different compound statements.

```
if ( temp>90 )
{
    cout << "Too hot" << endl;
    changeTemp = temp - 90;
}
else if ( temp>32 )
{
    cout << "I feel good" << endl;
    changeTemp = 0;
}
else
{
    cout << "Too cold" << endl;
    changeTemp = 32 - temp;
}
```

Warmup Exercise

The federal income tax that a person pays is a function of the person's taxable income. The following table contains the formulas for computing a single person's tax (from the 1993 IRS Tax Rate Schedule, Form 1040).

Bracket	Taxable Income	Marginal Tax Rate	Tax Paid
1	$22,100 or less	15%	15%
2	Between 22,100 and 53,500	28%	3,315 + 28% of the amount over 22,100
3	Between 53,500 and 115,000	31%	12,107 + 31% of the amount over 53,500
4	Between 115,000 and 250,000	36%	31,172 + 36% of the amount over 115,000
5	Over 250,000	39.6%	79,772 + 39.6% of the amount over 250,000

The marginal tax rate is the tax rate that you pay on the last dollar you earned. This rate gives you an idea of how much tax would have to be paid on any additional earnings you might make.

Complete the following program by filling in the missing C++ code. A shell for this program is given in the file *taxrate.shl*.

```
// Computes federal income tax for a single person using the
// 1993 Tax Rate Schedule from Form 1040.

#include <iostream.h>

int main()
{
    double income,    // Taxable income
           tax;       // Tax to be paid

    cout << endl << "Enter your taxable income: ";
    cin >> income;
    cout << "Your marginal tax rate is ";
    if (_____)
    ____
        cout << "39.6%" << endl;
        tax = 79772 + 0.396 * (income - 250000);

    ____
    else if ( income > 115000 )
    {
        cout << "36%" << endl;
        tax = 31172 + 0.36 * (income - 115000);
    }
    else if ( income > 53500 )
    {
        cout << "31%" << endl;
        tax = _____
    }
```

```
        else if ( income > 22100 )
        {
            _____

            tax = 3315 + 0.28 * (income - 22100);
        }
        else
        {
            _____

            _____

        }
        cout << "Your approximate tax is " << tax << endl;

        return 0;
    }
```

APPLICATION EXERCISE: Good for the Sol

On a cold winter day the sun can provide you with more than just light. The sun streaming through a window during the day can contribute significantly to a rise in the average daily indoor temperature. You can compute the average indoor temperature in a well-insulated room as

$$avgInTemp = \frac{\text{HGF} \cdot windowArea}{\text{HLF} \cdot roomArea} + avgOutTemp,$$

where the identifiers have the following meanings.

Identifier	Meaning
avgInTemp	Average daily indoor temperature
avgOutTemp	Average daily outdoor temperature
HGF	Heat gain factor
HLF	Heat loss factor
windowArea	Area of window in square feet
roomArea	Area of room in square feet.

On a clear January day in Chicago the average outdoor temperature is 28.9°F and the HGF and HLF for single- and double-paned windows are as follows.

Window Type	HGF	HLF
Single-paned	1540	13
Double-paned	1416	9.7

See the "Engaged Learning for Programming in C++" link on **http://www.jbpub.com/cs** for links to more information on window heat gain and loss.

Step 1: Create a program that computes the average daily indoor temperature in a well-insulated room as a result of the sun streaming through the window. Use the preceding formula and data for a clear January day in Chicago. Prompt the user to input the type of window (single- or double-paned) and the dimensions of both the window and the room. An appropriate message should be displayed if the user specifies an invalid window type.

Input: Type of window (1 for single-paned, 2 for double-paned)
Width of the window (in ft)
Height of the window (in ft)
Width of the room (in ft)
Length of the room (in ft)

Output: Average indoor temperature in °F

Step 2: Save your program as *sunshine.cpp*.

Step 3: Complete the following test plan.

Test Plan for *sunshine*

Test case	Sample data	Expected result	Checked
Single pane Small window (5 × 5) Medium room (20 × 25)	1 5 5 20 25	Avg temperature with single-paned window: 34.82 F	
Double pane Small window (5 × 5) Medium room (20 × 25)		Avg temperature with double-paned window: 36.2 F	
Single pane Large window (10 × 10) Medium room (20 × 25)		Avg temperature with single-paned window: 52.59 F	
Double pane Large window (10 × 10) Medium room (20 × 25)		Avg temperature with double-paned window: 58.1 F	

Step 4: Execute your program in the file *sunshine.cpp*.

Step 5: Check each case in your *sunshine* test plan and verify the expected result. If you discover mistakes in your program, correct them and execute the test plan again. Your results may differ slightly in the number of decimal digits displayed. In Lab 5 you will learn how to format output to a specified number of digits.

LABORATORY 4: Core Exercise 3—Logical Operators

Background

You can use logical operators to combine conditional expressions. The C++ **logical operators** are as follows.

Operator	Meaning
!	NOT (Reverse the truth value of a condition.)
&&	AND (Both conditions must be true.)
||	OR (At least one condition must be true.)

Suppose that you want to determine whether an `int` variable `number` contains a value between 10 and 40. You can express this condition by using the logical expression

```
number > 10  &&  number < 40
```

which yields true only when both conditional expressions are true—that is, when `number` is greater than 10 and less than 40. Similarly, you can determine whether a `char` variable `ch` contains the letter `'a'` or the letter `'A'` by using the following logical expression

```
ch == 'a'  ||  ch == 'A'
```

In this case, only one conditional expression needs to be true for the entire expression to be true.

The `!` operator is used to reverse truth values. Suppose that you have an `int` variable `speed` and literal constant SPEED_LIMIT. The logical expression

```
( speed > SPEED_LIMIT )
```

tests whether it is not true that speed is greater than SPEED_LIMIT. This is the same as the logical expression

```
( speed <= SPEED_LIMIT )
```

C++ is very efficient in evaluating logical expressions. It involves the use of what is called short-circuit evaluation—that is, evaluation is done left-to-right and is stopped as soon as the final value of the expression is known, even if all conditional expressions haven't been evaluated. For example, if the value of `ch` is `'a'`, evaluation of the logical expression

```
ch == 'a'  ||  ch == 'A'
```

terminates—and yields true—as soon as the first conditional expression is evaluated as true. There is no need to evaluate the second conditional expression because the `||` operator will yield true whenever one of its operands is true, regardless of the other operand. Similarly, if the value of `number` is 5, evaluation of the logical expression

```
number > 10  &&  number < 40
```

terminates, yielding false as soon as the first conditional expression yields false. If the value of number is 20, however, both conditional expressions will need to be evaluated to determine whether the logical expression is true or false.

Warmup Exercise

In card games, a pair is defined as two cards of the same rank—two queens, two aces, two tens, and so on. You can represent a playing card's rank by using the following characters.

Card	Character
Ace	'1'
2–9	'2'-'9'
10	'T'
Jack	'J'
Queen	'Q'
King	'K'
Joker	'*'

The phrase "jokers wild" means that you can treat a joker as though it is any card in the deck. If jokers are wild, a pair of aces can be formed in several ways: two aces, an ace and a joker, and two jokers.

Complete the following program that determines whether two cards form a pair of aces by filling in the missing C++ code. Use the preceding card rank representation. A shell for this program is given in the file *aces.shl*.

```cpp
// Determines if two cards entered by the user qualify as a pair of aces.

#include <iostream.h>

int main()
{
    char card1, card2;

    cout << endl << "Enter the character for the first card: ";
    cin >> card1;
    cout << "Enter the character for the second card: ";
    cin >> card2;

    if (_____)
        cout << "Pair of aces — both cards are aces" << endl;
    else if (_____)
        cout << "Pair of aces — both cards are jokers" << endl;
    else if (_____)
        cout << "Pair of aces — one card is an ace, the other is a "
             << "joker" << endl;
    else
        cout << "Not a pair of aces" << endl;

    return 0;
}
```

APPLICATION EXERCISE: Rollin', Rollin', Rollin'

When architects design building lobbies and corridors, their plans often must meet the requirements of the Uniform Federal Accessibility Standards (UFAS). The dimensions required by the standards for a turn around an obstruction in a corridor are as follows.

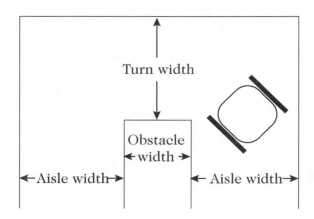

Obstacle Width	Aisle Width	Turn Width
>= 48"	Must be at least 36"	Must be at least 36"
< 48"	Must be at least 42"	Must be at least 48"

At first glance, it may seem strange that the narrower the obstacle is, the wider both the aisles and the turn must be. However, consider what a person in a wheelchair must do to complete a turn around a narrow obstacle. Rather than making a pair of shallow turns—one turn on one side of the obstacle and another turn on the other—the person must make a single, sharp U-turn. A U-turn takes significantly more room than a shallow turn—thus the need for wider aisles and turn space.

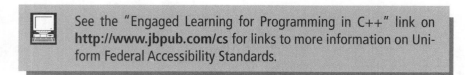

See the "Engaged Learning for Programming in C++" link on **http://www.jbpub.com/cs** for links to more information on Uniform Federal Accessibility Standards.

Step 1: Create a program to determine whether the design specifications for a turn meet the UFAS requirements as outlined.

Input: Width of the obstacle (in.)
Width of the aisle (in.)
Width of the turn (in.)

Output: A message indicating whether the dimensions for the turn meet the UFAS requirements.

Step 2:   Save your program as *rolling.cpp*.

Step 3:   Complete the following test plan.

Test Plan for *rolling*

Test case	Sample data	Expected result	Checked
Large obstacle (50″) Wide aisle (40″) Wide turn (40″)	50 40 40	Turn meets UFAS requirements	
Large obstacle (50″) Wide aisle (40″) Narrow turn (30″)	50 40 30	Turn fails UFAS requirements	
Small obstacle (30″) Wide aisle (45″) Wide turn (50″)	30 45 50		
Small obstacle (40″) Narrow aisle (35″) Wide turn (50″)	40 35 50		
Large obstacle boundary case		Turn meets UFAS requirements	
Small obstacle boundary case		Turn meets UFAS requirements	

Step 4:   Execute your program in the file *rolling.cpp*.

Step 5:   Check each case in your *rolling* test plan and verify the expected result. If you discover mistakes in your program, correct them and execute the test plan again.

LABORATORY 4: Core Exercise 4—`switch` Statements

Background

Often a program must take one of several actions, depending on some variable or expression. Using the `if-else` structure can become tedious and cumbersome for such programs. In C++, a `switch` statement that uses a multiple case selection structure handles certain types of data for a multiple alternative structure. Its general form is

```
switch  (expression)
{
case label1:
    statement1;
    break;
case label2:
    statement2;
    break;
case label3:
    statement3;
    break;
default:
    default statement;
}
```

where `label1`, `label2`, ... are integer or character literal constants. The result of the `switch` statement's `expression` is compared with each of the case labels; if the comparison with `label1` is true, `statement1` is executed; if the comparison is false, the next case is evaluated; and so on. If no match occurs, the default statement is executed; you should end each case structure with a break statement to ensure that only one statement sequence is executed. Otherwise, "fall-through" occurs with a match and all remaining statements after the match are executed.

In the following program from the file *switch1.cpp*, a letter grade is used to determine which case is to be executed.

```
// Sample program using switch statement.

#include <iostream.h>

int main ()
{
    char letterGrade;
    cout << endl << "Enter a letter grade: ";
    cin >> letterGrade;

    // Execute the selected test.
    switch ( letterGrade )
    {
        case 'A' : cout << "1st case" << endl; break;
        case 'B' : cout << "2nd case" << endl; break;
        case 'C' : cout << "3rd case" << endl; break;
        default  : cout << "Invalid input" << endl;
    }
```

```
      return 0;
   }
```

One last note on `switch` statements: Each `statement` associated with a `case label` doesn't have to be a single statement. As with the `if-else` structure, compound statements (a block of statements delimited by { and }) can also be used.

Warmup Exercise

Complete the following program by filling in the missing C++ code. A shell for this program is given in the file *discount.shl*.

```
// Determine the final total price for purchasing multiple items
// at an initial full price minus a discount applied.
// Discount on 1 item is 0%, discount on 2 items is 5%,
// discount on 3 items is 10%, discount on 4 or more items is 15%.

#include <iostream.h>

int main ()
{
    int itemsPurchased;     // User input number of items purchased
    double price,           // User input full price per item
           discount,        // Discount applied
           totalPrice;      // Calculated total price

    // Get full price per item and number of items purchased.
    cout << "Enter the full price of the item: ";
    cin >> price;
    cout << "Enter the number of items purchased: ";
    cin >> itemsPurchased;

    // Validate number of items purchased is positive.
    if ( _____ )
        cout << "Input Error - Zero or less items purchased." << endl;
    else
    {
        // Determine discount based on number of items purchased.
        switch ( _____ )
        {
            case __ : discount = 0.0;  _____;
            case __ : discount = 0.05; _____;
            case __ : discount = 0.10; _____;
            _____ : discount = 0.15;
        }

        // Calculate total purchase price.
        _____;

        // Output discount percentage and total purchase price.
        cout << "Discount=" << discount
             << "  Total Price=$" << totalPrice << endl;
    }

    return 0;
}
```

APPLICATION EXERCISE: Gung Hay Fat Choy

In the Chinese calendar, every year is associated with a particular animal. The 12-year animal cycle is rat, ox, tiger, rabbit, dragon, snake, horse, ram (or goat), monkey, rooster, dog, and boar. The year 1900 was a Year of the Rat; thus 1901 was a Year of the Ox, and 1912 was another Year of the Rat. If you know in what year a person was born, you can compute the offset from 1900 and determine the animal associated with that person's year of birth.

 See the "Engaged Learning for Programming in C++" link on **http://www.jbpub.com/cs** for links to more information on the Chinese calendar.

Step 1: Create a program that determines the animal corresponding to an input year of birth. Assume that the input year is 1900 or later.

> *Input:* Year of birth
>
> *Output:* Corresponding animal from the Chinese calendar

Step 2: Save your program as *animal.cpp*.

Step 3: Complete the following test plan.

Test Plan for *animal*

Test case	Sample data	Expected result	Checked
Base year	1900	Year of the rat	
Mid-cycle year	1942	Year of the horse	
Current year			
Your birth year			
A friend's birth year			

Step 4: Execute your program in the file *animal.cpp*.

Step 5: Check each case in your *animal* test plan and verify the expected result. If you discover mistakes in your program, correct them and execute the test plan again.

LABORATORY 4 Reinforcement Exercise—Logical Operator Practice

Open Sesame

Automatic doors are controlled by three sensors. One sensor detects whether someone is standing on the door's front pad, the second detects whether someone is standing on the door's rear pad, and the third detects whether the door is open or closed. The motor controlling the door is activated—to open the door and/or hold the door open—based on the data produced by these sensors.

You can use 1 to represent that a pad is occupied and 0 to represent that it isn't. Similarly, you can use 1 to represent that the door is open and 0 to represent that it is closed. Using the state (0 or 1) of the pads and the door, you can then determine whether the door should be activated.

As the figure shows, the door's motor should not be activated when both pads are empty. However, it should be activated if the front pad is occupied, the rear pad is unoccupied, and the door is closed, or if the front pad is unoccupied, the rear pad is occupied, and the door is open.

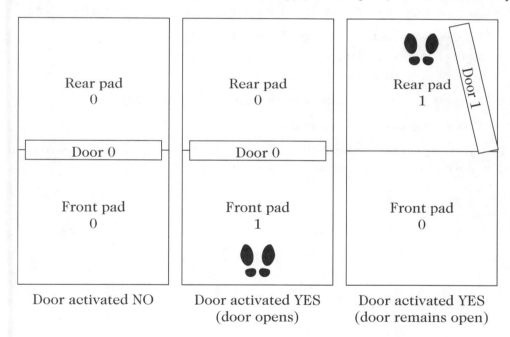

| Door activated NO | Door activated YES (door opens) | Door activated YES (door remains open) |

The following conditions describe when the door should (or should not) be activated.

Front pad	Rear pad	Door	Activate Door
0	0	0	No
0	0	1	No
0	1	0	No
0	1	1	Yes
1	0	0	Yes
1	0	1	Yes
1	1	0	No
1	1	1	Yes

 See the "Engaged Learning for Programming in C++" link on **http://www.jbpub.com/cs** for links to more information on the Boolean expressions.

Step 1: Create a program that determines whether to activate an automatic door.

Input: State of front pad (0 = empty; 1 = occupied)
State of rear pad (0 = empty; 1 = occupied)
State of door (0 = closed; 1 = open)

Output: A message stating whether the door should be activated

Step 2: Save your program as *opendoor.cpp*.

Step 3: Test your program by using the following the test plan. If you discover mistakes in your program, correct them and execute the test plan again.

Test Plan for *opendoor*

Test case	Sample data	Expected result	Checked
Front pad empty Back pad empty Door closed	0 0 0	`Do not activate the door`	
Front pad empty Back pad occupied Door open	0 1 1	`Activate the door`	
Front pad occupied Back pad occupied Door closed	1 1 0	`Do not activate the door`	
Front pad occupied Back pad occupied Door open	1 1 1	`Activate the door`	

LABORATORY 4: Analysis Exercise

Analyzing Selection Structures

Name _____

Hour/Period/Section _____

Date _____

Part A

The following program is supposed to display the message "Head to the beach" if the sun is shining and the temperature is at least 70°F outside. If it isn't sunny, the program should display the message "Bring your umbrella" regardless of the temperature. Note that no message should be displayed if it is sunny and less than 70°F.

```
#include <iostream.h>
int main ()
{
    char sunny;
    int temp;
    cout << endl << "Is it sunny out (Y/N)? ";
    cin >> sunny;
    cout << "What's the temperature outside? ";
    cin >> temp;
    if ( sunny == 'Y'  ||  sunny == 'y' )
    if ( temp >= 70 )
        cout << "Head to the beach" << endl;
    else
        cout << "Bring your umbrella" << endl;

    return 0;
}
```

Unfortunately, the program doesn't work as intended. The message "Bring your umbrella" is displayed when it is sunny and cooler than 70°F, and nothing is displayed when it isn't sunny. What's wrong with this program and how would you correct it?

Part B

The following code fragment classifies a score between 0 and 100 as one of five grades.

```
if ( score >= 90  &&  score <= 100 )
    cout << 'A' << endl;
else if ( score >= 80  &&  score < 90 )
    cout << 'B' << endl;
else if ( score >= 70  &&  score < 80 )
    cout << 'C' << endl;
else if ( score >= 60  &&  score < 70 )
    cout << 'D' << endl;
else if ( score >= 0  &&  score < 60 )
    cout << 'F' << endl;
```

Will the following code fragment yield the same results?

```
if ( score < 0  ||  score > 100 )
    cout << "Out of range" << endl;
else if ( score >= 90 )
    cout << 'A' << endl;
else if ( score >= 80 )
    cout << 'B' << endl;
else if ( score >= 70 )
    cout << 'C' << endl;
else if ( score >= 60 )
    cout << 'D' << endl;
else
    cout << 'F' << endl;
```

Explain why the results are the same or why they are different.

File I/O and Streams

OVERVIEW

In the programs that you have written so far, you have entered data interactively from the keyboard and displayed output on the screen. In this lab, you learn how to read input from a file and output results to a file. You also examine some of the additional functions and manipulators provided in the C++ stream libraries and the `apstring` class.

In Core Exercises 1 and 2, you learn how to read data from an input file and how to write data to an output file. Starting in Core Exercise 2, you also learn how to output to a file in HTML format that can be viewed via a Web browser. In Core Exercise 3, you explore use of the `getline()` function to read in strings with embedded blanks. In Core Exercise 4, you use the `setw`, `setprecision`, and `setiosflags` stream manipulators to give you more control over how output—particularly, numeric output—is displayed.

LABORATORY 5: Cover Sheet

Name _____

Hour/Period/Section _____

Date _____

Place a check mark (✔) in the Assigned column next to the exercises that your instructor has assigned to you. Have this sheet ready when your lab instructor checks your work. If your exercises are being checked outside the laboratory session, attach this sheet to the front of the packet of materials that you submit.

Exercise		Assigned	Completed
Core 1	File Input *Imagine That (image.cpp)*		
Core 2	File Output *Alphabet Soup (alpha.cpp)*		
Core 3	`getline()` *What's My Line? (comic.cpp)*		
Core 4	Output Manipulators *Sights and Sounds (thunder.cpp)*		
Reinforcement	File I/O Without `cin` and `cout` *A Cut Above (honors.cpp)*		
Analysis	Analyzing Stream Processing		
Total			

LABORATORY 5: Core Exercise 1—File Input

Background

So far, your programs have used the `cin` stream to read data from the keyboard and the `cout` stream to display output to the screen. Many programs, however, require large amounts of input data and produce results that need to be recorded for future reference—either by you or by another program. For these applications, you need to be able to read data from a file and output data to file. C++ provides support for file input/output in the *fstream.h* library.

You read data from a file using an **input file stream** (or `ifstream`). The following statement declares an input file stream object named `inFile`, which is just like declaring a variable.

```
ifstream inFile;
```

After declaring the input file stream object, you must open the file. The following statement opens the file *values.dat* for input by associating it with an input file stream object named `inFile`.

```
inFile.open("values.dat");
```

You deal with possible file opening errors in Laboratory 7. For now assume that the input file exists and contains the appropriate type and number of input values.

You read data from the file by applying the extraction operator (`>>`) to the input file stream `inFile`. The code fragment

```
ifstream inFile;
int num1;
inFile.open("values.dat");
inFile >> num1;
```

reads an integer value from the input file *values.dat* and stores it in `num1`. Note the similarity of this process to reading data from the `cin` input stream. The following program, found in *fileio1.cpp*, reads three real values from the file *values1.dat* and displays their average on the screen.

```
// Reads three real values from the file values1.dat and displays
// their average on the screen.

#include <iostream.h>   // For cin, cout
#include <fstream.h>    // For file input/output

int main()
{
    ifstream inFile;              // Declare the input file stream object
    double num1, num2, num3,      // Numbers read from file
           avg;                   // Average of numbers read in
    inFile.open("values1.dat");   // Open input file

    // Read in numbers and compute their average.
    inFile >> num1 >> num2 >> num3;
    avg = (num1 + num2 + num3) / 3.0;
```

```
    // Output the average.
    cout << "Average = " << avg << endl;

    // Close the input file stream.
    inFile.close();

    return 0;
}
```

When the input process is complete, close the input file stream (and the associated file), using the `close()` function. Note that the header file *fstream.h* must be included in any program that uses input/output file streams.

The input file *values1.dat* used in the preceding example must exist in the same directory as the C++ program *fileio1.cpp*. You can open and edit it by using most development environments, Microsoft Windows Notepad™, or similar means. Currently the file contains the following data in the format shown.

```
5.0 10.0 13.0
```

You don't need to enter all three real numbers on the same line in the input file *values1.dat*. As when you're reading data with the `cin>>` input stream, you need to separate input data with white space (spaces, tabs, and newline markers). Edit the file *values1.dat* and change the format to

```
5.0
10.0    13.0
```

Rerun *fileio1.cpp* and verify that the result is the same.

Warmup Exercise

Complete the following program by filling in the missing C++ code. A shell for this program is given in the file *sales1.shl*.

```
// Reads commission rate and sale amount for an employee from a file
// and outputs the sales commission to the screen.

#include <iostream.h>
#include <fstream.h>    // For file input

int main()
{
    ifstream salesData;        // Declare the input file stream object
    double saleAmount,         // Individual sale
           commissionRate,     // Commission rate
           commission;         // Employee commission

    // Open the file sales1.dat and associate it with an input file
    // stream named salesData.
    _____;

    // Read in the commission rate and sale amount.
    _____;
```

```
// Calculate the employee's sales commission.
commission = commissionRate * saleAmount;

// Output the commission to the screen.
_____ << "Commission: $" << commission << endl;

// Close the input file.
salesData.close();

return 0;
}
```

APPLICATION EXERCISE: Imagine That

You can save a picture in any of the many different image formats available. The bit mapped picture format (BMP) offers no compression, the graphic image file format (GIF) uses a compression technique that basically works by removing redundancies in information in the image, and the Joint Photographic Experts Group format (JPG) is optimized for speed, not necessarily quality. JPG compresses the picture by removing information to reduce file size.

Web designers must take into account the trade-offs between image quality and image size for pictures displayed on a web site. Three image properties contribute to how the image looks on the screen and how much storage space it requires.

1. Bit depth—The number of bits used to store color, intensity, and the like for each pixel on the screen.

2. Total number of pixels—Width in pixels times height in pixels (area of an image).

3. Compression Factor—BMP image files have a compression factor of 1 (no compression), GIF image files, on average, have a compression factor of about 0.4, and you can choose JPG image file compression factors of 0.14 (highest quality, least compression) to 0.01 (lowest quality, most compression). These compression factors are estimates.

A simple formula to estimate the size of an image file is

$$\text{size of file in kilobytes} = \frac{\text{width} \cdot \text{height} \cdot \text{bit depth}}{8{,}192} \cdot \text{compression factor.}$$

(With 8 bits in a byte and $2^{10} = 1{,}024$ bytes in a kilobyte, there are 8,192 bits in a kilobyte.)

 See the "Engaged Learning for Programming in C++" link on **http://www.jbpub.com/cs** for links to more information on image formats.

Look at the following sample image files and compare their quality and file size.

  Image_01bit_nocompress.bmp—1 bit black/white BMP; no compression; width = 320, height = 240
  Image_08bit_nocompress.bmp—8 bit BMP; no compression; width = 320, height = 240
  Image_24bit_nocompress.bmp—24 bit BMP; no compression; width = 320, height = 240
  Image_08bit_0.4compress.gif—8 bit GIF; compression factor = 0.4; width = 320, height = 240
  Image_24bit_0.01compress.jpg—24 bit JPG; compression factor = 0.01; width = 320, height = 240
  Image_24bit_0.04compress.jpg—24 bit JPG; compression factor = 0.04; width = 320, height = 240
  Image_24bit_0.14compress.jpg—24 bit JPG; compression factor = 0.14; width = 320, height = 240

Step 1: Create a program that reads in an image format (BMP, GIF, or JPG) as an `apstring`, an image pixel width and pixel height as integers, a bit depth as an integer, and a compression factor as a floating-point number from an input file. Then calculate the size of the file in kilobytes with an appropriate message. Use a constant for bits in a kilobyte (8,192). Assume that the input file contains valid data for the image format, image height and width, bit depth, and compression factor.

  Input: Image format, image width and height, bit depth, and compression factor from an input file (*image.dat*)

  Output: The size of the file in kilobytes, with an appropriate message

Step 2: Save your program as *image.cpp*.

Step 3: Complete the following test plan.

Test Plan for *image*

Test case	Sample data	Expected result	Checked
Image_08bit_nocompress.bmp	image.dat	Image width = 320, image height = 240 Compression factor = 1 BMP 8-bit image file size = 75 KB	

Step 4: Execute your program in the file *image.cpp*.

Step 5: Check each case in your *image* test plan and verify the expected result. If you discover mistakes in your program, correct them and execute the test plan again.

LABORATORY 5: Core Exercise 2—File Output

Background

Once you have seen how file input works, file output seems obvious. You write data to a file using an **output file stream** (or `ofstream`). The following statement declares an output file stream object named `outFile`.

```
ofstream outFile;
```

After declaring the output file stream object, you must open the file. The following statement opens the file *results.out* for output by associating it with an output file stream object named `outFile`.

```
outFile.open("results.out");
```

The output file *results.out* will exist in the same directory as the C++ program that opens it. You write data to the file by applying the insertion operator (`<<`) to output file stream `outFile`, as in

```
outFile << "The sum is " << sum << endl;
```

When the output process is complete, close the output file stream (and the associated file), using the `outFile.close()` function call. Note that the header file *fstream.h* must be included in any program that uses input/output file streams.

If you run the program a second time, the output stream file is reopened at the beginning of the file, all current data in the output file are erased, and new results are written to the file.

Warmup Exercise

Complete the following program by filling in the missing C++ code. A shell for this program is given in the file *sales2.shl*.

```cpp
// Reads sales data for an employee for 5 days from a file and outputs the
// employee's total sales and sales commission to a file.

#include <iostream.h>
#include <fstream.h>     // For file input/output

int main()
{
    ifstream salesData;        // Input file of sales data
    ofstream commOut;          // Output file of commissions

    double sales1, sales2, sales3, sales4, sales5,    // Daily sales
           totalSales = 0.0,                          // Total sales
           commissionRate,                            // Commission rate
           commission;                                // Commission

    // Read in the commission rate from the keyboard.
    cout << "Enter the commission rate (as a % of 1.0): ";
    cin >> commissionRate;
```

```
// Open the file sales2.dat and associate it with an input file
// stream named salesData.
_____;

// Read in 5 days sales numbers.
_____;

// Calculate the employee's total sales and sales commission.
totalSales = sales1 + sales2 + sales3 + sales4 + sales5;
commission = commissionRate * totalSales;

// Open the file commiss.out and associate it with an output
// file stream named commOut.
_____;

// Output the total sales and the commission to commiss.out.
_____ << "Total sales: $" << totalSales << endl
         << "Commission: $" << commission << endl;

// Close the input file.
_____;

// Close the output file.
_____;

   return 0;
}
```

One of the advantages of using an output file is that you can save the results from running your program and view them at any time in the future. A second advantage is the ability to output text to a file in a particular format—for example, in HyperText Markup Language (HTML). By outputting basic text in HTML syntax, you can create output files that, when viewed via an HTML browser, contain different fonts, colors, layouts, and images, such as the following.

Chicago

The HTML necessary to create the document containing the image *chicago.jpg* and caption Chicago is fairly simple.

```
<html><body>
<img src=chicago.jpg><br>
<h2>Chicago</h2>
</body></html>
```

The `<br>` tag is an HTML carriage return.

 See the "Engaged Learning for Programming in C++" link on **http://www.jbpub.com/cs** for links to more information on HTML syntax.

Suppose that the name of the image *chicago.jpg* is stored in an `apstring` object such as `imageFilename`. We need to write C++ code to write output (the HTML code just shown) to a file named *caption.html*. Complete the following program by filling in the missing C++ code. A shell for this program is given in the file *caption.shl*.

```
// Asks the user for an image filename.
// Opens a file and writes HTML code to display a picture and a caption.

#include <iostream.h>
#include <fstream.h>      // For file input/output
#include <apstring.h>     // For image filename
#include <apstring.cpp>   // For image filename

int main ()
{
    _____ HTMLfile;                  // Output file of HTML with image
    apstring _____;            // Input image filename

    // Opens the file caption.html for output
    // HTMLfile is output stream name
    _____.open("caption.html");

    // Read in the image filename from the keyboard.
    cout << "Enter the image filename: ";
    cin >> imageFilename;

    // Write the HTML code out to the HTMLfile.
    _____ << "<html><body>" << endl;
    _____ << _____ << endl;
    _____ << "<h2>Chicago</h2>" << endl;
    _____ << "</body></html>" << endl;
    HTMLfile.close();           // Close the file caption.html

    return 0;
}
```

APPLICATION EXERCISE: Alphabet Soup

To make the HTML image and caption more interesting, you want to be able to enter from the keyboard the name of the image you want to display and some words that you can combine, upon output, into a caption.

Step 1: Create a program that reads in an image filename (something like *apple.jpg* or *blueberry.jpg* or *cantaloupe.jpg* images given), a word describing the image, and the first letter of the word describing the image. We use these three input values (all stored in objects of type `apstring`) to create a caption for the image (something like: A as in apple), and then output the HTML code previously shown to the file *alpha.html*.

> *Input:* An image filename
>
> A word describing the image
>
> The first letter of the word describing the image

> *Output:* An HTML formatted file containing the image and a caption to the file *alpha.html*

Step 2: Save your program as *alpha.cpp*.

Step 3: Complete the following test plan.

Test Plan for *alpha*

Test case	Sample data	Expected result	Checked
apple.jpg image	*apple.jpg* apple A	 `A as in apple`	

Step 4: Execute your program in the file *alpha.cpp*.

Step 5: Check each case in your *alpha* test plan and verify the expected result. If you discover mistakes in your program, correct them and execute the test plan again.

LABORATORY 5: Core Exercise 3—`getline()`

Background

When reading in individual characters, the extraction operator (`>>`) ignores any white space (spaces, tabs, and newline markers) it encounters in an input stream. For instance, the statement

```
char ch1, ch2;
cin >> ch1 >> ch2;
```

reads two characters from the `cin` input stream. Whether the input is

```
ab
```

or

```
a b
```

or

```
a
b
```

the result is the same: `'a'` is assigned to `ch1` and `'b'` is assigned to `ch2`.

White space presents a different problem in terms of reading multiple `apstring`s. The extraction operator (`>>`) treats white space as an `apstring` delimiter. This approach is fine when you're reading in a pair of one-word names or a series of one-word commands. It causes problems, however, when the `apstring` that you're attempting to read in contains spaces—a sentence or a phrase, for instance. Fortunately, C++ provides a function, `getline()`, that reads a sequence of characters—including white space—from an input stream.

The `getline()` function for `apstring` has two parameters:

```
getline ( input file stream, apstring phrase )
```

The first parameter is the input file stream name (`cin` for keyboard input or a previously opened input file stream name for file input). The second parameter is the `apstring` object that will return the characters read from the input stream. The `getline()` function reads characters from the input stream until the newline (`'\n'`) character is encountered.

The following code fragment uses `getline()` to read a sentence from the keyboard.

```
apstring textString;
cout << endl << "Enter a sentence: " << endl;
getline(cin, textString);
```

For example, the input sentence

```
Hi there!
```

produces `textString = "Hi there!"`.

In this case, the `getline()` function stopped reading characters when it encountered the new-line marker.

When using `getline()` to read from an input file, you must be careful to avoid extra blank lines in the input file, especially blank lines at the end of the input file. Whereas blank lines are ignored when using the extraction operator (`>>`), `getline()` actually reads them and the result is an empty `apstring`.

Warmup Exercise

A file list often includes each filename, followed on the next line by a short description of the file's contents or purpose. Note that the name and description are separated by exactly one newline character. Microsoft Windows 95™ and most operating systems allow filenames to have blank spaces within the filename. Therefore you shouldn't use `cin >>` to read an `apstring` filename such as

```
my file.cpp
Driver program for the project
```

Complete the following program by filling in the missing C++ code. A shell for this program is given in the file *filelist.shl*.

```
// Reads in a file name followed by a short description of the file's
// contents.

#include <iostream.h>
#include <apstring.h>
#include <apstring.cpp>

int main ()
{
    apstring filename,          // User input file name
             description;       // User input description of file

    cout << "Enter a filename:" << endl;

    // Read in the name of the file using getline.
    _____;

    cout << "Enter a description of its contents:" << endl;

    // Read in the description of the file using getline.
    _____;

    cout << endl << "File: " << filename << endl
         << "Description: " << description << endl;

    return 0;
}
```

APPLICATION EXERCISE: What's My Line?

Step 1: Create a program that asks a user to input an image filename (something like the *golfer.jpg* or *swimmer.jpg* or *umpire.jpg* images given) and then asks the user for two funny captions for the image. Use `getline()` to read the image filename and each caption. Remember that you need to hit the Enter key between each input value. Finally, output HTML code for the image twice—once with each caption—to the file *comic.html*.

Input: An image filename

Two funny captions to display with the image

Output: An HTML formatted file (*comic.html*) containing the image and caption1 and the image again with caption2

Step 2: Save your program as *comic.cpp*.

Step 3: Complete the following test plan.

Test Plan for *comic*

Test case	Sample data	Expected result	Checked

swimmer.jpg	*swimmer.jpg*
	I'm Superman!
	Just wait til I get in the water
		
		`I'm Superman!`
		
		`Just wait til I get in the water.`	

Step 4: Execute your program in the file *comic.cpp*.

Step 5: Check each case in your *comic* test plan and verify the expected result. If you discover mistakes in your program, correct them and execute the test plan again.

LABORATORY 5: Core Exercise 4—Output Manipulators

Background

The C++ `cout` output stream uses a group of settings to specify how data are to be displayed by the output stream insertion operator (`<<`). You can change these settings by using the output stream **input/output manipulators** declared in the file *iomanip.h* and thus control the way in which your output is formatted.

Let's begin by examining the following program from the file *car1.cpp*.

```
// Calculates the total cost of a car purchase and displays the result.

#include <iostream.h>        // For cin, cout
#include <iomanip.h>         // For output manipulators

int main()
{
    int modelNum;            // Four-digit model number
    double basePrice,        // Base price of car
           taxRate,          // Tax rate
           finalPrice;       // Total cost of the car

    // Prompt the user for the car purchase data.
    cout << endl << "Enter the car's 4-digit model number: ";
    cin >> modelNum;
    cout << "Enter the car's base price: ";
    cin >> basePrice;
    cout << "Enter the tax rate (as a % of 1.0): ";
    cin >> taxRate;

    // Calculate the total cost of the purchase.
    finalPrice = basePrice * (1 + taxRate);

    // Output the model number and the purchase price (w/ headings).
    cout << endl << "Model #    Final Price" << endl;
    cout << modelNum << "     " << finalPrice << endl;

    return 0;
}
```

The output produced by a sample run of this program is

```
Enter the car's 4-digit model number: 1234
Enter the car's base price: 9995.95
Enter the tax rate (as a % of 1.0): 0.07

Model #    Final Price
1234     10695.7
```

This output suffers from several defects. Not only are the columns not properly aligned, but also the final price is rounded to one decimal place, rather than two—the final price should read

`10695.67`. Things get even uglier if we try to price a very expensive car—a million-dollar antique, for instance.

```
Enter the car's 4-digit model number: 1234
Enter the car's base price: 1000000
Enter the tax rate (as a % of 1.0): 0.07

Model #    Final Price
1234    1.07e+06
```

Now not only are the columns out of alignment, but the price is displayed in scientific notation rather than the fixed-point form that most people are accustomed to using.

To solve the alignment problem, use the `setw` manipulator to specify the **field width** for the next output value—that is, the number of columns (character positions) reserved for displaying the value. Replacing the last `cout` statement in *car1.cpp* with

```
cout << setw(7) << modelNum << "    "
     << setw(11) << finalPrice << endl;
```

sets the field width for `modelNum` to 7 and the field width for `finalPrice` to 11. The values 7 and 11 are based on the lengths of the headings `"Model #"` and `"Final Price"`, respectively. The resulting output is

```
Enter the car's 4-digit model number: 1234
Enter the car's base price: 9995.95
Enter the tax rate (as a % of 1.0): 0.07

Model #    Final Price
   1234        10695.7
```

Note that each output value is right-justified within its field. Note also that `setw` changes only the field width for the next value output to `cout`. After the value is output, the field width reverts to its default value and must be set again.

To display the final price in the form wanted, use the `setprecision` manipulator to specify the number of digits that should be displayed to the right of the decimal point. The call

```
setprecision(2)
```

indicates that all subsequent floating-point values should be output with two digits to the right of the decimal point. Use the `setiosflags` manipulator to specify the **formatting flags** (settings) that further control the output of floating-points values. The call

```
setiosflags( ios::fixed | ios::showpoint )
```

specifies that all subsequent floating-point values are to be displayed in fixed-point form (`ios::fixed`) and forces display of the decimal point and any trailing zeros (`ios::showpoint`)—even if a floating-point value is a whole number. Note that, unlike `setw`, the settings specified by the `setprecision` and `setiosflags` manipulators remain in effect until they are explicitly changed by another call to `setprecision` or `setiosflags`.

Replacing the last cout statement in *car1.cpp* with

```
cout << setprecision(2)
     << setiosflags( ios::fixed | ios::showpoint )
     << setw(7) << modelNum << "      "
     << setw(11) << finalPrice << endl;
```

produces the following sets of output for base prices of 9,995.95

```
Enter the car's 4-digit model number: 1234
Enter the car's base price: 9995.95
Enter the tax rate (as a % of 1.0): 0.07

Model #     Final Price
   1234         10695.67
```

and 1,000,000, respectively.

```
Enter the car's 4-digit model number: 1234
Enter the car's base price: 1000000
Enter the tax rate (as a % of 1.0): 0.07

Model #     Final Price
   1234       1070000.00
```

The updated version of *car1.cpp* is given in the file *car2.cpp*.

Warmup Exercise

Complete the following program by filling in the missing C++ code. A shell for this program is given in the file *sales3.shl*.

```
// Calculates an employee's sales commission and displays the result
// using formatted output.

#include <iostream.h>        // For cin, cout
#include _____         // For output manipulators

int main()
{
    int IDNum;               // Four digit employee ID number
    double totalSales,       // Total sales
           commissionRate,   // Commission rate
           commission;       // Employee's sales commission

    // Prompt the user for the employee data.
    cout << endl << "Enter the employee's four-digit ID number: ";
    cin >> IDNum;
    cout << "Enter the employee's total sales: ";
    cin >> totalSales;
    cout << "Enter the commission rate (as a % of 1.0): ";
    cin >> commissionRate;

    // Calculate the employee's sales commission.
    commission = commissionRate * totalSales;
```

```
        // Output the employee ID and commission earned (w/ headings).



        return 0;
    }
```

APPLICATION EXERCISE: Sights and Sounds

You can make a rough estimate of your distance (in miles) from a lightning strike by counting the number of seconds between when you see the lightning flash and when you hear the thunder clap, and dividing the result by 5. In this exercise, you explore the basis for this estimation technique by comparing the length of time it takes the flash of light from the strike to reach you with the length of time it takes the sound of the thunderclap to reach you.

You can compute the length of time for light to cover a given distance by using the formula

$$\text{time}_\text{light} = \frac{\text{distance}}{\text{speed of light}},$$

where time_light is measured in seconds, distance is measured in miles, and the speed of light is 186,000 mi/sec. Similarly, you can compute the length of time for sound to cover a given distance by using the formula

$$\text{time}_\text{sound} = \frac{\text{distance}}{\text{speed of sound}},$$

where time_sound is measured in seconds, distance is measured in miles, and the speed of sound is 0.206 mi/sec (that is, 1/5 mi/sec).

 See the "Engaged Learning for Programming in C++" link on **http://www.jbpub.com/cs** for links to more information on the speed of light and speed of sound.

Step 1: Create a program that computes the length of time for light and sound to cover a given distance. The time for light should be displayed in scientific notation, and the time for sound should be displayed in fixed-point form with two decimal places to the right of the decimal point.

Input: Distance (in miles)

Output: Columns showing the distance (in miles), the length of time for light to travel this distance, and the length of time for sound to travel this distance (both times in seconds)

Step 2: Save your program as *thunder.cpp*.

Step 3: Complete the following test plan.

Test Plan for *thunder*

Test case	Sample data	Expected result			Checked
One mile	1	Distance (mi)	Time for light (sec)	Time for sound (sec)	
		1	5.376e-06	4.85	
Eleven miles	11	Distance (mi)	Time for light (sec)	Time for sound (sec)	
		11	5.914e-05	53.40	

Step 4: Execute your program in the file *thunder.cpp*.

Step 5: Check each case in your *thunder* test plan and verify the expected result. If you discover mistakes in your program, correct them and execute the test plan again.

LABORATORY 5: Reinforcement Exercise—File I/O Without `cin` and `cout`

A Cut Above

At Watsamata U., the magna cum laude, summa cum laude, and cum laude honors recognize graduating students who have completed at least the 120 credit hours needed to graduate *and* have achieved at least a 3.0 grade point average (GPA).

Honor	*Minimum GPA*
Magna cum laude	3.75
Summa cum laude	3.5
Cum laude	3.0

GPA is calculated by using the formula

$$GPA = \frac{4 \cdot A \text{ credit hours} + 3 \cdot B \text{ credit hours} + 2 \cdot C \text{ credit hours} + 1 \cdot D \text{ credit hours}}{\text{credit hours taken}}$$

where A credit hours is the number of credit hours for which the student received an A, B credit hours is the number of credit hours for which the student has received a B, and so on, and credit hours taken is calculated by summing the credit hours for all classes the student has taken.

Step 1: Write a program that will read a file (*student.dat*) containing one student transcript and determine whether the student has graduated and then, if so, whether the student made honors. (In reality, the file probably would contain many student grade records, but you're interested in handling just one for now.) The program should output to a file (*diploma.out*) the student's name, total number of credit hours, and GPA, along with a message indicating whether the student has graduated. If the student has graduated, output the appropriate honor.

Input: Student first name (`apstring`)
Student last name (`apstring`)
A credit hours (integer)
B credit hours (integer)
C credit hours (integer)
D credit hours (integer)
F credit hours (integer)

Output: Diploma (if enough credit hours) showing honors, if applicable

Step 2: Save your program as *honors.cpp*.

Step 3: Test your program by using the following the test plan. If you discover mistakes in your program, correct them and execute the test plan again.

Test Plan for *honors*

Test case	Sample data	Expected result	Checked
Robert Smith 90 30 6 3 0 Mary Lamb 100 18 3 0 0 Chrissie Snow 30 70 15 6 3 John Johnson 50 3 3 3 3	student.dat	Robert Smith Credit Hours = 129 GPA = 3.60465 Graduated summa cum laude	

LABORATORY 5: Analysis Exercise

Analyzing Stream Processing

Name _____

Hour/Period/Section _____

Date _____

Part A

The following program from the file *sumscore.cpp* is designed to sum a set of four scores.

```cpp
#include <iostream.h>
#include <fstream.h>

int main ()
{
    ifstream inFile;
    int score1, score2, score3, score4,
        sum = 0;

    inFile.open("scores.dat");

    inFile >> score1 >> score2 >> score3 >> score4;
    sum = score1 + score2 + score3 + score4;

    cout << "The sum is " << sum << endl;

    inFile.close();

    return 0;
}
```

Explain why this program produces an incorrect sum for the scores in the data file *scores.dat*.

Part B

Describe the output produced by the following program from the file *mystery.cpp*. What output do the characters `'\t'`, `'\n'`, and `'\a'` produce?

```cpp
#include <iostream.h>
#include <math.h>
#include <apstring.h>
#include <apstring.cpp>

int main ()
{
    apstring temp;

    cout << "Number\tSquare Root";

    cout << '\n'<< 5 << '\t' << sqrt(5);
    cout << '\n'<< 4 << '\t' << sqrt(4);
    cout << '\n'<< 3 << '\t' << sqrt(3);
    cout << '\n'<< 2 << '\t' << sqrt(2);
    cout << '\n'<< 1 << '\t' << sqrt(1);

    cout << "\nHit <RETURN> to continue\n";
    getline(cin, temp);
    cout << "\a\n";

    return 0;
}
```

LABORATORY 6

Iteration I

OVERVIEW

In Laboratory 4, you altered the sequential execution of a program by using `if` statements to choose between alternative paths through the program. However, additional control structures are needed in order for you to repeat a statement multiple times. These control structures are called **loops**. In this lab, you explore two types of loops: counter-controlled loops and event-controlled loops. A **counter-controlled loop** executes a predetermined number of times. An **event-controlled loop** executes until some event occurs that terminates the loop.

In Core Exercise 1, you use the `while` loop to create counter-controlled loops. In Core Exercise 2, you use `while` loops to develop event-controlled loops. In Core Exercise 3, you create `while` loops that are both counter- and event-controlled. In Core Exercise 4, you use a `for` loop to create a counter-controlled loop.

LABORATORY 6: Cover Sheet

Name _____

Hour/Period/Section _____

Date _____

Place a check mark (✔) in the Assigned column next to the exercises that your instructor has assigned to you. Have this sheet ready when your lab instructor checks your work. If your exercises are being checked outside the laboratory session, attach this sheet to the front of the packet of materials that you submit.

Exercise		Assigned	Completed
Core 1	Counter-Controlled `while` Loops *Hit the Links (index.cpp)*		
Core 2	Event-Controlled `while` Loops *Triskaidekaphobia (stones.cpp)*		
Core 3	Combined Counter- and Event-Controlled Loops *Your Mileage May Vary (oilauto.cpp)*		
Core 4	`for` Loops *Going Up? (balloon.cpp)*		
Reinforcement	Sentinel-Controlled Loops *Statistically Speaking (stats.cpp)*		
Analysis	Analyzing Loops		
Total			

LABORATORY 6: Core Exercise 1—Counter-Controlled `while` **Loops**

Background

In a counter-controlled loop, the number of times that the loop is executed is predetermined. Sometimes the problem itself describes how many times the loop will execute, and sometimes data that you input will determine how many times the loop will execute. Either way, the number of times the loop will execute is predetermined before the loop is entered. In the following program from the file *evens.cpp* the `while` loop counts from 1 to 50 by 1s.

```cpp
// Displays the first 50 positive even integers five to a line.

#include <iostream.h>

const int MAX_COUNT = 50;      // Loop termination constant

int main()
{
    int count = 1,               // Loop control index initialized to 1
        evenNumber;              // Calculated even number for output

    // Execute the loop while count is less than or equal to MAX_COUNT.
    while ( count <= MAX_COUNT )
    {
        evenNumber = count * 2;
        cout << evenNumber << " ";

        // If count is evenly divisible by 5, output a line feed.
        if ( count % 5 == 0 ) cout << endl;

        count++;               // Increment loop control index
    }

    return 0;
}
```

A `while` loop begins by checking whether `count` is less than or equal to `MAX_COUNT`. The initial value of `count` is 1—which is certainly less than `MAX_COUNT`–and the compound statement that forms the body of the loop is executed once. The new value of `count` is then compared with `MAX_COUNT`, and the loop is executed a second time. This process continues until the `while` condition is false—that is, until count is greater than MAX_COUNT—at which point the loop terminates. The output produced by the program is

```
2  4  6  8  10
12  14  16  18  20
22  24  26  28  30
32  34  36  38  40
42  44  46  48  50
52  54  56  58  60
62  64  66  68  70
72  74  76  78  80
82  84  86  88  90
92  94  96  98  100
```

Counter-controlled loops do not have to start counting at 1. Nor do they have to count upward by 1s. Counter-controlled loops can count upward or downward, by integer or real number increments, and into negative numbers. In the following program (*odds.cpp*), for instance, the while loop counts from 9 to −9 by negative 2s.

```cpp
// Displays the odd integers between -9 and 9 in descending order.

#include <iostream.h>

int main()
{
    const int MIN_ODD_NUMBER = -9;   // Loop termination constant
    int oddNumber = 9;               // Loop control index initialized to 9

    // Execute the loop while oddNumber is
    // greater than or equal to MIN_ODD_NUMBER.
    while ( oddNumber >= MIN_ODD_NUMBER )
    {
        cout << oddNumber << " ";
        oddNumber = oddNumber - 2;       // Decrement loop control index
    }

    return 0;
}
```

The output produced by the program is

```
9  7  5  3  1  -1  -3  -5  -7  -9
```

Warmup Exercise

Suppose that when a ball is dropped it bounces from the pavement to a height one-half its previous height. You want to write a program that will simulate the behavior of the ball when it is dropped from a user input height (in meters) for a user input number of bounces. It should display the number of each bounce and the height of that bounce.

Complete the following program by filling in the missing C++ code. A shell for this program is given in the file *bounce.shl*.

```cpp
// Computes the height of each bounce of a ball that bounces to a height
// one-half of the previous bounce height.

#include <iostream.h>
#include <iomanip.h>        // Needed for formatted output, setw()

int main()
{
    double height;              // User input starting height
    int bounceCount=1,         // Loop control index initialized to 1
        maxBounces;            // User input loop termination value

    // Get the starting height and number of bounces.
    cout << "Enter the starting height (in meters): ";
    cin >> height;
    cout << "Enter the max number of bounces: ";
    cin >> maxBounces;

    // Output the column headings for the table.
    cout << "Bounce #     Height(meters)" << endl;

    // Execute the loop for maxBounces number of bounces.
    while ( _____ )
    {
        _____;        // Calculate new bounce height

        // Column formatted output of bounce number and height.
        cout << setw(8) << bounceCount << "       "
             << setw(14) << height << endl;

        bounceCount++;                // Increment loop control index
    }

    return 0;
}
```

APPLICATION EXERCISE: Hit the Links

In Laboratory 5, Core Exercises 2 and 3, you learned how to output HTML formatted files that contain images by using the `<img src=chicago.jpg>` HTML tag. Now you learn how to create links to other HTML files in an HTML file that you create with the HTML link tag

```
<a href=animal1.html>Speak no evil.</a><br>
```

`"Speak no evil."` is a caption for the HTML link and `animal1.html` is the file that the link points to.

 See the "Engaged Learning for Programming in C++" link on **http://www.jbpub.com/cs** for links to more information on HTML syntax.

Step 1: Create a program that asks the user for five `apstring` captions—one at a time, using a counter-controlled `while` loop—that each describe one of the five HTML files provided (*animal1.html*, *animal2.html*, *animal3.html*, *animal4.html*, and *animal5.html*). Create an HTML formatted output file (*index.html*) that contains the five captions and HTML links.

> *Input:* Five `apstring` captions, each read from the user with `getline()`
>
> *Output:* An HTML formatted file (*index.html*) containing five captions and links

Step 2: Save your program as *index.cpp*.

Step 3: Complete the following test plan.

Test Plan for *index*

Test case	Sample data	Expected result	Checked
Our captions	Speak no evil. The winner, by a neck! Polly wants a cracker. I think we go that way. Slow and steady.	Speak no evil. The winner, by a neck! Polly wants a cracker. I think we go that way. Slow and steady.	
Your own captions			
A friend's captions			

Step 4: Execute your program in the file *index.cpp*.

Step 5: Check each case in your *index* test plan and verify the expected result. If you discover mistakes in your program, correct them and execute the test plan again.

LABORATORY 6: Core Exercise 2—Event-Controlled `while` Loops

Background

In an event-controlled loop, the number of times that the loop is executed is not predetermined. Instead, termination of the loop is triggered by the occurrence of some event. In the following program from the file *cubes.cpp*, for instance, the loop terminates when the cube of an integer exceeds the value MAX_CUBE.

```cpp
// Displays a table of positive integers and their cubes.

#include <iostream.h>
#include <iomanip.h>

int main()
{
    const int MAX_CUBE = 99; // Loop termination constant
    int num = 1,             // Number counter initialized to 1
        numCubed = 1;        // Calculated cube of number initialized to 1

    // Output column headings.
    cout << endl << "Number  Cube" << endl;

    // Execute the loop while numCubed does not exceed MAX_CUBE.
    while ( numCubed <= MAX_CUBE )
    {
        // Output number and cube of number.
        cout << setw(6) << num << "   " << setw(4) << numCubed << endl;

        num++;                      // Increment number
        numCubed = num * num * num;    // Calculate cube of number
    }

    return 0;
}
```

The `while` loop begins by checking whether numCubed is less than or equal to MAX_CUBE. The initial value of numCubed is 1—which is certainly less than MAX_CUBE—and the compound statement that forms the body of the loop is executed once. The new value of numCubed is then compared with MAX_CUBE, and the loop is executed a second time. This process continues until the `while` condition is false—that is, until numCubed is greater than MAX_CUBE—at which point the loop terminates. The output produced by the program is

```
Number  Cube
     1     1
     2     8
     3    27
     4    64
```

When the conditions that terminate a loop's execution become complicated, you may want to use a Boolean flag to control loop execution. You create a flag by using a bool (a standard C++ data type) variable in which you store one of two values: false or true. The following program from the file *dataflag.cpp* uses a Boolean flag to indicate that the user has entered a number outside the acceptable range of values.

```
// Demonstrates use of a Boolean flag and summation within loop.

#include <iostream.h>

int main()
{
    bool validData = true;    // Boolean flag, true while data in range
    int num,                  // Input value
        count = 0;            // Number of input values
    double sum = 0.0;         // Sum of input values

    cout << endl;
    cout << "Enter numbers between 0 and 100 (out of range to stop):"
         << endl;

    // Loop until the input is value out of range.
    while ( validData )
    {
        cin >> num;

        // Check to see if data entered is valid.
        if ( num >= 0  &&  num <= 100 )
        {
            sum = sum + num;
            count++;
        }
        else
            validData = false;
    }
    cout << "Average is " << sum / count << endl;

    return 0;
}
```

The bool variable validData is initialized to true in its declaration, which guarantees that the loop will be executed at least once. So long as you enter data in the range 0 to 100, the loop's conditional expression remains true and the loop is executed. The flag validData is set to false when you enter an out-of-range value. The loop's conditional expression then evaluates to false, and execution transfers to the statement following the loop. The following is a sample run.

```
Enter numbers between 0 and 100 (out of range to stop):
50 95 77 -1
Average is 74
```

Also, note in the preceding program the use of `sum=sum+num;` within the `while` loop to sum the valid numbers entered. We also count the number of valid numbers input with `count++;` within the `while` loop.

Warmup Exercise

Computer guessing games often require an event-controlled loop. In the game Guess My Letter, a player guesses a letter "chosen" by the computer. In the versions you complete for this exercise, the game ends when the player correctly guesses the capital letter chosen by the computer.

Complete the following program by filling in the missing C++ code. A shell for this program is given in the file *gueslet1.shl*.

```cpp
// Letter guessing game (version 1).

#include<iostream.h>

int main()
{
    const char COMP_LET = 'M';   // Letter chosen by computer.

    char playerGuess;                // Player's guess

    cout << endl << "I am thinking of a CAPITAL letter..." << endl;
    cout << "What is your guess? ";
    cin >> playerGuess;

    // Loop until the user guesses the correct letter.
    while ( _____ )
    {
        if ( playerGuess > COMP_LET )
            cout << "Your guess is too high" << endl;
        else
            cout << "Your guess is too low" << endl;
        cout << "What is your guess? ";
        cin >> playerGuess;
    }

    cout << "Congratulations, you guessed my letter. "  << endl;

    return 0;
}
```

In the next version of the game, a Boolean flag is used for the loop condition. Complete the following program by filling in the missing C++ code. A shell for this program is given in the file *gueslet2.shl*.

```cpp
// Letter guessing game (version 2).

#include <iostream.h>

int main()
{
    const char COMP_LET = 'M';   // Letter chosen by computer

    bool guessed = _____;      // Boolean flag for game over
                                 // Initially letter is not guessed
    char playerGuess;            // Player's guess

    cout << endl << "I am thinking of a CAPITAL letter..." << endl;

    // Loop until the user guesses the correct letter.
    while ( _____ )
    {
        cout << "What is your guess? ";
        cin >> playerGuess;
        if ( playerGuess > COMP_LET )
            cout << "Your guess is too high" << endl;
        else if ( playerGuess < COMP_LET )
            cout << "Your guess is too low" << endl;
        else
            guessed = _____;    // Letter correctly guessed
    }

    cout << "Congratulations, you guessed my letter. "  << endl;

    return 0;
}
```

APPLICATION EXERCISE: Triskaidekaphobia

In this exercise you simulate the game of Thirteen Stones. In this game, two players alternate taking 1, 2, or 3 stones from a pile of 13 stones until no stones are left. The last player to pick up a stone is the winner.

Step 1: Create a program that simulates the Thirteen Stones game. Base your program on the program shell given in the file *stones.shl*. Your program should alternately ask the players to select the number of stones they want to remove from the pile. If a player enters an invalid number of stones, the program should display an error message and ask the player to select again. If the selection is valid, the selected number of stones should be removed from the pile.

Continue play until no stones are left and display a message indicating the winner (the last player to pick up a stone).

    Input: Number of stones (1, 2, or 3) chosen on a given turn

    Output: A message declaring the winner

Step 2:   Save your program as *stones.cpp*.

Step 3:   Complete the following test plan.

Test Plan for *stones*

Test case	Sample data	Expected result	Checked
Player 1 takes the last stone	3 1 2 2 1 3 1	Player 1 wins!	
Player 2 takes the last stone		Player 2 wins!	
Player 2 makes an illegal selection	1 3 2 4 1 3 3		

Step 4:   Execute your program in the file *stones.cpp*.

Step 5:   Check each case in your *stones* test plan and verify the expected result. If you discover mistakes in your program, correct them and execute the test plan again.

LABORATORY 6: Core Exercise 3—Combined Counter- and Event-Controlled Loops

Background

The conditional expression controlling a loop often monitors both a counter and an event. In this case, loop execution continues until the counter reaches some limit or until some event triggers loop termination. The following program from the file *words.cpp* includes an example of a combined counter- and event-controlled loop.

```
// Echoes a sequence of characters until a ! is encountered or the
// the number of characters output reaches MAX_COUNT.

#include <iostream.h>

const int MAX_COUNT = 10;          // Counter loop termination constant
const char STOP_CHARACTER = '!';   // Event loop termination constant

int main()
{
    char ch;                       // User input character
    int count = 1;                 // Loop control index initialized to 1

    // Ask the user for characters and read the first one.
    cout << "Enter a sequence of characters, then press enter:" << endl;
    cin >> ch;

    // Loop until MAX_COUNT characters read or STOP_CHARACTER is read.
    while ( count <= MAX_COUNT  &&  ch != STOP_CHARACTER )
    {
        cout << ch;
        count++;
        cin >> ch;
    }

    return 0;
}
```

This loop terminates whenever the number of characters exceeds MAX_COUNT, as in

```
Enter a sequence of characters:
12345678901
1234567890
```

or whenever the character '!' is read in, as in

```
Enter a sequence of characters:
Flag! test
Flag
```

Warmup Exercise

The computer letter guessing game that you developed in the Warmup Exercise of Core Exercise 2 never terminated if the user was unable to guess the letter—if the user kept guessing 'A', for example. In this exercise, you restrict the number of guesses that the user can make.

Complete the following program by filling in the missing C++ code. A shell for this program is given in the file *gueslet3.shl*.

```cpp
// Letter guessing game (version 3).

#include<iostream.h>

const char COMP_LET = 'M';     // Letter chosen by computer
const int MAX_GUESSES = 5;     // Max guesses allowed

int main()
{
    int numGuesses = ____; // Loop control index of player guesses
    bool guessed = _____; // Boolean flag for letter guessed,
                           // initially letter is not guessed
    char playerGuess;          // Player guess

    cout << endl << "I am thinking of a CAPITAL letter..." << endl;

    // Loop until the user guesses the correct letter or the number
    // of guesses reaches the maximum number allowed.
    while ( _____ )
    {
        cout << "What is your guess? ";
        cin >> playerGuess;
        numGuesses++;
        if (playerGuess > COMP_LET)
            cout << "Your guess is too high" << endl;
        else if (playerGuess < COMP_LET)
            cout << "Your guess is too low" << endl;
        else
            guessed = true;
    }

    // Check if letter was correctly guessed.
    if ( _____ )
      cout << "Congratulations, you guessed my letter in "
            << numGuesses << " guess(es)";
    else
      cout << "Sorry, you lose. The letter was " << COMP_LET << ".";
    cout << endl;

    return 0;
}
```

APPLICATION EXERCISE: Your Mileage May Vary

Automobile mechanics recommend that you change your oil every 3 mo., or when you have driven 3,000 mil since your last oil change, whichever occurs first (both reasons may occur at the same time). In this exercise, you create a program that determines when an oil change is needed and tells the user the reason for the needed oil change, based on the 3 mo./3,000 mi guideline.

Step 1: Create a program that determines when an oil change is needed. Your program should prompt for the odometer reading at the last oil change and then prompt for a series of month-by-month odometer readings. This process should continue until your program detects that an oil change is needed, based on the 3 mo/3,000 mi standard, at which point the process should terminate and an explanation of why the oil change is needed should be displayed.

> *Input:*   Odometer reading at last oil change
>
>   Month-by-month odometer readings
>
> *Output:*   A message explaining why the oil change is needed

Step 2: Save your program as *oilauto.cpp*.

Step 3: Complete the following test plan.

Test Plan for *oilauto.cpp*

Test case	Sample data	Expected result	Checked

Car driven at least 3,000 mi since last oil change
 	
Three months have passed since last oil change
	15000
	16500
	18250
		`Oil change needed--you have`
		`driven 3,250 mi since your last`
		`oil change.`	

Step 4: Execute your program in the file *oilauto.cpp*.

Step 5: Check each case in your *oilauto* test plan and verify the expected result. If you discover mistakes in your program, correct them and execute the test plan again.

LABORATORY 6: Core Exercise 4—for Loops

Background

A for loop executes a set of statements a fixed number of times. You typically use a for loop when you know in advance how many times you want to execute these statements. The following program from the file *for1.cpp* uses a for loop to control the size of a table of integers and their squares.

```cpp
// Displays a table of integers and their squares.

#include <iostream.h>

int main()
{
    int j;    // Loop control index

    // Display the headings for the table.
    cout << endl << "j" << "     Square" << endl;

    // Displays the squares for the positive integers that
    // are less than or equal to five.
    for ( j = 1; j <= 5; j++ )
       cout << j << "     " << j * j << endl;

    return 0;
}
```

The for statement begins by initializing the loop control variable j to 1. It then evaluates the test expression j<=5 for this value of j. The expression 1<=5 evaluates to true, so the cout statement that forms the **loop body** is executed once, outputting a line containing 1 and its square (also 1). The expression j++ completes the first pass through the loop by incrementing j by 1. A new pass begins by reevaluating the test expression j<=5 for the new value of j. The test expression is still true, and the loop body is executed again. This process is repeated until the value of j reaches 6. At this point, the test expression evaluates to false and the loop terminates. The output produced by *for1* is

```
j  Square
1    1
2    4
3    9
4    16
5    25
```

You can change *for1* to display only odd positive integers by changing the increment expression.

```cpp
for ( j = 1; j <= 5; j=j+2 )
```

Note that the expression j=j+2 increments j by 2 each time the loop is executed.

You can use the decrement operator in a `for` statement to cause the loop control variable to "count down" from an initial value. The following program from the file *for2.cpp* uses a `for` loop to display a list of positive integers in descending order.

```cpp
// "Counts down" to liftoff using a for loop.

#include <iostream.h>

int main()
{
    int j,          // Loop control index
        length;     // Length of countdown (in seconds)

    cout << endl << "Enter the length of the countdown (in secs): ";
    cin >> length;
    cout << "Countdown to liftoff: ";

    for ( j = length; j > 0; j-- )
        cout << j << " ";
    cout << endl << "***** Blast off! *****" << endl;

    return 0;
}
```

The expression `j--` decrements the value of `j` by 1 each time the loop is executed. Execution of the loop continues until the value of `j` is 0. The following is a sample execution of *for2*.

```
Enter the length of the countdown (in seconds): 10
Countdown to liftoff: 10 9 8 7 6 5 4 3 2 1
***** Blast off! *****
```

Another programming task, which is demonstrated in the program in the file *for3.cpp*, is to keep track of a maximum or minimum value among a series of values input or calculated within a loop.

```cpp
// Finds maximum value of 5 positive integers input by user.

#include <iostream.h>

int main()
{
    int j,          // Loop control index
        num,        // User input integer
        maximum=0;  // Variable to store maximum positive integer
                    // initialized to smallest positive integer 0

    for ( j = 1; j <= 5; j++ )
    {
        cout << "Enter a positive integer: ";
        cin >> num;
```

```
            // If the new num is larger than maximum
            // then store the new maximum
            if ( num > maximum )
                maximum = num;
        }
        cout << "Maximum integer = " << maximum;

        return 0;
    }
```

A sample execution of *for3* is shown below.

```
Enter a positive integer: 4
Enter a positive integer: 2
Enter a positive integer: 8
Enter a positive integer: 4
Enter a positive integer: 1
Maximum integer = 8
```

Warmup Exercise

A depreciation schedule is an accounting tool used to "write-off" the loss in value of something because of its regular use. A 7-yr, straight-line depreciation schedule means that each year (for 7 yrs) you deduct the same amount from the previous years value until the value is 0.

We are going to write a program to compute and output the 7-yr, straight-line depreciation schedule for a piece of computer hardware.

Assume that the user will input an integer initial purchase price for the computer hardware (between $1,000 and $50,000, and that you are going to depreciate integer values every year. Because the purchase price input by the user may not be evenly divisible by 7, you must deduct the nearest integer whole number the first 6 yr, and make up the remainder the final year.

Complete the following program by filling in the missing C++ code. A shell for this program is given in the file *deprecia.shl*.

```
// Computes a seven year depreciation table.

#include <iostream.h>
#include <iomanip.h>

int main()
{
    long purchasePrice;        // User input purchase price
    int yearlyDepreciation,    // Calculated 1/7 of purchase price
        endOfYearValue,        // Calculated value at the end of each year
        year;                  // Loop control index

    // Get user input initial purchase price.
    cout << "Enter the purchase price: ";
    cin >> purchasePrice;
    cout << endl << "Year Depreciation End-of-Year-Value" << endl;
```

```
    yearlyDepreciation = _____;
    endOfYearValue = purchasePrice;

    // Loop yearly for number of depreciation years.
    for (_____ )
    {
        // If the last year, depreciate the remaining value.
        if ( _____ )
            yearlyDepreciation = endOfYearValue;

        // Calculate the new end of year value.
        endOfYearValue = endOfYearValue - yearlyDepreciation;

        // Output year, value depreciated, and end of year value.
        cout << setw(4) << year << " "
             << setw(12) << yearlyDepreciation << " "
             << setw(17) << endOfYearValue << endl;
    }

    return 0;
}
```

APPLICATION EXERCISE: Going Up?

Weather balloons are used to gather temperature and pressure data at various altitudes in the atmosphere. Suppose that the following polynomial represents an estimate of the altitude (in meters) or height of a weather balloon in meters at any time t during the first 48 hr following launch of the balloon:

$$altitude(t) = -0.12t^4 + 12t^3 - 380t^2 + 4100t + 2200.$$

The units of t are in hours. The corresponding polynomial estimate for the velocity in meters per hour of the balloon is

$$velocity(t) = -0.48t^3 + 36t^2 - 760t + 4100.$$

Output a table of values of the altitude and the velocity of this weather balloon, using units of meters and meters/second. Let the user enter the starting time (in hours), the increment in time between the lines on the table (in hours), and the ending time (in hours), where all the time values must be less than 48 hr (you can assume that all three input values are valid). Also find and output the maximum altitude (or height) of the balloon that appears in the table and the corresponding time at which the maximum occurs.

Step 1: Create a program that computes a balloon altitude and velocity table.

Input: Starting time (in hours)

Increment in time between the lines on the table (in hours)

Ending time (in hours)

Output: Table of values of the altitude and the velocity of this weather balloon
Maximum altitude (or height) of the balloon that appears in the table
Corresponding time at which the maximum occurs

Step 2: Save your program as *balloon.cpp*.

Step 3: Complete the following test plan.

Test Plan for *balloon*

Test case	Sample data	Expected result	Checked
Starting time = 1 Increment time = 1 Ending time = 10	1 1 10	``` Time Height Velocity (hr) (m) (m/s) 1.0 5931.88 0.94 2.0 8974.08 0.76 3.0 11394.28 0.59 4.0 13257.28 0.45 5.0 14625.00 0.32 6.0 15556.48 0.20 7.0 16107.88 0.11 8.0 16332.48 0.02 9.0 16280.68 -0.05 10.0 16000.00 -0.11 Maximum balloon height was 16332.48 meters and it occurred at hour 8.0 ```	

Step 4: Execute your program in the file *balloon.cpp*.

Step 5: Check each case in your *balloon* test plan and verify the expected result. If you discover mistakes in your program, correct them and execute the test plan again.

LABORATORY 6: Reinforcement Exercise—Sentinel-Controlled Loops

In the Background section of Core Exercise 2 you learned how to use a Boolean flag to control loop execution when the event condition is complex. Another type of event-controlled loop is a sentinel-controlled loop. You use a **sentinel-controlled loop** when the number of values to be input by the user (or contained in an input file) is not predetermined and you want the user to enter a special value (or sentinel value) to signify the end of the input values. The sentinel value is determined in the problem description and needs to be outside the valid range for the input values.

Statistically Speaking

A common measurement of the spread or dispersion of data is the standard deviation. The standard deviation indicates how individual data items are scattered around the mean (average) of a sample data set. Formulae for computing the mean ($\bar{x}$) and standard deviation (s) for a set of data values $x_1, x_2, ..., x_n$ are

$$\bar{x} = \frac{\sum_{i=1}^{n} X_i}{n} \quad \text{and} \quad s = \sqrt{\frac{\sum_{i=1}^{n}(x_i - \bar{x})^2}{n-1}} = \sqrt{\frac{\sum_{i=1}^{n}(x_i)^2 - n \cdot \bar{x}^2}{n-1}}.$$

Applying these formulas to the 10 values

   20   14   23   16   15   18   12   20   22   17

yields a mean of 17.7 and a standard deviation of 3.56059. A small standard deviation (about 1) means that the individual data items generally are clustered near the mean.

Step 1: Create a program that computes the mean and standard deviation for a set of positive floating-point values input by the user. When the user wants to stop inputting numbers, have the user input a negative number. The negative number should not be included as a data value. The resulting mean and standard deviation should be output to the file *stats.out*.

Input: A set of positive floating-point values input by the user, ending with a negative number

Output: The mean and standard deviation of the input value

Step 2: Save your program as *stats.cpp*.

Step 3: Test your program using the following test plan. If you discover mistakes in your program, correct them and execute the test plan again.

Test Plan for *stats*

Test case	Sample data	Expected result	Checked
Large range of values	20 14 23 16 15 18 12 20 22 17 -1	Mean: 17.7 Std. dev.: 3.56059	
Small range of values	4 5 6 3 2 -1	Mean: Std. dev.:	

LABORATORY 6: Analysis Exercise

Loop Analysis

Name _____

Hour/Period/Section _____

Date _____

Part A

A common error when programming a loop is to create a loop that loops one too many or one too few times. This kind of logic error is referred to as an "off by one" error. The following program from the file *loopy.cpp* calculates an incorrect average for most data sets because of an "off by one" error.

```cpp
// Loop suffers from an "off by one" error.

#include <iostream.h>

int main ()
{
    int num,
        count = 1;
    double sum = 0.0;

    cout << endl;
    while ( count <= 3 )
    {
        cout << "Enter a number: ";
        cin >> num;
        sum = sum + num;
        count++;
    }
    cout << "Average is " << sum / count << endl;

    return 0;
}
```

Describe the program's "off by one" logic error and modify the program so that it correctly calculates the average.

Part B

Predict the output produced by the following code segments.

```
int i, k;
k = 13;
i = 1;
while (i <= k)
{
    i = i * 2;
    k--;
    cout << i << ' ' << k << endl;
}
```

```
double distance = 100;
while (distance > 0)
{
    cout << distance << endl;
    distance = distance / 2.;
}
```

```
int i = 10;
while ( i > 0 )
{
    cout << i << " ";
    i=i-2;
}
```

Rewrite the while loop in the last example as a for loop.

Iteration II

Overview

In this lab you continue learning about loops and encounter more advanced applications. In Core Exercise 1, you use loops to read and write to files. You also learn how to check the status of a file to verify that the reading or writing is going okay. In Core Exercise 2, you nest loops to develop programs that output tables of calculated values. In Core Exercise 3, you create do-while loops that are used when at least one iteration of the loop is required and for verifying that user input is valid.

LABORATORY 7: Cover Sheet

Name _____

Hour/Period/Section _____

Date _____

Place a check mark (✔) in the Assigned column next to the exercises that your instructor has assigned to you. Have this sheet ready when your lab instructor checks your work. If your exercises are being checked outside the laboratory session, attach this sheet to the front of the packet of materials that you submit.

Exercise		Assigned	Completed
Core 1	I/O Loops *Lights! Camera! Action! (film.cpp)*		
Core 2	Nested Loops *Hot Enough for Ya? (heatindx.cpp)*		
Core 3	do-while Loops *Random Thoughts (random.cpp)*		
Reinforcement	Applying I/O Loops *When You're Smilin' (smilquiz.cpp)*		
Analysis	Nested Loop Practice		
Total			

LABORATORY 7: Core Exercise 1—I/O Loops

Background

In Laboratory 5, Core Exercise 1, you learned how to read input data from a file instead of using the standard input stream operator `cin >>`. One advantage of reading input data from a file is that you can type in and save a large amount of input data in a file and have your program read it from the file. This approach is much easier than having to type in a large amount of input data each time you run the program.

When reading multiple values for the same variable from an input file—for example, reading in a set of numbers, summing them, and finding the average—you must use an iteration (loop) control structure. In Laboratory 6, you explored counter-controlled loops (the number of times that the loop is executed is predetermined) and event-controlled loops (termination of the loop is triggered by the occurrence of some event).

A good programming practice is to confirm that the data are read successfully from the file before you attempt to use the data. Many times, you may not know how many input data values are stored in a file. However, an input file stream object has a status associated with it. A conditional expression containing the input file stream object, for example, `inData`, evaluates to `true` if the status of `inData` is good—the last read was successful. The conditional expression containing `inData` evaluates to `false` if the status of the file stream is not good—the end-of-file has been reached. You can insert an input file stream object within a condition in a `while` (or `if`) statement, as shown in *ioloop1.cpp*.

```cpp
// Read in pairs of integers and display the larger of each pair
// to the screen.

#include <iostream.h>   // For cin, cout
#include <fstream.h>    // For file input/output

int main()
{
    ifstream inData;    // Declare the input file stream object
    int num1, num2;     // Pairs of integers read from file

    // Open input file numbers1.dat.
    inData.open("numbers1.dat");

    inData >> num1 >> num2;      // Priming read from input file
    while ( inData )
    {
        if ( num1 > num2 )
            cout << num1 << endl;
        else cout << num2 << endl;
        inData >> num1 >> num2;      // Attempt to read 2 more numbers
    }
```

```
        // Close the input file stream.
        inData.close();

        return 0;
    }
```

One situation in which the input file stream object has a bad status is when the open function can't locate the input file specified. Another situation in which the input file stream object has a bad status is when it reaches the end of a file. If the file contains more data than read by the program, all the unread data are ignored. If you run the program a second time, the file is reopened at the beginning of the file and the data are again read from the beginning of the file.

The following program, found in *ioloop2.cpp*, demonstrates use of a combined counter- and event-controlled `while` loop to read in (and sum) the first 50 numbers from the input file *numbers2.dat*. The event-control on the `while` loop is active while the status of the input file stream object `inData` is good.

```cpp
// Read in and sum 50 numbers from a file and display
// their average on the screen.

#include <iostream.h>  // For cin, cout
#include <fstream.h>   // For file input/output

int main()
{
    const int MAXCOUNT=50;    // Constant maximum number of numbers

    ifstream inData;     // Declare the input file stream object
    double num,          // Numbers read from file
           sum=0.0,      // Sum of numbers read in, initialized to 0.0
           avg;          // Average of numbers read in
    int count=0;         // Loop control index initialized to 0

    // Open input file numbers2.dat
    inData.open("numbers2.dat");

    inData >> num;
    while ( inData && count < MAXCOUNT )
    {
        sum = sum + num;
        count++;
        inData >> num;
    }

    // If at least one number was successfully read.
    if ( count > 0)
    {
        // Compute their average.
        avg = sum / count;
```

```
        // Output the count of how many numbers and their average.
        cout << "Count = " << count << "    Average = " << avg << endl;
    }
    else
        // Output an error message.
        cout << "No numbers could be read from numbers2.dat" << endl;

    // Close the input file stream.
    inData.close();

    return 0;
}
```

Recall from Laboratory 4 how a conditional expression containing the && logical operator, such as (inData && count < MAXCOUNT), is evaluated. Short-circuit evaluation of an && compound conditional expression begins by checking the first conditional expression. If it evaluates to false, there is no need to check the second conditional expression, and the entire conditional expression evaluates to false. Similarly, for a || compound conditional expression, if the first conditional expression evaluates to true, there is no need to check the second conditional expression, and the entire conditional expression evaluates to true.

Warmup Exercise

Complete the following program by filling in the missing C++ code. A shell for this program is given in the file *ioloop3.shl*.

```
// Reads integers from a file and counts the number of even integers and
// odd integers.  Reads until a zero is read for the file or the end of
// the file is reached.

#include <iostream.h>  // For cin, cout
#include <fstream.h>   // For file input/output

int main()
{
    ifstream inData;    // Declare the input file stream object
    int num,            // Numbers read from file
        evenCount=0,    // Count of even numbers read in, initialized to 0
        oddCount=0;     // Count of odd numbers read in, initialized to 0

    // Open input file numbers3.dat
    inData.open("numbers3.dat");
    _____;

    while ( _____ )
    {
        if (_____)
            evenCount++;
        else oddCount++;
        inData >> num;
    }
```

```
    // Output the count of how many even and odd numbers were read.
    cout << evenCount << " even numbers were read." << endl;
    cout << oddCount << " odd numbers were read." << endl;

    // Close the input file stream.
    inData.close();

    return 0;
}
```

Another good programming practice is to confirm that an output file has been successfully opened before you write to it. Both input and output file streams have a status associated with them. In other words, the call outFile returns the value true if the status of the file stream out-File is good (ready for writing) and the value false if the status of the file stream isn't good. The program

```
int main()
{
    ofstream outFile;
    outFile.open("result.out");

    if ( !outFile )
        cout << "result.out could not be opened for output" << endl;
    else
    {
        ... Read data from the screen, process the data,
            output result to the file and close the file ...
    }

    return 0;
}
```

tests whether the file *result.out* has been opened for output. If it hasn't—because no space is available on disk or the file has security set that prohibits writing, for instance—the program outputs an error message and terminates. If the status of outFile is good, the program is able to write data to the output file stream.

APPLICATION EXERCISE: Lights! Camera! Action!

In Laboratory 5, Core Exercises 2 and 3, you learned how to output HTML formatted files that contain images with the <img src=chicago.jpg> HTML tag. Now you become the film director as you create two output HTML files that contain a series of as many as eight images each. The *script.dat* file contains a sample script of which images to place in which output file. You can alter the order of the images or even repeat images listed in *script.dat*.

Step 1: Create a program that reads in from an input file a series of (output file code, image filename) pairs. The output file code (1 or 2) determines which output HTML file the image should be placed in. Your program should limit each output HTML file to eight images each.

Input: Output file code and image filename pairs from an input file (*script.dat*)

Output: 2 HTML formatted files (*film1.html* and *film2.html*) containing as many as 8 images each

Step 2: Save your program as *film.cpp*.

Step 3: Complete the following test plan.

Test Plan for *film*

Test case	Sample data	Expected result	Checked
script.dat input file	1 sail01.jpg 2 sail02.jpg 1 sail03.jpg . . .	`See film1.html and film2.html`	
Your own *script.dat* file			

Step 4: Execute your program in the file *film.cpp*.

Step 5: Check each case in your *film* test plan and verify the expected result. If you discover mistakes in your program, correct them and execute the test plan again.

LABORATORY 7: Core Exercise 2—Nested Loops

Background

You learned in Laboratory 4 that you sometimes have to nest `if-else` control structures for more complex problems. So too you can nest loop control structures. The following program, *nested1.cpp*, demonstrates nested counter-controlled `while` loops. The outer loop control index is `i`, which ranges from 1 to 3 by 1s. For each value of `i`, the entire inner loop (control index `j`) is executed again, starting from the beginning (`j=1`), until `j>5`.

```cpp
// Demonstrate nested counter-controlled while loops.

#include <iostream.h>

int main()
{
    int i=1,                // Row loop control index (outer loop)
        j;                  // Column loop control index (inner loop)

    while( i <= 3 )         // Outer loop

    {
        cout << "i = " << i;

        j=1;
        while( j <= 5 )             // Inner loop
        {
            cout << "  j = " << j;
            j++;
        }
        cout << endl;

        i++;
    }                                   // End of outer loop

    return 0;
}
```

The output for this program would be

```
i = 1  j = 1  j = 2  j = 3  j = 4  j = 5
i = 2  j = 1  j = 2  j = 3  j = 4  j = 5
i = 3  j = 1  j = 2  j = 3  j = 4  j = 5
```

You can also nest `for` loops as shown in *nested2.cpp*:

```cpp
// Demonstrate nested for loops.

#include <iostream.h>

int main()
{
    int i,                  // Row loop control index (outer loop)
        j;                  // Column loop control index (inner loop)
```

```
for(i=1 ; i<=3 ; i++)              // Outer loop
{
    cout << "i = " << i;

    for(j=1 ; j<=5 ; j++)          // Inner loop
        cout << "  j = " << j;

    cout << endl;
}                                  // End of outer loop

return 0;
}
```

The following program, found in *multiply.cpp*, demonstrates the use of nested `for` loops to generate a multiplication table. Note how and when the column and row headings are output.

```
// Using nested loops to generate a multiplication table.

#include <iostream.h>
#include <iomanip.h>              // For column formatted output

const int SIZE = 12;             // Size of table

int main()
{
    int i,                       // Row loop control index (outer loop)
        j;                       // Column loop control index (inner loop)

    // Output table title.
    cout << endl << SIZE << " by " << SIZE
        << " Multiplication Table" << endl << endl;

    // Loop to output column headings.
    cout << endl << "    |";
    for(i=1; i<=SIZE; i++)
        cout << setw(3) << i << "  ";

    // Underline each heading.
    cout << endl;
    for(i=0; i<=SIZE; i++)
        cout << "_____";

    // Nested for loops.
    for(i=1; i<=SIZE; i++)                    // Outer loop for rows
    {
        cout << endl
            << setw(3) << i << " |";          // Output row label

        for(j=1; j<=SIZE; j++)                // Inner loop to output the row
            cout << setw(3) << i*j << "  ";

    }                                         // End of outer loop
```

```
    cout << endl;

    return 0;
}
```

Note, also, that the inner loop and outer loop don't have to be the same type of loops. Thus you can nest `while` loops inside `for` loops and vice versa.

Warmup Exercise

A factor of a positive integer n is a positive integer smaller than n that divides evenly into n (leaves no remainder, using the modulus operator `%`). Another type of nested loop is when the inner loop is doing some calculation that requires a loop (finding the factors of an integer) and the outer loop is allowing the program to execute its main task (finding factors) multiple times on different user input.

Complete the following program by filling in the missing C++ code. A shell for this program is given in the file *factors.shl*. The program prompts the user for an integer n, finds all the integer factors of n, and then asks the user if he or she wants to factor another integer. Even though the user is specifically asked to reply `y` or `n`, continuing the `while` loop probably is safer if the user enters `y` or `Y`.

```cpp
// Computes the factors of an integer.
// Asks the user if he or she wants to factor another integer.

#include <iostream.h>

int main()
{
    char indicator = 'y';   // While loop event flag initialized to 'y'

    int factor,             // Loop control index, possible factor of n
        n;                  // Number whose factors are to be computed

    // Outer while loop to allow for user to find the factors
    // of multiple different user input integers (one after another).
    while( _____ )
    {
        // Ask the user for a positive integer.
        cout << endl;
        cout << "Enter a positive integer to factor: ";
        cin >> n;

        cout << "Factors of " << n << " are: ";

        // Initialize possible factor loop control index to 1.
        factor = 1;
```

```
      // Inner for loop to find factors.
      _____

      {
          if ( _____ )  // Does factor divide evenly into n?
              cout << factor << " ";
          factor++;
      }

      cout << endl << endl
          << "Do you want to factor another positive integer(y or n)? ";
      cin >> indicator;
   }

   return 0;
}
```

In Laboratory 5, you learned how to output text to a file in HTML format to create output files that, when viewed via an HTML browser, contain images. You now learn how to output HTML format text to create tables (rows and columns) and how to add color to the text. In the following table, the text in the first row is red, the second row is green, the third row is blue.

The Table

Row 1, Column 1	Row 1, Column 2	Row 1, Column 3	Row 1, Column 4
Row 2, Column 1	Row 2, Column 2	Row 2, Column 3	Row 2, Column 4
Row 3, Column 1	Row 3, Column 2	Row 3, Column 3	Row 3, Column 4

You can change the color of text in an HTML document by surrounding the text with `<font>` and `</font>` tags, as in

```
<font color=red>Row 1, Column 1</font>
```

where color specifies the color of the text between the tags. Some sample colors are listed below.

```
blue
brown
green
orange
purple
red
yellow
```

To specify an HTML table, use the `<table>` and `</table>` tags, as in

```
<table border=1 cellpadding=10>
<caption>The Table</caption>

. . .

</table>
```

where `border=1` indicates that the table borders should be 1 pixel wide and that `cellpadding=10` indicates that there should be a 10-pixel-wide blank space surrounding each cell in the table. The `<caption>` and `</caption>` tags define the text heading for the table.

Each row in the table is placed between `<tr>` and `</tr>` tags, as in

```
<tr>Row 1</tr>
<tr>Row 2</tr>
```

Similarly, each cell in a row is placed between `<td>` and `</td>` tags.

```
<td>Row 1, Column 1</td>
<td>Row 1, Column 2</td>
```

These table and font tags are combined in the following HTML code to produce the 3 row by 4 column table shown previously.

```
<html><body>
<table border=1 cellpadding=10>
<caption>The Table</caption>
<tr>
<td><font color=red>Row 1, Column 1</font></td>
<td><font color=red>Row 1, Column 2</font></td>
<td><font color=red>Row 1, Column 3</font></td>
<td><font color=red>Row 1, Column 4</font></td>
</tr>
<tr>
<td><font color=green>Row 2, Column 1</font></td>
<td><font color=green>Row 2, Column 2</font></td>
<td><font color=green>Row 2, Column 3</font></td>
<td><font color=green>Row 2, Column 4</font></td>
</tr>
<tr>
<td><font color=blue>Row 3, Column 1</font></td>
<td><font color=blue>Row 3, Column 2</font></td>
<td><font color=blue>Row 3, Column 3</font></td>
<td><font color=blue>Row 3, Column 4</font></td>
</tr>
</table>
</body></html>
```

 See the "Engaged Learning for Programming in C++" link on **http://www.jbpub.com/cs** for links to more information on HTML syntax.

You need to write C++ code to write text output (the preceding HTML code) to a file, *table.html*. Complete the following program by filling in the missing C++ code. A shell for this program is given in the file *table.shl*.

```cpp
// Outputs an HTML file with a 3 row by 4 column table with each
// row a different color text (red, green, blue).

#include <fstream.h>

int main ()
{
    ofstream HTMLfile;   // Output HTML file

    int row,             // Row loop control index
        column;          // Column loop control index
    HTMLfile.open("table.html");   // Opens file table.html
                                   // HTMLfile is output stream name
    if ( !HTMLfile )
       cout << "table.html could not be opened for output" << endl;
    else
    {
        // Write the HTML code out to the HTMLfile.
        HTMLfile << "<html><body>" << endl;
        HTMLfile << "<table border=1 cellpadding=10>" << endl;
        HTMLfile << "<caption>The Table</caption>" << endl;

        // Output the 3 rows by 4 columns table.
        for ( _____ )
        {
            HTMLfile << "<tr>" << endl;      // Output row begin tag

            for ( _____ )
            {
                _____;            // Output column begin tag

                // Output the font color tag for the row.
                if ( row == 1 )
                    HTMLfile << _____;
                else if ( row == 2 )
                    HTMLfile << _____;
                else HTMLfile << _____;

                // Output the Row x, Column y text
                // and close the font and column tags.
                _____
                _____
            }

            HTMLfile << "</tr>" << endl;      // Output row end tag
        }
```

```
        HTMLfile << "</table>" << endl;
        HTMLfile << "</body></html>" << endl;

        HTMLfile.close();              // Close the file table.html
    }

    return 0;
}
```

APPLICATION EXERCISE: Hot Enough for Ya?

People originally from cities such as New York and St. Louis who have moved to the Southwest often say that, despite higher temperatures in Arizona and New Mexico, they experience less discomfort than they did where they came from. This discomfort is due in large part to the high relative humidity in cities such as New York and St. Louis during the summer. A method for measuring the discomfort caused by humidity is the heat index (HI). The formula for computing the HI is

$$HI = -42.379 + 2.04901523 \cdot T + 10.14333127 \cdot RH - 0.22475541 \cdot T \cdot RH - 0.00683783 \cdot T^2 - 0.05481717 \cdot RH^2 + 0.00122874 \cdot T^2 \cdot RH + 0.00085282 \cdot T \cdot RH^2 - 0.00000199 \cdot T^2 \cdot RH^2,$$

where T is the temperature in °F and RH is the relative humidity in percent form—that is, if the relative humidity is 65%, use 65, not 0.65, for RH in the formula. The HI can be interpreted as follows.

Category	Apparent temperature (HI)	Dangers	Color
Safe	Less than 80	None	blue
Caution	80–90	Exercise more fatiguing than usual	yellow
Extreme caution	90–105	Heat cramps, exhaustion possible	orange
Danger	105–130	Heat exhaustion	red
Extreme danger	Greater than 130	Heat stroke imminent	brown

 See the "Engaged Learning for Programming in C++" link on **http://www.jbpub.com/cs** for links to more information on the heat index.

Step 1: Create a program to output an HTML formatted file (*heatindx.html*) that displays a color-coded HI table in which the relative humidity ranges from 40 to 100% and the temperature ranges from 80 to 100°F. Use an increment of 5 along each row and column.

Input: None

Output: HI table

Humidity

Temp.(F)	40	45	50	55	60	65	70	75	80	85	90	95	100
80	**79.93**	80.35	80.80	81.29	81.81	82.37	82.95	83.58	84.23	84.92	85.64	86.40	87.19
85	84.33	85.31	86.46	87.77	89.25	**90.89**	**92.70**	**94.67**	**96.81**	**99.11**	**101.58**	**104.21**	**107.01**
90	**90.68**	**92.49**	**94.60**	**96.99**	**99.68**	**102.65**	**105.92**	**109.48**	**113.33**	**117.47**	**121.90**	**126.62**	**131.64**
95	**98.99**	**101.90**	**105.22**	**108.95**	**113.09**	**117.65**	**122.61**	**127.99**	**133.78**	**139.99**	**146.60**	**153.63**	**161.07**
100	**109.26**	**113.52**	**118.32**	**123.64**	**129.49**	**135.87**	**142.78**	**150.21**	**158.17**	**166.67**	**175.69**	**185.23**	**195.31**

Under 80 Safe
80 - 90 Caution - Exercise more fatiguing than usual
90 - 105 Extreme caution - Heat cramps, exhaustion possible
105 - 130 Danger - Heat exhaustion
Over 130 Extreme danger - Heat stroke imminent

Step 2: Save your program as *heatindx.cpp*.

Step 3: Complete the following test plan.

Test Plan for *heatindex*

Test case	Sample data	Expected result	Checked
Low temperature Low humidity	80 45	HI = 80.35	
High temperature Low humidity	100 40	HI = 109.26	
High temperature High humidity	100 85	HI = 166.67	

Step 4: Execute your program in the file *heatindx.cpp*

Step 5: Check each case in your *heatindx* test plan and verify the expected result. If you discover mistakes in your program, correct them and execute the test plan again.

LABORATORY 7: Core Exercise 3—do-while Loops

Background

In Laboratory 6, Core Exercises 1 and 2, you learned how to use the while loop to repeat a statement (or statements) multiple times. A key thing to remember about while loops (both counter-controlled and event-controlled) is that the condition within the parentheses of a while loop is checked for a true value *before* the loop is executed (even the first time). Hence a while loop's compound statements (a block of statements delimited by { and }) may not even be executed.

C++ provides a do-while loop control structure to handle iteration problems when you want the loop's compound statements to be executed at least once. Its general form is

```
do
    statement;
while (condition);
```

As with the while loop, compound statements may replace the statement. Also, a do-while loop's condition can be an event-controlled and/or a counter-controlled condition. The do-while structure is similar to the while structure, but do-while evaluates its condition after the loop statement(s) are executed. A do-while loop is referred to as a *posttest* loop, and a while loop is called a *pretest* loop.

The following program, found in *doloop.cpp*, demonstrates the use of an event-controlled do-while loop to read in individual potato weights to pack in a potato sack that must contain at least 10 lb of potatoes (but the minimum number of potatoes).

```cpp
// Read in individual potato weights until 10 pounds total.
// Count and output number of potatoes and total weight.

#include <iostream.h>

double MIN_TOTAL_WEIGHT=10.0;

int main()
{
    double potatoWeight,      // Individual potato weight
           totalWeight=0.0;   // Total weight initialized to 0.0
    int count=0;              // Potato count initialized to 0

    do
    {
        // Read in individual potato weight
        cout << "Input potato weight: ";
        cin >> potatoWeight;

        // Count potato and sum potato weight
        count++;
        totalWeight=totalWeight+potatoWeight;
    }
    while (totalWeight < MIN_TOTAL_WEIGHT);
```

```
    // Output potato count and total weight.
    cout << "Number of potatoes is: " << count << endl;
    cout << "Total weight is: " << totalWeight << endl;

    return 0;
}
```

Warmup Exercise

Recall the bouncing ball Warmup Exercise in Laboratory 6, Core Exercise 1. When a ball is dropped, it bounces from the pavement to a height one-half of its previous height. We want to write a program that will simulate the behavior of the ball when it is dropped from a user input height (in meters) until the height of the bounce is less than 1 cm (instead of for a user input number of bounces). The program should display the number of each bounce and the height of that bounce (including the initial starting height as bounce # 0).

Complete the following program by filling in the missing C++ code. A shell for this program is given in the file *bounce1.shl*.

```
// Computes the height of each bounce of a ball that bounces to a height
// one-half of the previous bounce height.

#include <iostream.h>
#include <iomanip.h>        // Needed for formatted output, setw()

int main()
{
    const double MIN_HEIGHT=.01;    // Constant minimum height of bounce

    double height;                  // User input starting height
    int bounceCount=____            // Bounce counter initialized

    // Get the starting height and number of bounces.
    cout << "Enter the starting height (in meters): ";
    cin >> height;

    // Output the column headings for the table.
    cout << "Bounce #      Height(meters)" << endl;

    // Execute the loop until height is less than minimum height
    do
    {
        // Column formatted output of bounce number and height
        cout << setw(8) << bounceCount << "        "
            << setw(14) << height << endl;

        _____         // Calculate new bounce height
        bounceCount++;                // Increment bounce counter

    } while ( _____ );

    return 0;
}
```

APPLICATION EXERCISE: Random Thoughts

Lotteries, card games, and other forms of gambling usually rely on some sort of randomness in the game from which odds and payouts can be calculated. Any of many methods can be used to generate a list of random numbers, including

$$previous = seed$$
$$next = (previous \cdot b + 1)\%m$$

where seed, b and m are some arbitrary integers, all of which you set once. The result, next, is always an integer between 0 and $m - 1$. You can place the next = formula (followed by a new statement previous = next) inside a loop and generate as many random integers between 0 and $m - 1$ as you want. In general, to ensure randomness you should choose m as a large power of 10 or 2, choose b as an arbitrary integer with one less digit than m and with no pattern in its digits, except that the last three digits should be an even digit followed by 21, and choose seed as an arbitrary positive integer less than m.

 See the "Engaged Learning for Programming in C++" link on **http://www.jbpub.com/cs** for links to more information on the generating random numbers.

Step 1: Create a program that asks the user for values for seed, b, and m (integers) and generates and outputs (10 to a line) 100 random integers, using a counter-controlled loop (inner loop). Then ask the user if he or she wants to generate another list of random integers. If the reply is 'y', ask the user for new values for seed, b and m, which will require an outer do-while loop.

Input: Values for seed, b, and m (possibly more than one set)

Output: List of 100 random integers

Step 2: Save your program as *random.cpp*.

Step 3: Test your program by using the following test plan. If you discover mistakes in your program, correct them and execute the test plan again.

Test Plan for *random*

Test case	Sample data	Expected result	Checked
Good randomness	12 3621 10000		
Bad randomness	0 19 381		
Try your own			

LABORATORY 7: Reinforcement Exercise—Applying I/O Loops

APPLICATION EXERCISE: When You're Smilin'

In this exercise you write a program that reads a set of "smiley" questions and answers from a data file. After reading in a (question, answer) pair, the program should display the question, wait for the user to hit the Enter key, display the answer, and wait for the user to hit the Enter key again. See Laboratory 5, Core Exercise 3 if you need help with getline(). The following is a sample display.

```
-----------------------------------------------------------------
QUESTION: What does this smiley mean? :-)

ANSWER: I am smiling
-----------------------------------------------------------------
QUESTION: What does this smiley mean? :-<

ANSWER: I am sad
-----------------------------------------------------------------
. . .
```

Step 1: Create a program that quizzes a user on the meaning of various smiley icons.

Input: A set of (question, answer) pairs from a data file

Output: The following steps are performed after each (question, answer) pair is read from the data file.

Display the question.
Wait for the user to hit the Enter key.
Display the answer.
Wait (again) for the user to hit the Enter key.

Step 2: Save your program as *smilquiz.cpp*.

Step 3: Test your program by using the following test plan. If you discover mistakes in your program, correct them and execute the test plan again.

Test Plan for *smilquiz*

Test case	Sample data	Expected result	Checked
Smiley states of mind	Data file *smileya.dat*	A series of (question, answer) pairs	
Smiley beings	Data file *smileyb.dat*	A series of (question, answer) pairs	

LABORATORY 7: Analysis Exercise

Nested Loop Practice

Name _____

Hour/Period/Section _____

Date _____

Part A

Predict the output produced by the following code segments.

```
int i=0, j;
while ( i <= 5 )
{
    j = 0;
    while ( j < i )
    {
        cout << "*";
        j++;
    }
    cout << endl;
    i++;
}
```

```
int i, j;
for (i = 1; i < 4; i++)
{
    cout << i;
    for (j = i; j >= 1; j--)
        cout << j << endl;
}
```

```
int i, j;
for (i = 5; i > 0; i--)
{
    cout << i << endl;
    for (j = 1; j <= i; j++)
        cout << j << endl;
}
```

Part B

A common programming error is to create a loop that never terminates. The resulting loop is referred to as an *infinite loop*. The following program from the file *forever.cpp* is designed to display 10 rows of five stars, but instead displays stars forever. Explain why the nested loops never terminate and then correct the program.

```cpp
// Fix the infinite loop.

#include <iostream.h>

int main ()
{
    int j;
    for ( j = 0; j < 10; j++ )
    {
        for ( j = 0; j < 5; j++ )
            cout << '*';
        cout << endl;
    }

    return 0;
}
```

Functions I

OVERVIEW

When asked to define a program, a C aficionado is likely to respond: A program is a collection of functions. Ask the same question of a C++ programmer and you are likely to hear: A program is a collection of interacting objects that contain functions. In this lab, you lay the groundwork for a modular (or structured) approach to programming in which you divide among several functions the tasks that your programs must perform. In later labs, you extend this modular approach into an object-oriented programming style based on the use of classes and objects.

The programs that you wrote in previous labs were relatively short, consisting of a single function—main(). However, most applications yield programs that comprise many functions, each playing a different role within a program. This division of a complex task into simpler subtasks makes it easier for you to design, debug, and maintain programs. Moreover, the functions that you create for one program are likely to be reused in later programs, further shortening the time required to develop a program.

In Core Exercise 1, you begin creating your own functions. In Core Exercise 2, you focus on development of void functions—functions that perform a task without returning a value. In Core Exercise 3, you use the pass-by-reference method to create functions that return multiple values.

LABORATORY 8: Cover Sheet

Name _____

Hour/Period/Section _____

Date _____

Place a check mark (✔) in the Assigned column next to the exercises that your instructor has assigned to you. Have this sheet ready when your lab instructor checks your work. If your exercises are being checked outside the laboratory session, attach this sheet to the front of the packet of materials that you submit.

Exercise	Assigned	Completed
Core 1 Creating Functions *Low, Low Monthly Payments (testpay.cpp)*		
Core 2 Void Functions *IOU (testloan.cpp)*		
Core 3 Pass-by-Reference *Standin' on Shaky Ground (testquak.cpp)*		
Reinforcement Applying Functions That Return a Value *Triskaidekaphobia Revisited (slystone.cpp)*		
Analysis Scope of Variables		
Total		

LABORATORY 8: Core Exercise 1—Creating Functions

Background

In addition to providing a rich set of predefined functions, as demonstrated in Laboratory 3, Core Exercise 3, C++ gives you the ability to create your own functions. The sumSequence() function in the file *sumseq.cpp* computes the sum of a sequence of integers.

```cpp
// Displays the sum of the integers from 1 to a number entered by the
// user.

#include <iostream.h>

long sumSequence ( int n );    // Function prototype

int main()
{
    int num;    // Final term of sequence

    cout << endl << "Enter the final term of the series: ";
    cin >> num;

    // Display the sum.
    cout << "The sum of the integers from 1 to " << num << " is "
        << sumSequence(num) << endl;

    return 0;
}

// Function implementation
long sumSequence ( int n )
// Returns the sum of the integers from 1 to n.
{
    long sum = 0;  // Stores sum
    int j;

    for ( j = 1; j <= n; j++ )
        sum = sum + j;
    return sum;
}
```

Let's examine the mechanics of creating a function. You begin by creating a function prototype. The prototype for sumSequence() is

```cpp
long sumSequence( int n );
```

This prototype informs the compiler that the sumSequence() function has a single integer argument and returns a long integer value. Note that this prototype must appear before any call to the sumSequence() function.

The function prototype is used by the compiler when processing the call

```cpp
sumSequence(num)
```

When this call is made, sumSequence() will receive (as input) a copy of the current value of variable num via parameter n. The compiler verifies that the number of arguments and their respective data types are the same in both the function call and the function prototype's parameter list. Note that the name of the argument in the function call (num) is different from the name of the parameter in the function prototype (n)—they can have the same name, but need not have to.

By convention, implementation of the sumSequence() function is placed after main(). The function declaration is repeated—note that this time there is no semicolon (;) at the end. The statements in the **function body** use the value of parameter n to compute the sum of the sequence of integers from 1 to n. This sum is returned to the calling function—in this example, the function main()—by the statement

```
return sum;
```

The variable sum in function sumSequence() stores the sum as it is calculated. Variables such as sum that are declared within a function are referred to as **local variables**. They can be used only within the function in which they are defined. You could not use sum in main(), for example. You examine the scope of local variables in the Analysis Exercise.

You have actually been writing a function since the first program you wrote in Laboratory 1. The main() function is the function that the operating system calls to start your program. When your program finishes, the main() function returns a value that indicates to the operating system why the program terminated. Returning a value of 0 indicates that your program completed its tasks and terminated normally.

Warmup Exercise

A function prototype tells the compiler what it needs to know in order to compile calls to the function. To understand what the function does, you often need some more information about the function's parameters, the value returned by the function, and the output the function produces. We present this information as a **function specification** in which the function prototype is supplemented with text descriptions of parameters, returned values, and the like.

The following specification describes a function that computes factorials.

```
long factorial ( int n )
```
Input parameter
n: the number whose factorial is to be computed
Returns
The factorial of n

The factorial of a positive integer n is the product of the integers from 1 to n. Factorials are commonly used in probability and statistics to calculate the number of ways in which elements can be selected from a set.

You can express the factorial of a positive integer *n*—written as *n!*—using the formula

$$n! = 1 \cdot 2 \cdot \cdots \cdot (n - 2) \cdot (n - 1) \cdot n.$$

For example, 4! is 1·2·3·4.

Complete the following program by filling in the missing C++ code. A shell for this program is given in the file *factfunc.shl*.

```cpp
// Computes n!

#include <iostream.h>

long factorial( int n );    // Function prototype (declaration)

int main()
{
    int num;     // Number whose factorial is to be computed

    cout << endl << "Input the number: ";
    cin >> num;

    // Display the factorial of the number.
    cout << num << "! is " << _____ << endl;

    return 0;
}


// Implementation of factorial()

_____    // Function return type, name and
                                // formal parameters.
{
    long fact = 1;    // Stores factorial
    int j;

    for ( j = 1; j <= n; j++ )
        fact = fact * j;
    return _____;
}
```

APPLICATION EXERCISE: Low, Low Monthly Payments

You can compute the monthly payment on a fully amortized loan if you know the amount borrowed (principal), the annual interest rate, and the length of the loan. The following formula computes a monthly loan payment, where *mpr* is the monthly percentage (interest) rate and *t* is the length of the loan in months:

$$\text{monthly payment} = mpr \cdot \frac{\text{principal}}{1 - \dfrac{1}{(1 + mpr)^t}}.$$

Step 1: Create a function, `monthlyPayment()`, that computes the monthly payment on a fully amortized loan. Base your function on the following specification.

```
double monthlyPayment ( double principal, double annualRate,
                        int numYears                         )
```

Input parameters
`principal`: amount borrowed (in dollars)
`annualRate`: annual interest rate (as a % of 1.0)
`numYears`: length of the loan (in years)
Returns
The monthly payment (in dollars and cents)

Note that the monthly percentage rate is $\frac{1}{12}$ the annual interest rate.

Step 2: Add your `monthlyPayment()` function to the test program *testpay.cpp*.

Step 3: Complete the following test plan.

Test Plan for *monthlyPayment()*

Test case	Sample data	Expected result	Checked
$1,000 borrowed 10% interest 1 yr	1000 0.1 1	Monthly payment: $87.92	
$5,000 borrowed 5% interest 2 yr	5000 0.05 2	Monthly payment: $219.36	
$10,000 borrowed 8.9% interest 10 yr		Monthly payment: $126.14	

Step 4: Execute your program in the file *testpay.cpp*.

Step 5: Check each case in your *monthlyPayment()* test plan and verify the expected result. If you discover mistakes in your program, correct them and execute the test plan again.

LABORATORY 8: Core Exercise 2—Void Functions

Background

Certain functions, called **void functions**, perform tasks that do not result in a value being returned to the calling routine. One example of a void function is a routine that displays information. The void function `lineOfChars()` from the file *linechar.cpp* displays a line by outputting a specified character a number of times.

```cpp
// Demonstrates the use of a void function to display a line of
// characters.

#include <iostream.h>

void lineOfChars ( char borderChar, int size );    // Function prototype

int main()
{
    char lineChar;      // Character used to form line
    int lineLength;     // Length of line

    // Display a line of 30 asterisks.
    lineOfChars('*', 30);

    cout << "Enter character and length: ";
    cin >> lineChar >> lineLength;

    // Display the line of characters specified by the user.
    lineOfChars(lineChar,lineLength);

    return 0;
}

// Implementation of lineOfChars()

void lineOfChars ( char borderChar, int size )
// Displays a line by displaying borderChar size times.
{
    int j;
    for ( j = 0; j < size; j++ )
        cout << borderChar;
    cout << endl;
}
```

Two calls are made to `lineOfChars()`. In the first call,

```cpp
lineOfChars('*', 30);
```

the character constant `'*'` and the integer constant 30 are passed to `lineOfChars()`, and the function displays a line containing 30 asterisks. In the second call,

```cpp
lineOfChars(lineChar,lineLength);
```

the values of the variables `lineChar` and `lineLength` are passed to function `lineOfChars()`. Note that because `lineOfChars()` doesn't return a value, the calls to `lineOfChars()` are statements by themselves. The following is a sample execution of *linechar.cpp*.

```
******************************
Enter character and length: = 27
===========================
```

Warmup Exercise

Void functions are commonly used to output information. The following function displays a table showing how an investment grows over time.

```
void investmentTable ( double principal,
                       double interestRate,
                       int timePeriod        )
```
Input parameters
`principal`: amount invested (in dollars)
`interestRate`: annual interest rate (as a % of 1.0)
`timePeriod`: length of the investment (in years)
Outputs
A table showing for each year of the investment the amount of interest earned during that year and the value of the investment at the end of the year. Based on the assumption that interest is compounded annually.

Functions aren't limited to being called within `main()`, so functions can call other functions. The following function is called by `investmentTable` to calculate the simple interest earned on a principal amount for a stated yearly interest rate for 1 yr.

```
double simpleInterest ( double principal, double interestRate)
```
Input parameters
`principal`: amount invested (in dollars)
`interestRate`: annual interest rate (as a % of 1.0)
Returns
The interest earned (in dollars and cents)

Complete the following program by filling in the missing C++ code. A shell for this program is given in the file *invest.shl*.

```
// Displays a table showing yearly interest earned on an investment
// and the updated balance. Assumes interest compounded annually.

#include <iostream.h>
#include <iomanip.h>
#include <math.h>
```

```
// simpleInterest() prototype
double simpleInterest( double principal, double interestRate);

// investmentTable() prototype
void investmentTable( double principal, double interestRate,
                      int timePeriod                      );

int main ()
{
    double amtInvested,     // Original investment (in dollars)
           intRate;         // Annual interest rate (as a % of 1.0)
    int numYears;           // Length of the investment (in years)

    // Prompt the user and read in the amount invested, the interest
    // rate, and the duration of the investment.
    cout << endl << "Enter the amount invested: ";
    cin >> amtInvested;
    cout << "Enter the annual interest rate (as a % of 1.0): ";
    cin >> intRate;
    cout << "Enter the length of the investment (in years): ";
    cin >> numYears;

    // Display table.
    investmentTable( _____ , _____ , _____ );

    return 0;
}


//-------------------------------------------------------------------

double simpleInterest( double value, double interestRate)

// Computes and returns simple interest on a given value for
// a given interestRate.

{
    return _____ ;
}


//-------------------------------------------------------------------

void investmentTable( double principal,
                      double interestRate,
                      int timePeriod        )
// Displays a table showing interest earned each year and the value of
// the investment.

{
    double interestEarned,  // Yearly interest earned
           value;           // Investment plus interest earned
    int j;
```

```
// Display the investment table.
cout << endl;
cout << "  Year        Interest Earned     Updated Value " << endl;
cout << "  ----        ---------------     ------------- " << endl;

// Set output formatting for floating-point values to display
// two digits of precision to the right of the decimal point.
cout << setprecision(2) << setiosflags(ios::fixed|ios::showpoint);

// Set the value equal to the initial investment.
value = principal;

// Display yearly accumulated interest and updated value.
for ( j = 1; j <= timePeriod; j++ )
{
    interestEarned = _____;
    value = _____ ;
    cout << setw(6) << j
         << setw(20) << interestEarned
         << setw(18) << value << endl;
}
}
```

APPLICATION EXERCISE: IOU

Part of each payment on a loan goes toward paying off the interest and part goes toward paying off the principal. With a typical amortized loan, a borrower pays much more toward interest at the start of the loan period and much more toward principal at the end. The following formulas compute the amount paid in interest and principal for a given month

$$interest\ paid = mpr \cdot balance$$

and

$$principal\ paid = monthly\ payment - interest\ paid,$$

where *mpr* is the monthly percentage (interest) rate, *balance* is the balance due on the loan at the start of the month, and *monthly payment* is the amount of monthly payment on the loan.

A loan schedule is a table showing the interest paid, principal paid, and balance remaining for each month during the life of a loan. The following is an outline of a sample loan schedule (user input in bold).

```
Enter the amount borrowed: 1000
Enter the annual interest rate (as a % of 1.0): .1
Enter the length of the loan (in years): 1
Monthly payment = $87.92
```

Month	Interest Paid	Principal Paid	Remaining Balance
1	8.33	79.58	920.42
2	7.67	80.25	840.17
.	.	.	.
.	.	.	.
12	0.73	87.19	0.00

Step 1:   Create a function, `loanSchedule()`, that displays a loan schedule for a fully amortized loan. Base your function on the following specification.

```
void loanSchedule ( double principal, double annualRate,
                    int numYears                         )
```

Input parameters

`principal`: amount borrowed (in dollars)

`annualRate`: annual interest rate (as a % of 1.0)

`numYears`: length of the loan (in years)

Outputs

A loan schedule for a fully amortized loan.

Note that the `monthlyPayment()` function you created in Core Exercise 1 computes the monthly payment on a fully amortized loan.

Step 2:   Add your `loanSchedule()` function to the file *testloan.cpp*.

Step 3: Complete the following test plan.

Test Plan for *loanSchedule( )*

Test case	Sample data	Expected result	Checked
$5,000 borrowed 5% interest 2 yr	5000 0.05 2	Monthly payment: $219.36 Interest Principal Remaining Month Paid Paid Balance 1 20.83 198.52 4801.48 2 20.01 199.35 4602.13 . . . . 24 0.91 218.45 0.00	
$100,000 borrowed 7.9% interest 20 yr	100000 0.079 20	Monthly payment: $830.23 Interest Principal Remaining Month Paid Paid Balance 1 658.33 171.89 99828.11 2 657.20 173.03 99655.08 . . . . 240 5.43 824.80 0.00	
$1,000 borrowed 15% interest 1 yr			

Step 4: Execute your program in the file *testloan.cpp*.

Step 5: Check each case in your *loanSchedule()* test plan and verify the expected result. If you discover mistakes in your program, correct them and execute the test plan again.

LABORATORY 8: Core Exercise 3—Pass-by-Reference

Background

Sometimes you need to return more than a single value from a function—when a function computes a set of results, for instance. One way to return multiple values from a function is to pass the results back to the calling routine by using the arguments in the function call. The call

```
rectangleProperties(length,width,area,perimeter);
```

passes the length and width of a rectangle to the function rectangleProperties() and returns with arguments area and perimeter containing the rectangle's area and perimeter, respectively.

The argument passing mechanism you used in Core Exercises 1 and 2 don't allow you to change an argument's value in this way. This mechanism, called **pass-by-value**, copies an argument's value and passes the copy to the function via the corresponding function parameter. Any changes made to the parameter within the function affect only the parameter, not the original argument.

Fortunately, C++ provides another argument passing mechanism, called **pass-by-reference**, in which the address in memory where an argument is stored is passed to a function. As a result, changes made to the corresponding parameter change the argument also. The following program from the file *params.cpp* demonstrates how to return information using pass-by-reference.

```cpp
// Comparing pass-by-value and pass-by-reference.

#include <iostream.h>

void paramFun ( int &x, int &y, int z );   // x and y are reference
                                           // parameters
int main()
{
    int a = 1,
        b = 3,
        c = 4;

    cout << "In main(), before call to paramFun()" << endl;
    cout << "a:" << a << " b:" << b << " c:" << c;
    cout << endl << endl;
    paramFun(a,b,c);
    cout << "In main(), after call to paramFun()" << endl;
    cout << "a:" << a << " b:" << b << " c:" << c;
    cout << endl << endl;

    return 0;
}

void paramFun ( int &x, int &y, int z )
{
```

```
    x++;
    y = y + 2;
    z = z * 3;
    cout << "Inside paramFun()" << endl;
    cout << "x:" << x << " y:" << y << "z:" << z;
    cout << endl << endl;
}
```

Variables a and b in main() are passed to parameters x and y in the function paramFun() using pass-by-reference. You designate a parameter as a **reference parameter** by placing an ampersand (&) between the parameter type and the parameter name in the function prototype. The prototype for paramFun()

```
    void paramFun ( int &x, int &y, int z );
```

indicates that x and y are reference parameters. Note that parameters x and y are actually nothing more than aliases, or second names, for variables a and b in main(). Thus any changes made to x and y in paramFun() are actually made to a and b. This use of pass-by-reference is reflected in the following sample output.

```
    In main(), before call to paramFun()
    a:1 b:3 c:4

    Inside paramFun()
    x:2 y:5 z:12

    In main(), after call to paramFun()
    a:2 b:5 c:4
```

In contrast, parameter z is a **value parameter**—a copy of argument c is passed to paramFun(), not the address of argument c. As a result, changing the value of z to 12 has no impact on argument c—it remains 4.

Reference parameters, on the one hand, provide a form of two-way communication between functions. Value parameters, on the other hand, only allow information to be communicated one-way—into a function. In our function specifications, we categorize parameters as follows: Any parameter that carries information into a function is an **input parameter**, any parameter that returns information from a function is an **output parameter**, and any parameter that does both is an **input/output parameter**. Input parameters can be either value or reference parameters, output and input/output parameters must be reference parameters.

Warmup Exercise

You frequently need to exchange the values of two variables in your programs. The function `swap()` uses a pair of reference parameters to exchange two integers.

```
void swap ( int &x, int &y )
```
Input/output parameters
`x, y:` (input) two integers
          (output) the integers exchanged

Complete the following program by filling in the missing C++ code. A shell for this program is given in the file *swapref.shl*.

```cpp
// Exchanges the values of two integer variables using the pass-by-
// reference mechanism.

#include <iostream.h>

void swap ( _____ );    // Prototype

int main ()
{
    int a, b;

    cout << endl << "Enter two integers separated by a space: ";
    cin >> a >> b;
    cout << "Before swap" << endl;
    cout << "a:" << a << " b:" << b << endl << endl;

    // Exchange the values of a and b.
    _____
    cout << "After swap" << endl;
    cout << "a:" << a << " b:" << b << endl;

    return 0;
}

void swap ( _____ )
// Exchanges the integers.
{
    int temp;
    temp = _____;
    _____ = _____;
    _____ = temp;
}
```

APPLICATION EXERCISE: Standin' on Shaky Ground

The Richter scale expresses the intensity of an earthquake on a scale from 1 to 10. Unlike most scales that you are familiar with, the Richter scale is logarithmic, not linear. Thus an earthquake that produces a reading of 5.0 on the Richter scale is 10 times more powerful than an earthquake that produces a reading of 4.0.

You can compute the relative magnitude and the relative energy release of two earthquakes (quake 1 and quake 2) by using the formulas

$$relative\ magnitude = 10^{richter1-richter2}$$

and

$$relative\ energy = 30^{richter1-richter2},$$

where *richter1* and *richter2* are the Richter scale readings for quake 1 and quake 2, respectively. Note that the *relative magnitude* is the magnitude of quake 1 compared to quake 2—that is, the ratio (magnitude of quake 1/magnitude of quake 2)—and the *relative energy* is the amount of energy released by quake 1 compared to quake 2.

See the "Engaged Learning for Programming in C++" link on **http://www.jbpub.com/cs** for links to more information on the Richter scale.

Step 1:   Create a function `compareQuakes()` that calculates the relative magnitude and relative energy of two earthquakes. Base your function on the following specification.

```
void compareQuakes ( double richter1, double richter2,
                     double &relMagnitude,
                     double &relEnergy                  )
```
Input parameters
`richter1, richter2`: Richter scale readings for a pair of earthquakes
Output parameters
`relMagnitude`: magnitude of the first quake compared to the second
`relEnergy`: amount of energy released by the first quake compared to the second

Step 2:   Add your `compareQuakes()` function to the test program in the file *testquak.cpp*.

Step 3: Complete the following test plan.

Test Plan for *compareQuakes( )*

Test case	Sample data	Expected result	Checked
Quake1: Southern Alaska, 1964 Quake2: San Francisco, 1906	8.5 (est.) 8.3 (est.)	Quake 1 was 1.58 times the magnitude of quake 2. Quake 1 released 1.97 times the energy of quake 2.	
Quake1: Northwest Iran, 1990 Quake2: Central Mexico, 1985	7.7 8.1	Quake 1 was 0.4 times the magnitude of quake 2. Quake 1 released 0.26 times the energy of quake 2.	
Quake1: Shaanxi Province, China, 1556 Quake2: Los Angeles, 1994	8.6 (est.) 6.6	Quake 1 was 100 times the magnitude of quake 2. Quake 1 released 900 times the energy of quake 2.	

Step 4: Execute your program in the file *testquak.cpp*.

Step 5: Check each case in your *compareQuakes()* test plan and verify the expected result. If you discover mistakes in your program, correct them and execute the test plan again.

LABORATORY 8: Reinforcement Exercise—Applying Functions

Triskaidekaphobia Revisited

In this exercise, you add *functionality* to the Thirteen Stones program you developed in Laboratory 6, Core Exercise 2, Application Exercise. In the new version of the game, your program replaces one of the players (player 1) and the remaining human player competes against your program. Rather than asking player 1 to enter a move, your program calls the following function to determine player 1's move.

```
int player1Pick ( int numStones, int player2Pick )
```
Input parameters

`numStones`: number of stones remaining

`player2Pick`: number of stones player 2 (the human player) took on her or his last move

Returns

The number of stones (1, 2, or 3) that player 1 wants to pick up

Having your program take the place of player 1 is no coincidence. Player 1 will always win if your program picks the correct number of stones on each move. See if you can determine player 1's strategy from the following sample game (user input in bold).

```
Number of stones remaining: 13
Player 1's pick: 1
Number of stones remaining: 12
Player 2's pick: 1
Number of stones remaining: 11
Player 1's pick: 3
Number of stones remaining: 8
Player 2's pick: 2
Number of stones remaining: 6
Player 1's pick: 2
Number of stones remaining: 4
Player 2's pick: 3
Number of stones remaining: 1
Player 1's pick: 1
The winner is player 1!
```

If you noticed that the player 1 took one stone on the first move and (4 - player 2's last pick) stones on each subsequent move, you are very clever indeed!

Step 1: Create the function `player1Pick()`, which should ensure a victory by player 1 by using the optimal selection strategy just outlined.

Step 2: Modify your *stones.cpp* program from Laboratory 6 so that the program takes the place of player 1. Use your `player1Pick()` function to generate player 1's moves. Save the new version of your program as *slystone.cpp*.

Step 3: Test your program by using the following test plan (user input in bold). If you discover mistakes in your program, correct them and execute the test plan again.

Test Plan for *slystone*

Test case	Sample data	Expected result	Checked
Player 1 selects the last stone	1 **3** 1 **2** 2 **3** 1	Player 1 wins!	
Player 1 selects the last stone		Player 1 wins!	
Includes illegal move by player 2	1 **1** 3 **2** 2 **4** 2 2		

LABORATORY 8: Analysis Exercise

Scope of Variables

Name _____

Hour/Period/Section _____

Date _____

Since now you have written programs with multiple functions, it is a good time to discuss the scope of variables in your programs. Scope is defined to be the statement block of the program, designated by open and close braces {}, where the variable is declared and, therefore, where the variable can legally be used. A variable is **local** to the statement block it is declared in. Variables in function parameter lists are local to that function. Variables declared before `main()` are **global** and can be used anywhere in the program, including within functions. When a variable goes out of scope, the program has finished executing the statement block where the variable was declared, the variable is deleted and no longer accessible.

Part A

The following program from the file *fun1.cpp*

```cpp
#include <iostream.h>

int square ();

int main()
{
    int k = 5;
    cout << endl << k << " squared is " << square() << endl;

    return 0;
}

int square ()
{
    int k;
    return k * k;
}
```

outputs an incorrect answer when run. Why isn't the output correct? What would you do to fix the program?

Part B

The following program from the file *fun2.cpp*

```cpp
#include <iostream.h>

void foo();

int main()
{
    int j = 5;
    cout << endl << "j in main() is " << j << endl;
    foo();
    cout << "j in main is " << j << endl;

    return 0;
}

void foo()
{
    int j = 10;
    cout << "j in foo() is " << j << endl;
}
```

produces the output

```
j in main() is 5
j in foo() is 10
j in main() is 5
```

Explain why the value displayed for j in `main()` is 5 and the value displayed for j in `foo()` is 10.

APCS Classes I: Arrays and the apvector Class

OVERVIEW

Most of the data encountered in everyday life occurs in groups rather than in individual pieces. People tend to collect these related data items into conceptual units and then assign them names—a group of birds is a flock, a collection of students is a class, and so on. In C++, arrays are used to store groups of similar items in a named collection. What makes arrays particularly useful is the ease (and efficiency) with which you can access individual items, particularly when all (or some) of the items in the array are accessed as part of an iterative process—when finding the largest bird in a flock, for instance.

In Laboratory 2, Core Exercise 3, you used the apstring class and learned some of the basics about declaring and using objects of the type apstring. The Advanced Placement board has also developed an array class called apvector, a safe and easy implementation of arrays. In this lab (and Laboratories 10 and 11) you will learn more about classes and their use, including templated classes, constructors and destructors, operator overloading, and class member functions. In Laboratories 14 and 15 you will learn to write your own classes.

A **class** is an entity that *combines* data elements with functions that operate on them. Thus a class is different from the built-in data types (i.e., int, double, char, etc.) that consist of data alone.

A **templated class** contains a parameterized data type; that is, objects of the templated class consist of individual elements of whatever type you declare in the program. The apvector class is a templated class. Because apstring objects contain strings consisting of individual elements of type char only, apstring is not a templated class.

A **constructor** is a special function associated with a class that is automatically called whenever you declare an object of a class type. A constructor initializes the class object—allocates storage, sets its data elements to default or specified values, and so on.

A **destructor** is a function that is called automatically when the class object goes out of scope and is used to deallocate storage.

Operator overloading in C++ lets you redefine the meaning of standard operators (arithmetic, comparison, and input/output) for class objects. It allows you to perform these operations on class objects with the standard operators.

A **class member function** is a function defined specifically to assist with the management and manipulation of the data contained in a class object.

In Core Exercise 1, you examine how to declare an array and how to reference individual array elements. In Core Exercise 2, you learn about the `apvector` version of the array and its advantages over the standard C++ array. In Core Exercise 3, you look at how to pass `apvector` arrays to functions.

See the "Engaged Learning for Programming in C++" link on **http://www.jbpub.com/cs** for more information on the `apvector` class.

LABORATORY 9: Cover Sheet

Name _____

Hour/Period/Section _____

Date _____

Place a check mark (✔) in the Assigned column next to the exercises that your instructor has assigned to you. Have this sheet ready when your lab instructor checks your work. If your exercises are being checked outside the laboratory session, attach this sheet to the front of the packet of materials that you submit.

Exercise		Assigned	Completed
Core 1	Standard Array Processing *Do Ya Feel Lucky? (dice.cpp)*		
Core 2	Using the `apvector` Class *A Picture's Worth a Thousand Values (bar1.cpp)*		
Core 3	Passing `apvector`s to Functions *Raisin' the Bar (bar2.cpp)*		
Reinforcement	Resizing an `apvector` *Queue Tips (bankline.cpp)*		
Analysis	`apvector` Constructors		
Total			

LABORATORY 9: Core Exercise 1—Standard Array Processing

Background

An **array** is a named collection of data items. All the items in an array must be of the same type, but you can create arrays of integers, arrays of characters, and the like. An array declaration specifies the name of the array, the type of **elements** stored in the array, and the number of array elements (the size of the array). In the following program from the file *arrayio.cpp*, the array polLevel is used to store a set of pollution level readings.

```cpp
// Reads six integers into array polLevel and displays them to
// the screen three per line.

#include <iostream.h>

int main()
{
    int polLevel[6];    // Array of six pollution level readings
    int j;              // Loop control index

    // Input six integers into the pollution level array.
    cout << "Enter the six pollution level readings: ";
    for ( j = 0; j < 6; j++ )
        cin >> polLevel[j];

    // Display the readings three values per line.
    for ( j = 0; j < 6; j++ )
    {
        if ( j % 3 == 0 )
            cout << endl;
        cout << polLevel[j] << " ";
    }
    cout << endl;

    return 0;
}
```

The declaration

```cpp
    int polLevel[6];
```

creates an array of integers named polLevel and reserves enough memory to store six integers. This requirement of arrays—the need to fix the number of elements in the array when you declare the array variable—can be troublesome because sometimes the number of elements you need to store may change within the program. You can safely access only as many array elements as you declare. In Core Exercise 2, you will see how apvector arrays correct this problem.

The elements in an array are numbered, beginning with zero. You refer to an individual array element by placing its number—called its **subscript**, or **array index**—within brackets immediately after the array name. In the polLevel array you denote the first element polLevel[0], the second element polLevel[1], and so on.

In the program *arrayio.cpp*, a series of pollution levels is read by means of a loop in which the loop counter, j, ranges from 0 to 5. For each value of j, the statement

```
cin >> polLevel[j];
```

reads in a pollution level and stores it in array element polLevel[j]. For example, if you entered the integer values

```
40 25 15 12 31 43
```

as the six pollution level readings, your input data would be stored in polLevel as

```
polLevel[0]  40
polLevel[1]  25
polLevel[2]  15
polLevel[3]  12
polLevel[4]  31
polLevel[5]  43
```

Warmup Exercise

Complete the following program by filling in the missing C++ code. A shell for this program is given in the file *scoreavg.shl*.

```cpp
// Finds the average of up to 100 scores.

#include <iostream.h>
#include <iomanip.h>

const int MAX_NUM_SCORES = _____;    // Max number of scores

int main ()
{
    int count,                       // Actual number of scores
        j;                           // Loop counter
    double score[_____],    // Array of size MAX_NUM_SCORES
           sumOfScores=0.0;          // Sum of array elements

    // Prompt the user for the number of scores.
    cout << endl << "Enter the number of scores: ";
    cin >> count;

    // Read in the scores and store them in the array.
    cout << "Enter the scores: " << endl;
    for ( j = ___; j < _____ ; j++ )
        cin >> _____;
    cout << endl;
```

```
// Find and display the average of the scores.
for ( j = ___; j < _____ ; j++ )
    _____;      // Sum the scores
cout << "The average is " << setprecision (2)
    << sumOfScores / count << endl;

return 0;
}
```

If the user enters a value for number of scores (count) larger than MAX_NUM_SCORES, you can't be sure that the program will work correctly. A runtime error may occur when the user is actually entering the scores into the array, or the program may sometimes seem to work fine. In Core Exercise 2, you will see how apvector arrays correct this problem.

APPLICATION EXERCISE: Do Ya Feel Lucky?

In Laboratory 7, Core Exercise 3, you learned how to write a program to generate integers randomly. C++ also provides a function to generate a random integer. The *stdlib.h* header file includes the following prototype for the C++ random number generator.

```
int rand();
```

The function rand() requires no parameters and returns one random integer from 0 to the largest integer allowed (usually a constant RAND_MAX=32,768). You can call rand() multiple times in one program—maybe within a loop—and it will return a random integer each time. In Laboratory 7, Core Exercise 3, you let the user define a "seed" for the random number generator you wrote. The *stdlib.h* header file includes the following prototype for the C++ random number generator seed function.

```
void srand(int);
```

This prototype allows the user, or program, to seed the function rand() so that each run of the program will potentially return a new set of random numbers. You need only call srand once at the beginning of your program to set the seed for that run. One way to let the program set the seed and ensure that a different seed is used for each program run is to use the *time.h* function time(). The function prototype

```
int time(NULL);
```

returns the current time in integer format from your computer's clock. Ask your instructor if there is a different way to get the current time in integer format on your system. Combining the srand() and time() functions in a single call is usually done once at the beginning of a program that is going to call the random number generator rand(), as in

```
srand(time(NULL));
```

At times you will need to generate random numbers in a range other than 0 to 32,768. You can easily use the % (mod or remainder) function to translate a random integer from 0 to 32,768, to a random integer in any integer range. To get a random number between 1 and 10, use

```
number = rand()%10 + 1;
```

The term `rand()%10` will always be an integer between 0 and 9 (inclusive) because that is the range of possible remainders when you divide an integer by 10. Add 1 and you have a random integer between 1 and 10 (inclusive).

Now that you know how to generate random integers in a fixed range, you can use this knowledge to play the game of Elimination.

Rules of Elimination

Elimination is a one-player game. The board consists of a set of 12 tiles, numbered 1 through 12. The player rolls a pair of dice and removes tiles based on the numbers shown on the dice. For each roll, the player can remove either the two tiles corresponding to the numbers shown on the dice or a single tile corresponding to the sum of the numbers on the dice. If the player rolls doubles (the same number on both dice), the player can remove only the tile corresponding to the sum of the dice. Play continues until the player cannot make a legal move or all the tiles have been removed. The sum of the remaining tiles is the player's score. The goal is to have a low score.

Here is a sample game:

```
1  2  3  4  5  6  7  8  9 10 11 12

.  .  .  .  .  .  .  .  .  .  .  .


Dice roll: 1  6                    Player chooses to remove two tiles.
1  2  3  4  5  6  7  8  9 10 11 12
X  .  .  .  .  X  .  .  .  .  .  .


Dice roll: 6  2                    Player chooses to remove sum.
1  2  3  4  5  6  7  8  9 10 11 12
X  .  .  .  X  .  X  .  .  .  .  .


Dice roll: 5  5                    Player chooses to remove sum—the only legal
                                   move with doubles.
1  2  3  4  5  6  7  8  9 10 11 12
X  .  .  .  X  .  X  .  X  .  .  .


Dice roll: 2  4                    Player chooses to remove two tiles.
1  2  3  4  5  6  7  8  9 10 11 12
X  X  .  X  .  X  .  X  .  X  .  .


Dice roll: 3  1                    Player quits—cannot make a legal move.
                                   Final score is 47.
1  2  3  4  5  6  7  8  9 10 11 12
X  X  .  X  .  X  .  X  .  X  .  .
```

Step 1: Create a program to play the game of Elimination.

Repeat the following steps until the user has removed all the tiles or quit.
- Display the board.
- Roll the dice.
- Let the user pick a move (D = dice, S = sum, Q = quit). Ensure that the user makes a legal choice.

Display the final board and the sum of the remaining tiles.

Step 2: Save your program as *dice.cpp*.

Step 3: Complete the following test plan.

Test Plan for *dice*

Test case	Sample data	Expected result	Checked
Play the game!		See sample play	

Step 4: Execute your program in the file *dice.cpp*.

Step 5: Check each case in your *dice* test plan and verify the expected result. If you discover mistakes in your program, correct them and execute the test plan again.

LABORATORY 9: Core Exercise 2—Using the `apvector` Class

Background

The Advanced Placement Board has developed an array class called `apvector`, a safe and easy implementation of arrays. This section focuses on operations that you can use with the Advanced Placement board implementation of arrays.

To use the `apvector` data type, you must include the following preprocessor directive at the beginning of your program, along with any other preprocessor directives.

```
#include <apvector.h>
```

The angle brackets tell the compiler to look in the standard include directory—this directory contains all the standard header files for C++. You do not need to include `apvector.cpp` because the Advanced Placement board has already added `#include <apvector.cpp>` at the end of `apvector.h`.

 See the "Engaged Learning for Programming in C++" link on **http://www.jbpub.com/cs** for information on using `apvector` in different programming environments.

An `apvector` is a named collection of data items of the same type, just like the standard C++ array. Because `apvector` is a templated class, you can construct `apvectors` of integers, of floating-point numbers, of characters, and the like. The data type within the `apvector<` and `>` specifies the type of the elements stored in the `apvector`. In the following program from the file *mileage.cpp*, the `apvector` `mileage` is used to store and average a week's set of daily mileage readings for a truck driver.

```
// Reads seven real numbers into the apvector mileage and displays
// the numbers and their average to screen.

#include <iostream.h>
#include <apvector.h>

int main()
{
    apvector<double> mileage(7);   // apvector of seven mileage readings
    double sum=0.0;                // Calculated sum of mileage readings
    int j, k;                      // Loop control indices

    // Input seven floating point numbers into the mileage apvector.
    cout << "Enter the seven mileage readings: ";
    for ( j = 0; j < 7; j++ )
        cin >> mileage[j];

    // Display the readings and sum them.
    cout << endl << "Daily Mileages" << endl;
```

```
    for ( k = 0; k < 7; k++ )
    {
        cout << mileage[k] << " ";
        sum = sum + mileage[k];
    }

    cout << endl << "Average daily mileage = " << sum/7.0 << endl;

    return 0;
}
```

An `apvector` declaration specifies the name of the `apvector` object, the type of **elements** stored in the `apvector`, and, optionally, the number of `apvector` elements (the size of the `apvector`) and, optionally, the initialization value for all elements in the `apvector`. When you declare objects of a particular class (`apstring`, `apvector`, etc.), the appropriate constructor for the class is automatically called. The `apvector` class has four constructor functions.

The declaration

```
    apvector<double> mileage(7);
```

creates an `apvector` of floating-point numbers named `mileage` and reserves enough memory to store seven real numbers.

The declaration

```
    apvector<int> scores;
```

creates an empty `apvector` of integers named `scores`. This declaration calls the **default constructor** for `apvector`, but because no memory is reserved yet to store data, the `apvector` is essentially unusable. You will see shortly how to enlarge and shrink the size of an `apvector`.

The declaration

```
    apvector<char> middleInitial(10, ' ');
```

creates an `apvector` of characters named `middleInitial`, reserves enough memory to store 10 characters, and initializes the 10 `apvector` elements to a single blank space.

And, finally, the preceding declaration followed by the declaration

```
    apvector<char> firstInitial = middleInitial;
```

creates an `apvector` of characters named `firstInitial` and copies the size and contents of the `apvector` of characters named `middleInitial`. This declaration calls the **copy constructor** for `apvector`.

When the program flow goes outside the block of statements (demarcated by { and }) in which an `apvector` is declared, the class destructor is automatically called to delete the class object and deallocate memory.

As with the standard C++ array, the elements in an `apvector` are numbered, beginning with zero. You also refer to an individual `apvector` element by placing its number—called its **subscript** or `apvector` **index**—within brackets immediately after the `apvector` name. You designate the first element in the `mileage` apvector as `mileage[0]`, the second as `mileage[1]`, and so on. The C++ array index operator `[ ]` is said to be overloaded in the `apvector` class. That is, the operator has been defined for the class to work the same way as the standard C++ array index operator `[ ]`.

The overloaded `[ ]` operator for `apvectors` also has the additional functionality (not supported in C++ arrays) of checking at runtime that each subscript value used falls within the legal range. A detailed runtime error message will be generated if the program tries to access an array index beyond the `apvector` size.

Warmup Exercise

Besides constructors, the destructor, and the overloaded `[ ]` operator, the `apvector` class has two **class member functions**: `resize(...)` and `length()`. Class member functions are called by using the object name followed by a dot operator (`.`) and the class member function name (with parentheses and containing parameters if required).

One advantage of using an `apvector` instead of the standard C++ array is the ability to declare an `apvector` object and not have to specify how many elements the `apvector` will hold. You can use the `apvector` function `resize(newsize)` to resize the `apvector`. Doing so allows you to declare the `apvector` as size `0` initially and then, once you know how many elements the `apvector` needs (maybe based on user input), you can use `resize(newsize)` to lengthen (or shorten) the `apvector`, as with

```
apvector<double> score;        // apvector of initial size 0
. . .
score.resize(userInputSize);   // apvector resized
```

Calling the `apvector` `resize` member function, while convenient for programs in which you want to allow the user to define the size of the `apvector`, should be minimized because of the increased resource consumption (memory and CPU time).

Because you can resize an `apvector` during the course of a program, the `apvector` function `length()` is provided to get the current integer length of the `apvector`, as in

```
apvector<double> score;    // apvector of initial size 0
int arraySize=0;
. . .
arraySize=score.length();
```

Sensor readings from engineering equipment sometimes need to be summarized into statistical measures, such as the number of sensor readings, the maximum reading (and at what time it occurred), and the minimum reading (and at what time it occurred). Complete the following program by filling in the missing C++ code. A shell for this program is given in the file *sensors.shl*.

```
// Finds the maximum and minimum, and the time each occurred, for
// a user specified number of sensor readings.

#include <iostream.h>
#include <apvector.h>
```

```
int main ()
{
    apvector<double> sensor;    // Apvector of sensor readings,
                                // initial size 0
    double maximumSensor,       // Maximum sensor reading
           minimumSensor;       // Minimum sensor reading
    int count,                  // Actual number of sensor readings
        j,                      // Loop control index
        maximumTime,            // Time of maximum sensor reading
        minimumTime;            // Time of minimum sensor reading

    // Prompt the user for the number of sensor readings.
    cout << endl << "Enter the number of sensor readings: ";
    cin >> count;

    sensor._____;        // apvector resized to count

    // Read in the sensor reading and store them in the apvector.
    for ( j = ___; j < _____; j++ )
    {
        cout << "Enter sensor reading at " << j+1 << " second: ";
        cin >> _____;
    }

    // Initialize the maximum and minimum sensor readings
    // and when they occurred.
    maximumSensor = _____;
    maximumTime = ____;
    minimumSensor = _____;
    minimumTime = ____;

    // Find the maximum and minimum sensor readings and when they occurred.
    for ( j = ___; j < _____; j++ )
    {
        if ( _____ )
        {
            maximumSensor = _____;
            maximumTime = ____;
        }
        if ( _____ )
        {
            minimumSensor = _____;
            minimumTime = ____;
        }
    }

    cout << "Number of sensor readings was " << count << endl;
    cout << "Maximum sensor reading was " << maximumSensor
         << " and it occurred at second " << maximumTime << endl;
    cout << "Minimum sensor reading was " << minimumSensor
         << " and it occurred at second " << minimumTime << endl;

    return 0;
}
```

APPLICATION EXERCISE: A Picture's Worth a Thousand Values

Data are often easier to interpret when displayed in graphical form. Pie charts, line graphs, and bar charts are all examples of graphical representations of data. The following is an example of an HTML bar chart that you can create with a C++ program.

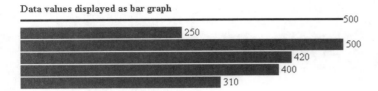

Data values displayed as bar graph

The HTML necessary to create this bar graph is fairly simple.

You draw the "scale" line by "stretching" a basic .gif image (*scale.gif*), using the `width=500` parameter on the `<img ...>` HTML tag. A `width=500` will fill the width of most computer screens. Similarly, you draw the data bars themselves by stretching a basic .gif image (*bar.gif*), using the `width=???` parameter on each `<img ...>` HTML tag. The ??? will be actual data values (between 0 and 500) input by the user. The data value is displayed to the right of the bar by inserting the data value after each `<img . . >` HTML tag.

 See the "Engaged Learning for Programming in C++" link on **http://www.jbpub.com/cs** for more information on these HTML tags.

The following HTML code is contained in *bargraph.html*.

```
<html><head><title>Bar Graph</title></head>
<body><p><b>Data values displayed as bar graph</b><br>
<img src=scale.gif height=20 width=500 align=top>500<br>
<img src=bar.gif height=20 width=250 align=top> 250<br>
<img src=bar.gif height=20 width=500 align=top> 500<br>
<img src=bar.gif height=20 width=420 align=top> 420<br>
<img src=bar.gif height=20 width=400 align=top> 400<br>
<img src=bar.gif height=20 width=310 align=top> 310<br>
</p></body></html>
```

Step 1: Create a program that produces an HTML formatted output file (*bar1.html*) bar graph from a set of integer values entered by the user. The user first enters the number of bars in the graph, followed by a set of integer values (one per bar), which you store in an `apvector`. Your program then displays an HTML bar graph, as just explained. Assume that the bars have integer values in the range from 0 to 500.

Input: The number of bars

A list of integer values in the range 0 to 500

Output: A bar graph

Be sure to display the bar graph scale (0–500), as shown on the graph.

Step 2: Save your program as *bar1.cpp*.

Step 3: Complete the following test plan.

Test Plan for *bar1*

Test case	Sample data	Expected result	Checked
Bar graph with the max data value	5 250 500 420 400 310	See the image presented at the beginning of this exercise.	
Bar graph with one bar			
Bar graph with many bars (>10) and a wide range of data values			

Step 4: Execute your program in the file *bar1.cpp*.

Step 5: Check each case in your *bar1* test plan and verify the expected result. If you discover mistakes in your program, correct them and execute the test plan again.

LABORATORY 9: Core Exercise 3—Passing `apvectors` to Functions

Background

As you learned in Laboratory 8, when a function argument does not include an ampersand (&), a copy of the argument is created and this copy is passed to the function via the corresponding function parameter. This process is called **pass-by-value** argument passing. You also encountered **pass-by-reference** argument passing, which uses the pass-by-reference symbol (&), in which the address in memory where an argument is stored is passed to a function. As a result, changes made to the corresponding parameter within the function also change the argument.

Passing `apvectors` (or arrays) by pass-by-value is quite costly in terms of both the time needed to create the copy and the memory required to store the copy. For greatest efficiency, then, use pass-by-reference argument passing to pass `apvector` (or array) arguments to functions. The `apvector` requires the pass-by-reference symbol, &, to be explicitly stated. The standard C++ array implicitly assumes inclusion of the pass-by-reference symbol.

When an `apvector` argument is passed to a function by using the pass-by-reference symbol (&), the function is given the address in memory where the first element in the `apvector` is stored. As a result, changes made to the corresponding `apvector` parameter also change the `apvector` argument. Although some functions need *not* change the contents of an `apvector` argument, you still will want to take advantage of the efficiency in using pass-by-reference. For this case you combine the use of the `const` keyword with the pass-by-reference symbol (&) for `apvector` arguments.

The following program from the file *arrpass.cpp* passes an `apvector` argument to two functions that modify the contents of the `apvector` and to one function that does not modify its contents.

```
// Passes an apvector to a function and doubles the values
// of the apvector.

#include <iostream.h>
#include <apvector.h>

const int MAX_PER_LINE = 5;    // Max values per line to display

void inputValues (apvector<int> &data, int count);
void doubleValues (apvector<int> &data, int count);
void displayValues (const apvector<int> &data, int count);

int main ()
{
    int numVals;               // Actual number of values to process
    apvector<int> value;       // Apvector of integers
```

```
    // Prompt the user for the number of data items.
    cout << endl << "Enter the number of values to process: ";
    cin >> numVals;

    //Resize apvector to size numVals.
    value.resize(numVals);

    // Read in the data.
    inputValues(value, numVals);

    // Double the value of each data element.
    doubleValues(value, numVals);

    // Display the data.
    cout << "Data doubled:";
    displayValues(value, numVals);
    cout << endl;

    return 0;
}


//--------------------------------------------------------------------
void inputValues (apvector<int> &data, int count)
// Read values into an apvector.
{
    int j;
    cout << "Enter the data: ";
    for ( j = 0; j < count; j++ )
        cin >> data[j];
}

//--------------------------------------------------------------------
void doubleValues (apvector<int> &data, int count)
// Double the values in the apvector.
{
    int j;
    for ( j = 0; j < count; j++ )
        data[j] = data[j] * 2;
}

//--------------------------------------------------------------------
void displayValues (const apvector<int> &data, int count)
// Display the values in the apvector.
{
    int j;
    for ( j = 0; j < count; j++ )
    {
        if ( j % MAX_PER_LINE  == 0 )
            cout << endl;
        cout << data[j] << " ";
    }
}
```

Let's look at the `inputValues()` function. Note the pass-by reference symbol, `&`, in the function prototype and function definition.

The function call

```
inputValues(value, numVals);
```

passes the `apvector value` to the parameter `apvector data`. In effect, `data` is nothing more than an alias, or a second name, for `value`. Any changes that are made to `data` in `inputValues()` are actually made to `value`. The same is true for the call

```
doubleValues(value, numVals);
```

Take a look at the `displayValues()` function and note the use of `const` in the function parameter list of the function prototype and function definition. The `displayValues()` function does not need to change any entries in the `apvector` passed to it. With pass-by-`const`-reference, the address of an argument—rather than a copy of it—is passed to the function. The `const` designation means that the function cannot alter the value of the argument. Note that in changing the function to use pass-by-`const`-reference we didn't change the body of the function, only its parameter list.

```
void displayValues (const apvector<int> &data, int count);
```

This use of pass-by-reference is reflected in the following sample output.

```
Enter the number of values to process: 7
Enter the data: 34 50 43 21 39 46 44
Data doubled
68 100 86 42 78
92 88
```

Warmup Exercise

The following specifications describe functions that read in mileage data for a series of trips, convert the distances traveled from miles to kilometers for each trip, and display the length of each trip in both miles and kilometers.

```
void readMileage ( apvector<double> &tripMiles, int count )
```
Input parameter
`count`: number of trips
Output parameter
`tripMiles`: (apvector) number of miles in each trip

```
void milesToKms ( const apvector<double> &tripMiles,
                  apvector<double> &tripKms, int count )
```
Input parameter
`tripMiles`: (apvector) number of miles in each trip
`count`: number of trips
Output parameter
`tripKms`: (apvector) number of kilometers in each trip

```
void displayData ( const apvector<double> &tripMiles,
                   const apvector<double> &tripKms, int count )
```
Input parameters
tripMiles: (apvector) number of miles in each trip
tripKms: (apvector) number of kilometers in each trip
count: number of trips
Outputs
Displays each trip in both miles and kilometers.

Complete the following program by filling in the missing C++ code. A shell for this program is given in the file *mile_km.shl*.

```
// Displays the distance traveled for up to 100 trips in both miles
// and kilometers.

#include <iostream.h>
#include <iomanip.h>
#include <apvector.h>

const double MILES_TO_KMS = 1.61; // Miles to kilometers conversion
                                  // factor
// Function prototypes
void readMiles (apvector<double> &tripMiles, int count);
void milesToKms ( const apvector<doubl e> &tripMiles,
                 apvector<double> &tripKms, int count);
void displayData (const apvector<double> &tripMiles,
                 const apvector<double> &tripKms, int count);

int main ()
{
    int numTrips;               // Actual number of trips
    apvector<double> miles,     // Miles data
                     kms;       // Kilometers data

    // Prompt the user for the number of trips
    cout << endl << "Enter the number of trips: ";
    cin >> numTrips;

    // Resize apvectors to size "numTrips".
    miles.resize(numTrips);
    kms.resize(numTrips);

    // Read the mileage for each trip.
    readMiles(_____);

    // Convert miles to kilometers.
    milesToKms(_____);
```

```
    // Display the data for each trip.
    displayData(_____);

    return 0;
}

//------------------------------------------------------------
void readMiles (apvector<double> &tripMiles, int count)
{
    int j;
    cout << "Enter the mileage for each trip: ";
    for ( j = 0; j < count; j++ )
        cin >>_____;
}

//------------------------------------------------------------------
void milesToKms (const apvector<double> &tripMiles,
                 apvector<double> &tripKms, int count)
{
    int j;
    for ( j = 0; j < count; j++ )
        _____ = _____ * MILES_TO_KMS;
}

//------------------------------------------------------------------
void displayData (const apvector<double> &tripMiles,
                  const apvector<double> &tripKms, int count)
{
    int j;
    cout << endl << setw(4) << "Trip" << setw(7) << "Miles"
                 << setw(12) << "Kilometers" << endl;
    for (_____)
    {
        cout << setw(4) << j + 1 << setw(7) << tripMiles[j]
             << setw(12) << tripKms[j] << endl;
    }
}
```

APPLICATION EXERCISE: Raisin' the Bar

The bar graph program that you created in Core Exercise 2 could display integer values only in the range 0 to 500. In this exercise, you generalize your program to support a much broader range of values by scaling the data before displaying it. The following formula scales the data values to the range 0–500:

$$\text{scaled value} = \frac{500 \cdot \text{data value}}{\text{maximum data value}}.$$

Scaling the values 800, 1000, 600, and 700 with this formula produces the scaled values 400, 500, 300, and 350, respectively. Note that the maximum data value (1,000) yields a scaled value of 500 and that the remaining values are reduced linearly in proportion to the maximum data value. The actual data values are still printed to the right of each bar. Even though the actual data values are declared as real numbers (`apvector<double>`), the scaled data values can be integers (`apvector<int>`) because the width=??? parameter on each <img ...> HTML tag accepts only integer values.

Your new program will then display the scaled data. The larger values listed produce the following scaled bar graph.

Data values displayed as bar graph

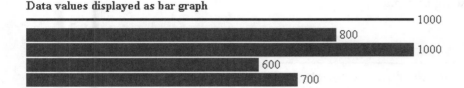

Step 1: Using your program *bar1.cpp* as a basis, create a program that displays a scaled bar graph. Base your new program on the functions specified.

```
void readData ( apvector<double> &data, int count )
```
Input parameters
`count`: number of data values
Output parameter
`data`: data values

```
double max ( const apvector<double> &data, int count )
```
Input parameters
`data`: data values
`count`: number of data values
Returns
The largest data value

```
void scaleValues ( const apvector<double> &data,
                   apvector<int> &scaledData,
                   double maxValue, int count )
```
Input parameters
`data`: data values
`maxValue`: largest data value
`count`: number of data values
Output parameter
`scaledData`: scaled data values

```
void displayBarGraph ( const apvector<double> &data,
                       const apvector<int> &scaledData,
                       double maxValue, int count )
```

Input parameters

data: data values

scaledData: scaled data values

maxValue: largest data value

count: number of data values

Outputs

A scaled bar graph

Step 2: Save your program as *bar2.cpp*.

Step 3: Complete the following test plan.

Test Plan for *bar2*

Test case	Sample data	Expected result	Checked
Bar graph scaled 500/1,000	5 800 800.8 1000 730 250		
Bar graph scaled 500/2,500			

Step 4: Execute your program in the file *bar2.cpp*.

Step 5: Check each case in your *bar2* test plan and verify the expected result. If you discover mistakes in your program, correct them and execute the test plan again.

LABORATORY 9: Reinforcement Exercise—Resizing an `apvector`

Queue Tips

A line (queue) of customers at the bank can be simulated with an `apvector` that will hold the arrival time of each customer in the line and an integer variable, `lineLength`, that will hold the current number of people in line (not the length of `apvector`). Position 0 in the `apvector` is the customer currently first in line. You simulate a customer being served by removing the first "arrival time" from the queue and by moving all the other customer "arrival times" forward in the queue (called a **dequeue**). You simulate the arrival of a new customer by placing the customer arrival time in the `lineLength` position (the next open position) in the `apvector` and increasing `lineLength` by 1 (called an **enqueue**). You calculate the **wait time** for each customer by finding the difference between when the customer arrived and when the customer left the queue. You can easily sum all these wait times and count all the customers to calculate the average wait time for a customer.

On average, customers arrive every 5 min (set a constant for this) in groups of a size that is randomly generated and **normally distributed** with a mean of 4 customers (ask the user to input the arrival mean) and standard deviation of 1 customer (ask the user to input the arrival STD). Every minute, one customer is served and leaves. The following function changes the `rand()` function—a uniformly distributed random number generator—to a random normal function.

```
int random_normal(int mean, int std)
// Returns a normally distributed random integer
// with the distribution mean and std given as parameters
{
    int i,num=0;
    double sum=0.0;

    while (num <= 0)
    {
        for (i=1; i<=12; i++)
            sum = sum + rand()/double(RAND_MAX);
        sum = sum - 6.0;
        num = mean + int(std * sum);
    }

    return num;
}
```

The following pseudocode will help.

1. For each minute of the simulation:

   a. If it is a 5-min interval, randomly generate how many customers have arrived, add their arrival times to the end of the queue one by one, and increase `lineLength` (don't forget to `resize()` the `apvector` queue to make it larger, if necessary).

b. If the queue is not empty, remove one customer from the queue, calculate the customer's wait time, and decrease `lineLength` by 1.

c. If it is a 60-min interval, calculate the average wait time for that interval (store this value in another `apvector`) and reset the total wait time and customer count to 0.

2. After completing the simulation, use the `max`, `scaleValues`, and `displayBarGraph` functions to generate a horizontal bar chart of the average customer wait time for each 60-min interval.

Step 1: Run the bank line simulation for 8 hrs. (480 min; set a constant for this length of time).

Step 2: Save your program as *bankline.cpp*.

Step 3: Test your program by using the following the test plan (because of randomness, your results may vary). If you discover mistakes in your program, correct them and execute the test plan again.

Test Plan for *bankline*

Test case	Sample data	Expected result	Checked
Arrival mean = 4 Arrival STD = 1	4 1		
Arrival mean = 4 Arrival STD = 2			
Arrival mean = 5 Arrival STD = 1			

See the "Engaged Learning for Programming in C++" link on **http://www.jbpub.com/cs** for more information on computer simulations of queues.

LABORATORY 9: Analysis Exercise

apvector **Constructors**

Name _____

Hour/Period/Section _____

Date _____

Part A

Describe in detail the type of apvector created with each of the following constructors and statements.

```
apvector <double> a;
```

```
apvector <apstring> a(50);
```

```
apvector <char> a(10,'X');
```

```
apvector <char> a(10,'X');
apvector <char> b;
b=a;
```

Part B

Describe what happens when you run each of the following programs.

```cpp
#include <iostream.h>
int main()
{
    int data[10];
    int j;

    for (j=1; j<=10; j++)
    {
        data[j] = j*2;
        cout << data[j] << " ";
    }

    cout << endl;

    return 0;
}
```

```cpp
#include <iostream.h>
#include <apvector.h>
int main()
{
    apvector<int> data(10);
    int j;

    for (j=1; j<=10; j++)
    {
        data[j] = j*2;
        cout << data[j] << " ";
    }

    cout << endl;

    return 0;
}
```

APCS Classes II: Strings and the `apstring` Class

OVERVIEW

Since Laboratory 2, you have used the Advanced Placement board class implementation of strings, the `apstring`. Now you will see some of the advantages in using this implementation of strings. These advantages include

- no need to fix the size of the `apstring` at declaration,

- automatic resizing of an `apstring` upon assignment,

- `apstring` addition,

- no need to worry about the null termination (`'\0'`) required in C-style strings, and

- both array-style access to the characters in strings and many easy-to-use string functions.

You will learn more about the `apstring` constructors and destructor, operator overloading, and class member functions. As mentioned in Laboratory 9, `apstring` is not a templated class because the individual elements of `apstring` can only be of type `char`.

In Core Exercise 1, you learn how to treat an `apstring` as an array of characters, how to apply the class member function `length()` and overloaded operator + (`apstring` addition/concatenation), and how to pass `apstring` objects to a function. In Core Exercise 2, you encounter the variety of `apstring` class member functions and use them to develop command line parsing programs. In Core Exercise 3, you create an `apvector` of `apstring`s and determine how to apply different `apvector` and `apstring` class member functions.

 See the "Engaged Learning for Programming in C++" link on **http://www.jbpub.com/cs** for more information on the `apstring` class, including the use of `apstring` in different programming environments.

LABORATORY 10: Cover Sheet

Name _____

Hour/Period/Section _____

Date _____

Place a check mark (✔) in the Assigned column next to the exercises that your instructor has assigned to you. Have this sheet ready when your lab instructor checks your work. If your exercises are being checked outside the laboratory session, attach this sheet to the front of the packet of materials that you submit.

Exercise	Assigned	Completed
Core 1 Using the `apstring` Class *Word of Fortune (hangman.cpp)*		
Core 2 Additional `apstring` Functions *Follow the Bouncing Ball (animate.cpp)*		
Reinforcement Applying `apstring`s *Forget Me Note (note.cpp)*		
Analysis `apstring` Constructors		
Total		

LABORATORY 10: Core Exercise 1—Using the `apstring` Class

Background

A **string** is a sequence of characters. You have been using the Advanced Placement board class implementation of strings, the `apstring`, since Laboratory 2. As with `apvector`, multiple constructors are available for the `apstring` class:

```
apstring firstName;            // Constructs an empty (zero-length) apstring
                               // (default constructor)
apstring month="January";      // apstring month is initialized to the
                               // literal string "January"
apstring birthdayMonth = month;  // apstring birthdayMonth is set equal to
                                 // the value of month (copy constructor)
```

You can access and manipulate `apstring`s as character arrays as follows:

```
apstring firstName;
firstName = "Bjarne";     // apstring overloaded assignment operator (=)
```

The characters in the resulting `apstring` are referenced as stored in an array, starting in element 0. The `apstring` "Bjarne" is stored in array `firstName` as

```
firstName[0] 'B'
firstName[1] 'j'
firstName[2] 'a'
firstName[3] 'r'
firstName[4] 'n'
firstName[5] 'e'
```

You can manipulate the characters in an `apstring` the same way you manipulate elements in any other array. The overloaded index operator `[]` for `apstring` allows you to access individual characters by using the `apstring` object name and the appropriate subscript. (As with `apvector`, the subscript must be in the valid range for the `apstring` object or a runtime error will be generated.) The following code fragment outputs the third character in the `firstName` `apstring` and changes the first character of the `apstring` to `'b'`.

```
cout << firstName[2];
firstName[0] = 'b';
```

The `apstring` class has many more functions and operators than `apvector`. We cover some now and some in Core Exercise 2.

One advantage of the `apstring` version of a string is the ability to declare an `apstring` object and not have to specify the length of string that it will hold. The `apstring` object automatically resizes itself if you assign a longer or shorter string to the object. You can use the `apstring` member function `length()` to get the current integer length of the `apstring`.

```
apstring name;         // apstring for name
int string_size=0;
cin >> name;    // input stream extraction operator overridden for apstring
string_size=name.length();
```

Note that the input stream extraction operator (>>) is available for apstrings, as is the output stream insertion operator (<<). Neither are available with entire apvector objects, but they are supported for individual apvector elements.

You can use the standard comparison operators (==, !=, <, <=, >, >=) to compare apstrings. You can also "add," or append, a character or apstring to the end of another apstring by using the apstring overloaded + operator.

```
apstring name, newname;        // apstring for name
char comma = ',';
name = "John";
newname = name;                // Copies name to newname
newname = newname + comma;     // Appends a copy of char comma to
                               // apstring newname
newname = newname + name;      // Appends a copy of apstring name to apstring newname
                               // newname will now equal "John,John"
```

Warmup Exercise

Complete the following program by filling in the missing C++ code. A shell for this program is given in the file *backword.shl*.

```
// Displays the letters in a word in reverse order.

#include <iostream.h>
#include <_____>
#include <_____>

void reverse ( const apstring &word );

int main()
{
        _____ word;    // apstring storing a word
    cout << endl << "Enter a word: ";
    cin >> word;
    reverse(word);

    return 0;
}

void reverse ( const apstring &word )
{
    int i,
        lastCharPos = 0; // Index of last letter in word

    // Find the end of the word.
    lastCharPos = _____;

    // Display the word backwards.
    cout << "The word written backwards is: ";
    for ( i = _____; i >= _____; i-- )
        cout << _____;
    cout << endl;
}
```

Note the use of `const apstring &` when an `apstring` is passed as a parameter to a function that doesn't need to change the `apstring` parameter. You drop the `const` keyword if the function needs to change the `apstring` parameter. This approach is similar to passing `apvector`s to functions.

APPLICATION EXERCISE: Word of Fortune

In this exercise, you create a two-person version of the Hangman word-guessing game. The Hangman game begins with one player entering a secret word. The secret word is then scrolled off the screen before the other player sits down to play. A blank guess template then appears on the screen. This template is the same length as the secret word but has dashes in place of the letters in the word.

The player attempting to guess the secret word enters letters one at a time. After each guess, the guess template is updated to show which letters in the secret word match the letter guessed (if any). For example, if the secret word is "paper," guessing the letter p results in the following changes in the guess template.

```
Enter the secret word: paper (This scrolls off the screen)
-----
Guess a letter: p
p-p--
```

This process continues until the guess template matches the secret word. The number of guesses is then output. The following is a sample game.

```
Enter the secret word: test (This scrolls off the screen)
----
Guess a letter: a
----
Guess a letter: e
-e--
Guess a letter: n
-e--
Guess a letter: s
-es-
Guess a letter: t
test=test
You guessed the word in 5 guesses
```

The program shell in the file *hangman.shl* contains the basic elements of the Hangman game. It is missing three key functions, however, which we provide here.

```
void createTemplate ( const apstring &secretWord,
                      apstring &guessTemplate )
```
Input parameter
`secretWord`: the secret word
Output parameter
`guessTemplate`: a guess template containing all dashes

```
void updateTemplate ( const apstring &secretWord,
                      char guessLetter,
                      apstring &guessTemplate )
```

Input parameters

`secretWord`: the secret word

`guessLetter`: letter guessed

Input/output parameters

`guessTemplate`: (input) a guess template showing the position of the letters guessed that match letters in the secret word (output) an updated guess template that includes the letters in the secret word that match `guessLetter`

```
bool matchTemplate ( const apstring &secretWord,
                     const apstring &guessTemplate )
```

Input parameters

`secretWord`: the secret word

`guessTemplate`: a guess template showing the position of the letters guessed that match letters in the secret word

Returns

Returns `true` if the guess template is the same as the secret word. Otherwise, returns `false`.

Step 1: Create the specified functions `createTemplate()`, `updateTemplate()`, and `matchTemplate()` and add them to the program shell in the file *hangman.shl*.

Step 2: Save your program in the file *hangman.cpp*.

Step 3: Complete the following test plan.

Test Plan for *hangman*

Test case	Sample data	Expected result	Checked

Test	a e n s t	```----```
		```----```
		```-e--```
		```-e--```
		```-es-```
		```test=test```
		```You guessed the word in 5 guesses.```	

Cryptic	a e i o u y n s t r h c p		
Your secret word			

Step 4: Execute your program in the file *hangman.cpp*.

Step 5: Check each case in your *hangman* test plan and verify the expected result. If you discover mistakes in your program, correct them and execute the test plan again.

LABORATORY 10: Core Exercise 2—Additional `apstring` Functions

Background

The `apstring` class member function `find(apstring str)` attempts to locate the first occurrence (if at all) of the string `str` in the `apstring` to which you applied the `find` function. The function returns the location, counting the first location as 0, if the string `str` was found. In

```
int i;
apstring word="because";
i = word.find("cause");
```

the variable `i` would contain the value 2. If the string is not found, the find function returns the value -1.

A second version of the `apstring` class member function `find` takes a `char` parameter. The `apstring` function `find(char ch)` attempts to locate the first occurrence (if at all) of the character `ch` in the `apstring`. The function returns the location, counting the first location as 0, if the character `ch` was found in the `apstring`. In

```
int i;
apstring word="hello";
i = word.find('o');
```

the variable `i` would contain the value 4. If the character is not found, the find function returns the value -1.

The `apstring` class member function `substr(int pos, int len)` extracts the substring from the `apstring`, starting at location `pos` and counting the first location as 0, for `len` length number of characters. The code fragment

```
apstring word="downward";
cout << word.substr(1,3);
```

outputs the string `own` to the screen.

By careful, repeated application of the `find()` and `substr()` functions to an `apstring`, you can separate multiple substrings from a larger string, as shown in Warmup Exercise A.

Finally, the `apstring` class member function `c_str()` converts the `apstring` to a C-style string. As mentioned in Laboratory 2, C++ does not provide a predefined data type to handle sequences of characters (strings). However, a C-style string can be used in C++. A C-style string is a null (`'\0'`) terminated array of type `char`. The Laboratory 10 Overview details some advantages of the apstring over C-style strings. Some C++ functions—the file stream open("externalfilename") function, for example—requires a C-style string for the external filename as in

```
ostream outFile;
apstring filename;
cout << "Enter the output filename: ";
cin >> filename;
outFile.open(filename.c_str());
```

Recall that apvector is a templated class. However, the apvector templated element type need not be one of C++'s built-in data types. The following declaration, for example, constructs the courseList object as an apvector of apstrings.

```
apvector<apstring> courseList(3);
```

You can assign apstrings to array positions in the apvector as follows (or use cin>> or getline()).

```
courseList[0]="Algebra II";
courseList[1]="U.S. History";
courseList[2]="British Literature";
```

All the apvector functions and apstring functions can still be applied, as in

```
// Output the number of courses in the list.
cout << courseList.length() << endl; // This will output 3

// Resize the course list to 2 courses
courseList.resize(2);

// Output the position of the first '.' in the second apstring.
cout << courseList[1].find('.') << endl;  // This will output 1

// Output the first 7 characters in the first apstring.
cout << courseList[0].substr(0,7) << endl;  // This will output "Algebra"
```

Warmup Exercise A

When you "surf" the Internet, are you ever curious about the significance of the different fields in the www address? Many Internet addresses have the three fields

```
www.name.type
```

where *name* is the name of the company or organization and *type* is the type of entity (e.g., com, edu, org, gov, etc.).

Complete the following program that displays the three fields in an Internet address by filling in the missing C++ code. A shell for this program is given in the file *internet.shl*.

```
// Displays the three fields of an Internet e-mail address.

#include <iostream.h>
#include <apstring.h>
#include <apstring.cpp>
```

```
int main ()
{
    apstring address;    // Internet address
    int j;               // '.' location in apstring

    // Read in the Internet address.
    cout << endl << "Enter the Internet address: ";
    cin >> address;

    // Display the individual fields.
    cout << "The address contains the following fields:" << endl;

    // Find the first '.'.
    j = _____ ;

    // Output the substring from the beginning to the '.'.
    cout << _____ << endl;

    // Reset the address as the remaining end of the old apstring.
    address = _____ ;

    // Find the next '.'.
    j = _____ ;

    // Output the substring from the beginning to the '.'.
    cout << _____ << endl;

    // Output the last substring.
    cout << _____ << endl;

    return 0;
}
```

Warmup Exercise B

Complete the following program, which displays a "favorites list" of URLs, by filling in the missing C++ code. A shell for this program is given in the file *bookmark.shl*.

```
// Outputs to the screen a list of URLs read from a file.

#include <iostream.h>
#include <fstream.h>
#include <apstring.h>
#include <apstring.cpp>
#include <apvector.h>

// Function prototypes
void outputFavs ( const apvector<apstring> &favList, int count);

//----------------------------------------------------------------
int main()
{
```

```
    ifstream URLFile;

    apvector<apstring> URLList(10);

    int index = 0;                    // URL index

    URLFile.open("urls.dat");

    getline(_____ );     // Get the URL.
    while ( _____ )
    {
        index++;                               // Update URL count.
        if ( index == URLList.length() )       // Resize apvector,
            URLList.resize(URLList.length()+10); // if necessary.
        getline(_____ );      // Get the URL.
    }

    URLFile.close();

    outputFavs(URLList, index);

    return 0;
}

void outputFavs ( const apvector<apstring> &favList, int count)
{
    int i;
    cout << "Favorites list: " << endl;
    for (i=0; _____ ; i++)
        cout << _____ << endl;
}
```

APPLICATION EXERCISE: Follow the Bouncing Ball

A Javascript enabled animation of an image is defined by an image (`imageFilename`), a path
(x1,y1 x2,y2 x3,y3 ... xn,yn), a time interval (`t`) between movements, and an output HTML
filename (`htmlFilename`). A user can enter a series of the following commands to define the animation (commands do not have to be entered in any order and can be repeated) such as

```
image imageFilename
path x1,y1 x2,y2 x3,y3 ... xn,yn
time t
create htmlFilename
quit
```

Read in each command line as an `apstring` and parse into pieces, depending on the first word
on the command line. When a user enters `create`, create an HTML file that animates an image
based on the following example (**user input values are shown in bold**).

```
<html>
<head><title>Animation</title>
<script>
var numPoints = n;
```

```
var pointX = new Array (x1,x2,x3,...);
var pointY = new Array (y1,y2,y3,...);
var interval = t;
</script>
<script src=move.js></script>
</head>
<body>
<form><input type=button value=Go onClick=move()></form>
<div id=Image style=position:absolute>
<img src=imageFilename></div>
</body>
</html>
```

The program shell in the file *animate.shl* contains the basic elements to output the HTML necessary to run the Javascript animation program in file *move.js*. It is missing three key functions, however, which we provide here.

```
void readCommandLine ( apstring &commandLine )
```
Output parameter
`commandLine`: an `apstring` containing the entire command line entered by the user

```
void parseCommandLine ( const apstring &commandLine,
                        char delim, apstring &command,
                        apstring &argument )
```
Input parameters
`commandLine`: an `apstring` containing the entire command line
`delim`: "character" used to separate the command and argument
Output parameters
`command`: command word of command line
`argument`: argument portion of command line

```
void parsePathArgument ( apstring &argument, int &pointCount,
                         apvector<apstring> &x,
                         apvector<apstring> &y)
```
Input parameters
`argument`: argument portion of command line
Output parameters
`pointCount`: number of points entered by user
`x`: apvector of x coordinates
`y`: apvector of y coordinates

Step 1: Create a program to implement the Javascript enabled animation program described, using an `apstring` to read in each command line. If the animation doesn't appear, try an HTML browser software that supports Javascript.

 See the "Engaged Learning for Programming in C++" link on **http://www.jbpub.com/cs** for more information on Javascript..

Step 2: Save your program in the file *animate.cpp*.

Step 3: Complete the following test plan.

Test Plan for *animate*

Test case	Sample data	Expected result	Checked
Balloon moves in a square.	image balloon.gif time 100 path 100,100 100,200 200,200 200,100 create out.html		
Smiley moves in a zig-zag manner.			

Step 4: Execute your program in the file *animate.cpp*.

Step 5: Check each case in your *animate* test plan and verify the expected result. If you discover mistakes in your program, correct them and execute the test plan again.

LABORATORY 10: Reinforcement Exercise— Applying `apstring`s

Forget Me Note

In this exercise you create a program that reads a set of notes from a data file and creates an HTML message board that displays these notes. A sample data file *notes.dat* contains one note per line, and your program randomly generates x and y coordinates for the upper left corner of each note to determine where each note will be placed on the screen.

Your program will read the notes from the data file and store them as an `apvector` of `apstring`s. It will then create an HTML message board file containing these notes. Base your HTML message board on the following template (**user input or random values are shown in bold**).

```
<html><head><title>Message Board</title>
<style>
.Note {
    background-color: yellow;
    position: absolute;
    width: 100;
    height: 100;
    padding: 10;
    border: 1pt;
}
</style>
</head>
<body bgcolor=black>
<img src=umpire.jpg>
<div class=Note style=left:x1; style=top:y1;>
Text note 1
</div>
<div class=Note style=left:x2; style=top:y2;>
Text note 2
</div>
...
</body></html>
```

Note that most of the HTML in this template is unchanged boilerplate that can be output by your program as simple string literals. The remaining content consists of a series of `<div>` elements, one `<div>` element per note.

Filling in this template with the notes in the file *notes.dat* and randomly generating upper left corner coordinates for each note yields the image shown. Use the C++ `rand()` function to generate upper left corner coordinates between 0 and 500. If the notes don't appear as shown, try a more recent HTML browser software that supports the HTML `<style>` and `<div>` tags.

 See the "Engaged Learning for Programming in C++" link on **http://www.jbpub.com/cs** for more information on these HTML tags.

Step 1: Create a program to implement the HTML message board program described, using an `apvector` of `apstrings` to store the notes. Your program should read the notes from the data file and store them in the `apvector`. Then it should create an HTML message board file that displays these notes.

Step 2: Save your program as *notes.cpp*.

Step 3: Test your program by using the following the test plan. If you discover mistakes in your program, correct them and execute the test plan again.

Test Plan for *notes*

Test case	Sample data	Expected result	Checked
notes.dat	Get school T-shirt for kid brother Call Chris about Saturday Simpson's special tonight When is the CS stuff due?	The HTML message board given	

LABORATORY 10: Analysis Exercise

apstring Constructors

Name

Hour/Period/Section

Date

Describe the result of each of the following `apstring` constructor declarations.

```
apstring a;
```

```
apstring a("Apple");
```

```
apstring a = "Apple";
```

```
apstring a = "A";
```

```
apstring a = 'A';
```

```
apstring <apvector> a (10,0);
```

APCS Classes III: Two-Dimensional Arrays and the `apmatrix` Class

OVERVIEW

Many problems require organizing data into the rows and columns of a table. In C++, two-dimensional arrays are used to store groups of similar items in a named collection. The `apmatrix` class is an easy-to-use implementation of two-dimensional arrays.

In Core Exercise 1, you examine how to declare the `apmatrix` class, how to reference individual `apmatrix` elements, how to use `apmatrix` functions, and how to use nested loops to iterate through the rows and columns of an `apmatrix`. In the Reinforcement Exercise, you learn about vector * matrix multiplication and graphic operation matrices.

 See the "Engaged Learning for Programming in C++" link on **http://www.jbpub.com/cs** for more information on the `apmatrix` class, including the use of apmatrix in different programming environments.

LABORATORY 11: Cover Sheet

Name _____

Hour/Period/Section _____

Date _____

Place a check mark (✔) in the Assigned column next to the exercises that your instructor has assigned to you. Have this sheet ready when your lab instructor checks your work. If your exercises are being checked outside the laboratory session, attach this sheet to the front of the packet of materials that you submit.

Exercise	Assigned	Completed
Core 1 Using the `apmatrix` Class *Your Name in Lights (board.cpp)*		
Reinforcement Applying Two-Dimensional Arrays *Moving Day (graphics.cpp)*		
Analysis More `apmatrix` Practice		
Total		

LABORATORY 11: Core Exercise 1—Using the `apmatrix` Class

Background

In many programming applications you naturally organize data into rows and columns. In C++ you can use a two-dimensional array to store data in this form. Here, we introduce you to the Advanced Placement board version of a two-dimensional array: `apmatrix`. The following is a declaration for a two-dimensional array of characters, consisting of 5 rows and 11 columns.

```
#include <apmatrix.h>
apmatrix<char> box(5, 11);
```

The first `apmatrix` subscript specifies the number of rows, and the second specifies the number of columns. You identify a particular element by specifying its row and column. For example, the assignment statement

```
box[2][3]='*';
```

stores an asterisk in the element specified by the third row and fourth column of `box`—recall that indexing for both the row and the column starts at zero.

You can declare `apmatrix` object that initializes every element, as in

```
#include <apmatrix.h>
apmatrix<char> box(5, 11, '*');
```

As with `apvector`, an advantage in using an `apmatrix` is the ability to construct an `apmatrix` object and not have to specify how many rows and columns the `apmatrix` will hold. The `apmatrix` class member function `resize(newRows, newCols)` can be used to resize the `apmatrix`. You still can't access `apmatrix` elements past the end of the declared (or resized) size of the `apmatrix`, and, if you try to do so, you will get a detailed runtime error message stating that you tried to access an `apmatrix` index beyond the declared size.

You can resize an `apmatrix` during the course of a program, so the `apmatrix` class member functions `numrows()` and `numcols()` are provided to get the current integer row length and column length of the `apmatrix`.

Finally, passing an object of type `apmatrix` to a function requires the pass-by-reference symbol, `&`, to be explicitly stated, as with `apvector`.

The following program, from the file *matrix.cpp*, demonstrates how to declare an `apmatrix`, how functions operate on an `apmatrix`, and how to pass an `apmatrix` argument to a function that modifies the contents of the `apmatrix`.

```
// Passes an apmatrix to a function and multiplies the row index times
// column index to set the values of the apmatrix.

#include <iostream.h>
#include <apmatrix.h>
```

```cpp
void calculateValues ( apmatrix<int> &data );
void displayValues ( const apmatrix<int> &data );

int main ()
{
    int numRows, numCols;      // Actual number of rows/columns to process
    apmatrix<int> table;       // apmatrix of integers

    // Prompt the user for the number of data items.
    cout << endl << "Enter the number of rows to process: ";
    cin >> numRows;
    cout << "Enter the number of columns to process: ";
    cin >> numCols;

    // Resize apmatrix to size numRows by numCols.
    table.resize(numRows, numCols);

    // Calculate the value as row * column.
    calculateValues(table);

    // Display the data.
    displayValues(table);
    cout << endl;

    return 0;
}

//-------------------------------------------------------------------

void calculateValues ( apmatrix<int> &data )
// Calculate the value as row * column.
{
    int i, j;
    for ( i = 0; i < data.numrows(); i++ )
       for ( j = 0; j < data.numcols(); j++ )
           data[i][j] = i * j;
}

//-------------------------------------------------------------------

void displayValues ( const apmatrix<int> &data )
// Display the values in the apmatrix.
{
    int i, j;
    for ( i = 0; i < data.numrows(); i++ )
    {
       for ( j = 0; j < data.numcols(); j++ )
           cout << data[i][j] << " ";
       cout << endl;
    }
}
```

The following is a sample run for a 4 × 3 matrix.

```
Enter the number of rows to process: 4
Enter the number of columns to process: 3
0 0 0
0 1 2
0 2 4
0 3 6
```

Warmup Exercise

A trait of square matrices (same number of rows and columns) that often needs to be verified is symmetry. A symmetric matrix is one whose entries are identical across the main diagonal. So if the element at row 2, column 3, `table[1][2]`, is the same as the element at row 3, column 2, `table[2][1]`, the matrix is symmetric on those elements. Complete the following program, which determines whether an entire matrix is symmetric, by filling in the missing C++ code. A shell for this program is given in the file *symmetry.shl*.

```cpp
// Checks to see if an apmatrix is symmetric.

#include <iostream.h>
#include <_____>

void displayValues ( const apmatrix<int> &data );
bool symmetric ( const apmatrix<int> &data );

int main()
{
    _____ data;    // Square apmatrix of integers

    data.resize(3,3);
    data[0][0] = 1;   data[0][1] = 2;   data[0][2] = 3;
    data[1][0] = 1;   data[1][1] = 2;   data[1][2] = 3;
    data[2][0] = 1;   data[2][1] = 2;   data[2][2] = 3;
    displayValues(data);

    if ( symmetric(data) )
       cout << "Matrix is symmetric. " << endl;
    else
       cout << "Matrix is not symmetric. " << endl << endl;

    data.resize(3,3);
    data[0][0] = 1;   data[0][1] = 2;   data[0][2] = 3;
    data[1][0] = 2;   data[1][1] = 3;   data[1][2] = 4;
    data[2][0] = 3;   data[2][1] = 4;   data[2][2] = 5;
    displayValues(data);

    if ( symmetric(data) )
       cout << "Matrix is symmetric. " << endl;
    else
       cout << "Matrix is not symmetric. " << endl << endl;
```

```
        return 0;
}

//------------------------------------------------------------------

void displayValues ( const apmatrix<int> &data )
// Display the values in the apmatrix.
{
    int i, j;
    for ( i = 0; i < data.numrows(); i++ )
    {
        for ( j = 0; j < data.numcols(); j++ )
            cout << data[i][j] << " ";
        cout << endl;
    }
}

//------------------------------------------------------------------

bool symmetric ( const apmatrix<int> &data )
{
    int i, j;
    for ( i = 0; i < _____ ; i++ )
        for ( j = 0; j <= _____ ; j++ )
            if (_____ != _____ )
                return false;

    return true;
}
```

APPLICATION EXERCISE: Your Name in Lights

In this exercise you use a two-dimensional array of characters to represent a message board. For example, you can display the message "I C U" on a 5 × 11 message board as follows.

```
...........
.I.CCC.U.U.
.I.CC..U.U.
.I.CCC.UUU.
...........
```

The function fillRectangle() fills in a specified rectangle on the message board with a given character.

```
void fillRectangle ( apmatrix<char> &board, int row, int col,
                     int width, int height, char fillChar )
```
Input parameters
row, col: row and column of the upper, left corner of the rectangle
width, height: rectangle dimensions
fillChar: character to fill the rectangle width

Input/Output parameter
`board`: (input) message board
      (output) updated message board, including specified rectangle

The `displayBoard()` function displays the message board.

```
void displayBoard ( const apmatrix<char> &board )
```
Input parameter
`board`: message board
Outputs
Displays the message board

The following calls

```
fillRectangle(board,0,0,11,5,'.');      // Set the board to all '.'s
fillRectangle(board,1,1,1,3,'I');       // Forms the block letter 'I'
```

produce part of the message board shown.

Step 1: Create the specified functions `fillRectangle()` and `displayBoard()` and add them to the program shell in the file *board.shl*.

Step 2: Save your program in the file *board.cpp*.

Step 3: Complete the following test plan.

Test Plan for *board*

Test case	Sample data	Expected result	Checked
Data in test program	See test program (in file board.shl).		
Your initials	Add `fillRectangle( )` calls to board.cpp.		

Step 4: Execute your program in the file *board.cpp*.

Step 5: Check each case in your *board* test plan and verify the expected result. If you discover mistakes in your program, correct them and execute the test plan again.

LABORATORY 11: Reinforcement Exercise—Applying Two-Dimensional Arrays

Moving Day

Multiplication of a vector times a matrix is a fairly straightforward operation with many interesting applications. This exercise demonstrates two-dimensional graphics operations.

If you want to multiply a vector times a matrix, the number of entries (columns) in the vector must match the number of rows in the matrix. The individual elements in the vector are first multiplied by their corresponding individual elements in the first matrix column. These products are then summed, and the result is placed in the first element in the result vector. This operation is repeated for the second and subsequent columns of the matrix as in

$$\begin{bmatrix} x & y & z \end{bmatrix} \cdot \begin{bmatrix} a_1 & a_2 & a_3 \\ b_1 & b_2 & b_3 \\ c_1 & c_2 & c_3 \end{bmatrix} = \begin{bmatrix} (x \cdot a_1 + y \cdot b_1 + z \cdot c_1) & (x \cdot a_2 + y \cdot b_2 + z \cdot c_2) & (x \cdot a_3 + y \cdot b_3 + z \cdot c_3) \end{bmatrix}$$

With careful application of nested loops, a vector * matrix multiplication is easy to implement in a C++ program.

In this exercise you use the standard graphics 3 × 3 matrices and vector * matrix multiplication to perform two-dimensional translation, rotation (about the origin), and spin (about the figure's center) on a figure (made up of a series of (x, y) points). By multiplying each point in the figure by the appropriate graphics matrix, the entire figure is appropriately translated, rotated, or spun.

To achieve translation of a point (x, y) by a distance Δx in the x direction and a distance Δy in the y direction (Δx and Δy can be positive or negative), use

$$\begin{bmatrix} x & y & 1 \end{bmatrix} \cdot \begin{bmatrix} 1 & 0 & 0 \\ 0 & 1 & 0 \\ \Delta x & \Delta y & 1 \end{bmatrix} = \begin{bmatrix} x + \Delta x & y + \Delta y & 1 \end{bmatrix}.$$

To achieve rotation of a point (x, y) through an angle θ around the origin $(0, 0)$ (positive θ rotates the point clockwise and negative θ rotates the point counterclockwise), use

$$\begin{bmatrix} x & y & 1 \end{bmatrix} \cdot \begin{bmatrix} \cos\theta & \sin\theta & 0 \\ -\sin\theta & \cos\theta & 0 \\ 0 & 0 & 1 \end{bmatrix} = \begin{bmatrix} x \cdot \cos\theta - y \cdot \sin\theta & x \cdot \sin\theta + y \cdot \cos\theta & 1 \end{bmatrix}.$$

To achieve spin of a point (x, y) through an angle θ around the center of the figure that the point is part of (positive θ rotates the point clockwise and negative θ rotates the point counterclockwise),

- find $(center_x, center_y)$ of the figure by finding the average of all the x coordinates and the average of all the y coordinates;

- translate each point (x, y) by a distance $-center_x$ in the x direction and a distance $-center_y$ in the y direction;

- rotate each point through an angle θ around the origin; and

- translate each point (x, y) by a distance $center_x$ in the x direction and a distance $center_y$ in the y direction.

The function, `translate()`, translates a point by a distance Δx in the x direction and a distance Δy in the y direction.

```
void translate ( const apvector<double> &point,
                 double deltaX, double deltaY,
                 apvector<double> &result )
```
Input parameters
`point`: point apvector $(x, y, 1)$
`deltaX, deltaY`: distances in x and y directions to move point
Output parameter
`result`: translated point apvector $(x', y', 1)$

```
void rotate ( const apvector<double> &point, double angle,
              apvector<double> &result )
```
Input parameters
`point`: point apvector $(x, y, 1)$
`angle`: angle to rotate the point clockwise around the origin $(0, 0)$
Output parameter
`result`: rotated point apvector $(x', y', 1)$

These functions, in turn, use the following function, which multiplies the point apvector by an apmatrix to produce the transformed point.

```
void vectorMatrixProduct ( const apvector<double> &vector,
                           const apmatrix<double> &matrix,
                           apvector<double> &result )
```
Input parameters
`vector`: point apvector $(x, y, 1)$
`matrix`: translation or rotation apmatrix
Output parameter
`result`: translated or rotated point apvector $(x', y', 1)$

Step 1: Create the specified functions `translate()`, `rotate()`, and `vectorMatrixProduct()` and add them to the program shell in the file *graphics.shl*. If the figures don't appear as shown, try an HTML browser software that supports the HTML `<span>` tag.

 See the "Engaged Learning for Programming in C++" link on **http://www.jbpub.com/cs** for more information on this HTML tag.

Step 2: Save your program in the file *graphics.cpp*.

Step 3: Test your program by using the following the test plan. If you discover mistakes in your program, correct them and execute the test plan again.

Test Plan for *graphics*

Test case	Sample data	Expected result	Checked

square.dat	t 50 100	`1 * * * * 2`
		`*         *`
		`*         *`
		`*         *`
		`4 * * * * 3`
		
		         `1 * * * * 2`
		         `*         *`
		         `*         *`
		         `*         *`
		         `4 * * * * 3`	

square.dat	r 45		
square.dat	s −30		

Step 4: Determine the appropriate graphics matrix to perform the following requested graphics operations on a figure. Recall that multiplying each point in a figure by the appropriate graphics matrix appropriately moves the entire figure. Draw a simple symbol on graph paper

and manually perform the graphics operation to help determine the graphics matrix. Then implement the functions in *graphics.cpp*.

Reflect the mirror image of a figure across the x axis ($y = 0$).

Reflect the mirror image of a figure across the y axis ($x = 0$).

 See the "Engaged Learning for Programming in C++" link on **http://www.jbpub.com/cs** for more information on graphics operations.

LABORATORY 11: Analysis Exercise

More `apmatrix` Practice

Name _____

Hour/Period/Section _____

Date _____

Part A

How do you determine the size (total number of elements) of an `apmatrix`?

Part B

Describe in pseudocode how to exchange the rows and columns in a square `apmatrix` (`numRows() == numCols()`).

Structures

OVERVIEW

In Laboratory 9 you used arrays to represent collections of elements in which each element is of the same type. In this lab you use structures (structs) to represent collections in which the elements can be of different types. These structures provide you with a way to create your own data types.

In Core Exercise 1, you examine how to define a structure, how to declare structure variables, and how to reference the individual elements in a structure variable. In Core Exercise 2, you learn how to pass structure variables to functions and how to create apvectors in which each element is a structure.

LABORATORY 12: Cover Sheet

Name _____

Hour/Period/Section _____

Date _____

Place a check mark (✔) in the Assigned column next to the exercises that your instructor has assigned to you. Have this sheet ready when your lab instructor checks your work. If your exercises are being checked outside the laboratory session, attach this sheet to the front of the packet of materials that you submit.

Exercise	Assigned	Completed
Core 1 Structure Basics *Fit for Life (fitness.cpp)*		
Core 2 `apvector` of Structures *Check the Label (bar3.cpp)*		
Reinforcement Using Structures *One Ringy-Dingy, Two Ringy-Dingy (tone.cpp)*		
Analysis Comparing `apvector`s and Structures		
Total		

LABORATORY 12: Core Exercise 1—Structure Basics

Background

A **structure** is a collection of elements of various types. Each of the elements in a structure is called a **data member** and is referred to by name rather than by number, as for arrays. Suppose that you want to construct a data type consisting of a pair of integers that specify the *x* and *y* coordinates of a two-dimensional point. You can use a structure to create your own `Point` data type as follows.

```
// Definition of the Point data type
struct Point
{
   int x,   // Point coordinates
       y;
};
```

The definition of the `Point` structure begins with the keyword `struct` followed by the structure name (`Point`). The declarations of the structure's data members (`x` and `y`) are enclosed within braces. Note that a semicolon follows the closing brace at the end of the structure definition. Take care not to forget to include this semicolon; omitting it will often cause the compiler to generate seemingly obscure error messages—especially when you break a program into multiple files (as you will do in Laboratory 14).

Once you have used a structure to define a data type, you declare a variable of this type just as you would declare a variable of any of C++'s built-in data types. For example, the declaration

```
Point pt1, pt2;
```

creates two variables (`pt1` and `pt2`) of type `Point`. You access a variable's data members by using the **dot operator** (.) followed by the name of a data member. The statement

```
pt1.x = 2;
```

assigns the value 2 to the `x` member of `pt1`. This value is used in the statement

```
pt1.y = pt1.x * pt1.x;
```

to specify the value of `pt1`'s *y* coordinate. The following diagram shows `pt1`'s data members after execution of these statements.

```
        x    y
      ┌─────────┐
pt    │  2    4 │
      └─────────┘
```

Warmup Exercise

Complete the following program by filling in the missing C++ code. A shell for this program is given in the file *sturec.shl*.

```cpp
#include <iostream.h>

// Computes a student's grade point average (GPA).

// Definition of the Student data type
struct Student
{
    int IDNum,        // Student ID
        creditPts,    // Credit points
        creditHrs;    // Credit hours
    double GPA;        // Grade point average
};

int main()
{
    _____ _____;    // Declare a variable of type Student

    cout << endl << "Enter the student's ID, credit points,"
            << " and credit hours earned : ";
    cin >> _____ >> _____ >> _____;

    // Calculate the student's GPA.

    _____;

    // Display the student data.

    cout << "Student ID:    " << _____ << endl;
    cout << "Credit points: " << _____ << endl;
    cout << "Credit hours:  " << _____ << endl;
    cout << "GPA:           " << _____ << endl;

    return 0;
}
```

APPLICATION EXERCISE: Fit for Life

You can base a person's fitness level on the time it takes the person to walk 3 mi *without* running. The following table gives the time standards for five general fitness levels for a woman 20–29 years old.

Fitness level (women, 20–29)	Time it takes to walk 3 miles
1	more than 48 min
2	more than 44, but less than or equal to 48 min
3	more than 40, but less than or equal to 44 min
4	more than 36, but less than or equal to 40 min
5	36 min or less

These standards can be extended to men by subtracting 2 min from each of the times listed and to people aged 13–19 by subtracting 1 min from each time.

Step 1:   Create a program that bases a person's fitness level on the standards outlined. Your program should read in the person's first name, last name, age, gender, and the length of time that it takes the person to walk 3 mi. It should store the input information in a fitness profile structure, complete the contents of the structure by determining the person's fitness level, and output the completed fitness profile (name, age, gender, walk time, and fitness level). If the person's age falls outside the 13–29-year-old range, your program should display a message indicating that the program cannot determine that person's fitness level.

Input: First and last name
Age (in years)
Gender ('M' or 'F')
Walk time (in minutes)

Output: Fitness profile (name, age, gender, walk time, and fitness level)

Step 2:   Save your program as *fitness.cpp*.

Step 3: Complete the following test plan.

Test Plan for *fitness*

Test case	Sample data	Expected result	Checked
Female, 22, 28-min walk, fitness level 5	Speedy Sara 22 F 28	Name: Speedy Sara Age: 22 years old Gender: F Walk time: 28 min Fitness level: 5	
Male, 18, 40-min walk, fitness level 3	Andy Average 18 M 40	Name: Andy Average Age: 18 years old Gender: M Walk time: 40 min Fitness level: 3	
Female, under 20, fitness level 2		Fitness level: 2	
Male, over 20, fitness level 4		Fitness level: 4	

Step 4: Execute your program in the file *fitness.cpp*.

Step 5: Check each case in your *fitness* test plan and verify the expected result. If you discover mistakes in your program, correct them and execute the test plan again.

LABORATORY 12: Core Exercise 2—`apvector` **of Structures**

Background

In this exercise, you explore the use of structures as function parameters and `apvector` (array) elements. You conclude by combining these concepts to create functions that process an `apvector` of structures.

You declare a structure variable as a function parameter the same way you declare any other function parameter—you specify the type of parameter and the parameter name. For example, the prototype

```
double distance ( Point pt1, Point pt2 );
```

specifies a function that receives two parameters of type `Point`. Note that the default parameter passing mechanism for a structure is pass-by-value.

The `distance()` function uses `pt1`'s and `pt2`'s data members to compute the distance between these points, as follows:

```
double distance ( Point pt1, Point pt2 )
// Returns the distance between two points.
{
    return  sqrt( pow((pt2.x - pt1.x),2) + pow((pt2.y - pt1.y),2) );
}
```

This function is used in the code fragment

```
Point alpha, beta;
...
cout << "Distance apart: " << distance(alpha,beta) << endl;
```

to compute the distance between two points `alpha` and `beta`.

In Laboratory 9 you created `apvector`s of integers, characters, and so forth. You declare an `apvector` in which each element is a structure—an `apvector` of structures—by specifying a structure type within the standard `apvector` declaration. The `apvector` declaration

```
apvector<Point> pt;
```

creates an `apvector` named `pt` (currently containing 0 points). Accessing the data members of an individual point in this `apvector` requires specifying the array index of the point followed by the name of a data member. The following loop assigns coordinate values to each point in the `pt` `apvector` after the user inputs the size of the `apvector`, `numPts`.

```
cin >> numPts;
cout << endl;
pt.resize(numPts);
```

```
// Read in the coordinates for each point in the apvector.
for ( j = 0 ; j < numPts ; j++ )
{
    cout << "Enter coordinates for point[" << j << "]: ";
    cin >> pt[j].x >> pt[j].y;
}
```

Suppose that numPts is 3. If the user enters the coordinate pairs

```
2 3
0 0
5 1
```

the pt apvector contains the data

```
        x   y
pt[0]   2   3
pt[1]   0   0
pt[2]   5   1
```

The function displayDistances() takes an apvector of points as input and outputs the distance between each pair of points in the apvector. Note that the pt apvector is passed to displayDistances() by the pass-by-const reference.

```
void displayDistances ( const apvector<Point> &pt, int count )
// Displays the distance between each pair of points in the array.
// Parameter count is the number of points in the array. Note that
// each pair is only processed one time.
{
    int j, k;
    for ( j = 0 ; j < count-1 ; j++ )
        for ( k = j+1 ; k < count ; k++ )
            cout << "Distance between points " << j << " and " << k
                << " : " << distance(pt[j],pt[k]) << endl;
}
```

The distance() and displayDistances() functions are included in the program given in the file *ptstruct.cpp*.

Warmup Exercise

Complete the following program by filling in the missing C++ code. A shell for this program is given in the file *stulist.shl*.

```
#include <iostream.h>
#include <iomanip.h>
#include <apvector.h>

// Displays information on a list of students.
```

```
// Definition of the Student data type
struct Student
{
    int IDNum,          // Student ID
        creditPts,      // Credit points
        creditHrs;      // Credit hours
    double GPA;         // Grade point average
};

// Function prototypes
void readStudentData ( apvector<Student> &stuList, int count );
void calculateGPAs ( apvector<Student> &stuList, int count );
void displayGPAs ( const apvector<Student> &stuList, int count );

int main()
{
    _____ ;    // apvector of students
    int numStudents;            // User input number of students

    cout << endl << "Enter the number of students: ";
    cin >> numStudents;
    stu.resize(numStudents);

    readStudentData(_____);
    calculateGPAs(_____);
    displayGPAs(_____);
    cout << endl;

    return 0;
}

//-----------------------------------------------------------------
void readStudentData ( apvector<Student> &stuList, int count )
// Reads in the ID numbers, credit points, and credit hours for a list
// of students and returns the information in the apvector stuList.
{
    int j;
    cout << endl << "Enter the ID number, credit points, and credit"
         << " hours for each student:" << endl;
    for ( _____ )
        cin >> _____ ;
}

//-----------------------------------------------------------------
void calculateGPAs ( apvector<Student> &stuList, int count )
// Calculates the GPA for each student in the apvector.
{
    int j;
    for ( _____ )
        _____ ;
}
```

```
//----------------------------------------------------------------
void displayGPAs ( const apvector<Student> &stuList, int count )
// Displays a table listing the ID number and GPA of each student in
// the apvector.
{
    int j;
    cout << endl << setw(4) << "ID #" << setw(6) << "GPA" << endl;
    for ( _____ )
        cout << setw(4) << _____ << setprecision(2)
            << setw(6) << _____ << endl;
}
```

APPLICATION EXERCISE: Check the Label

You used a bar graph in Laboratory 9 to represent scaled data graphically. In this exercise you add labels to the scaled bar graph to make the data more meaningful. The following is a labeled bar graph representing U.S. national debt.

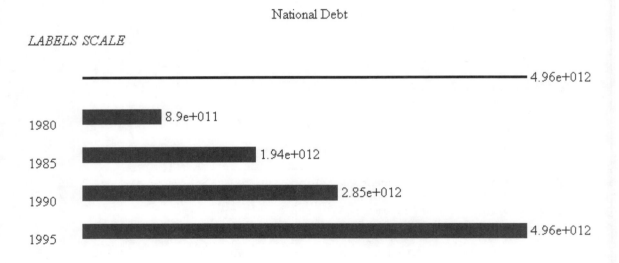

Step 1: Using your program *bar2.cpp* from Laboratory 9 (for the HTML bar chart example) and your program *heatindx.cpp* from Laboratory 7 (for the HTML table example), create a program that outputs an HTML file (file name specified by the user) with a labeled, scaled bar graph. A two-column HTML table is used, with the first column for data labels and the second column for data bars. Your program should begin by reading (from a file specified by the user) an apstring label for the graph—the label "US National Debt" in the case of the graph shown. Then the number of data/label values is read. Finally, read data (double), label (apstring) pairs for each bar into an array of structures. See *usdebt.dat*.

See the "Engaged Learning for Programming in C++" link on **http://www.jbpub.com/cs** for more information on HTML tables.

Recall that the stream function, `getline(stream_name, apstring)`, is used to read data that contains embedded blanks from a line input by the user or from an input file into one `apstring` object. Recall also that `getline()` reads to (and including) the end-of-line marker. Recall further that the standard stream extractor, `>>`, reads up to but *not* including whitespace (blanks, tabs, end-of-lines). Therefore, if the function is reading from an input file or from the user, one line at a time, and using both `>>` and `getline()` to read right after each other, you need a `get()` between each extraction operator input statement and each `getline()` to read the extra white space.

```
inFile >> data[j].value;
inFile.get();
getline(inFile,data[j].label);
```

Step 2: Save your program as *bar3.cpp*.

Step 3: Complete the following test plan.

Test Plan for *bar3*

Test case	Sample data	Expected result	Checked
U.S. National debt	usdebt.dat	See the U.S. debt bar graph.	
Population of the world's largest cities	citypop.dat		
Your own data			

Step 4: Execute your program in the file *bar3.cpp*.

Step 5: Check each case in your *bar3* test plan and verify the expected result. If you discover mistakes in your program, correct them and execute the test plan again.

LABORATORY 12: Reinforcement Exercise—Using Structures

One Ringy-Dingy, Two Ringy-Dingy

Each key on a telephone keypad generates a different pair of tones. One tone is determined by the row on which the key appears; the other is determined by the column. The frequencies of these tones are as follows.

	Key			Row tone (Hz)
1	2	3		697
4	5	6		770
7	8	9		852
*	0	#		941
Column tone (Hz)	1209	1336	1477	

For example, pressing the 8 key generates a row tone at 852 Hz and a column tone at 1336 Hz.

Step 1: To the shell program *tone.shl*, add a function `keyTones()` that returns a structure containing the row tone and column tone produced by a given key. Base your function on the following specification.

> **PhoneTones keyTones (char key)**
> **Input parameter**
> **key:** the key pressed (`'0'-'9'`, `'*'`, or `'#'`)
> **Returns**
> The tones produced by that key.

The `PhoneTones` structure is defined as

```
struct PhoneTones
{
   int rowTone,    // Frequencies of the tones generated by a key press
       colTone;
};
```

In Laboratory 4 you learned how to use the `switch` statement when a program must take one of several actions, depending on some variable or expression. A slightly different syntax allows multiple cases to be grouped as follows (which may be useful with this problem).

```
switch (expression)
{
case label1: case label2:
    statement1;
    break;
```

```
case label3: case label4:
    statement2;
    break;
 default:
    default statement;
}
```

Step 2:   Save your program in the file *tone.cpp*.

Step 3:   Test your `keyTones()` function by using the following test plan. If you discover mistakes in your function, correct them and execute the test plan again.

Test Plan for *keyTones()*

Test case	Sample data	Expected result	Checked
Row 1, Column 3	3	`Tones produced at 697 and 1477 Hz`	
Row 2, Column 2	5	`Tones produced at 770 and 1336 Hz`	

LABORATORY 12: Analysis Exercise

Comparing apvectors and Structures

Name _____

Hour/Period/Section _____

Date _____

In Laboratory 9 and this lab you examined two methods for forming collections of data—apvectors (arrays) and structures—that exist in one form or another in most modern programming languages. Use the following table to compare and contrast the properties and use of apvectors and structures in C++.

	apvectors	Structures
Must all the data items in an apvector/a structure be of the same type?		
How do you declare an apvector/a structure variable? Give an example of each.		
How do you access a data item in an apvector/a structure? Give an example of each.		
What form of parameter passing—pass-by-value or pass-by-reference—is used by default with apvectors/structures?		

Searching and Sorting

OVERVIEW

Searching for a particular element in an array (`apvector`) and sorting an array (`apvector`) based on a particular field are two very important functions needed to solve many business problems. Usually these arrays contain not just a single data type, but a user defined structure, as you saw in Laboratory 12.

In Core Exercise 1, you examine how to perform a linear search on both an unsorted array and a sorted array. In Core Exercise 2, you learn how sort an array with a basic sort algorithm called selection sort. In Core Exercise 3, you study a second search method, binary search, which exhibits an improved (faster) algorithm for locating a particular element in a sorted array.

LABORATORY 13: Cover Sheet

Name _____

Hour/Period/Section _____

Date _____

Place a check mark (✔) in the Assigned column next to the exercises that your instructor has assigned to you. Have this sheet ready when your lab instructor checks your work. If your exercises are being checked outside the laboratory session, attach this sheet to the front of the packet of materials that you submit.

Exercise	Assigned	Completed
Core 1 Linear Search *Everyday's a Holiday (holidays.cpp)*		
Core 2 Selection Sort *Behind Bars (upc.cpp)*		
Core 3 Binary Search *Splitting the Difference (binsrch.cpp)*		
Reinforcement More Selection Sort *Sorting Things Out (upc1.cpp)*		
Analysis Searching Efficiently		
Total		

LABORATORY 13: Core Exercise 1—Linear Search

Background

Many applications require that you find a particular element in an array. Suppose that you have the following unsorted array of integers (`apvector<int>`).

Array index	0	1	2	3	4	5	6	7	8	9
Array entry	24	57	71	89	23	46	35	15	42	63

You are asked to find the element with the value 71 (the searchKey). The array is unsorted, so the only systematic way that you can find the searchKey is by starting at the first element, at index=0, and checking the array element value to see if it is equal to the searchKey. If it is, you can stop looking; index is where you found the searchKey. If it isn't the same as the searchKey, increment index and repeat the check for the searchKey.

Array index	0	1	2	3	4	5	6	7	8	9
Array entry	24	57	71	89	23	46	35	15	42	63

↑
index=0, searchKey not found

Array index	0	1	2	3	4	5	6	7	8	9
Array entry	24	57	71	89	23	46	35	15	42	63

↑
index=1, searchKey not found

Array index	0	1	2	3	4	5	6	7	8	9
Array entry	24	57	71	89	23	46	35	15	42	63

↑
index=2, searchKey found

If you reach the end of the array and haven't found the searchKey, the search has failed.

The following function searches through the list array, element by element, until it finds an element that equals searchKey. If a matching element is found, the function returns its array index. Otherwise, the function returns -1. This type of search is called a **linear search**. Note that the function stops the search as soon as searchKey is found.

```
int search ( const apvector<int> &list, int count, int searchKey )
// Linear search. Returns the array index of the entry that
// matches searchKey. Returns -1 if searchKey is not in the array.
{
    int index = 0;   // Array index returned

    // Continue searching while there are more values left in the
    // array and searchKey has not been found.
    while ( index < count && list[index] != searchKey )
        index++;

    // If index equals count, then the search failed.
    if ( index == count )
        index = -1;

    return index;
}
```

Warmup Exercise

Searches are commonly performed on arrays of structures. Usually, the search process focuses on a data member that identifies the entries in the array. The following program, for instance, uses a linear search to locate the student who has a specified student ID number. Complete this program by filling in the missing C++ code. A shell for this program is given in the file *stusrch.shl*.

```
#include <iostream.h>
#include <apvector.h>

// Retrieves student data.

// Definition of the Student data type
struct Student
{
    int IDNum,        // Student ID
        creditPts,    // Credit points
        creditHrs;    // Credit hours
    double GPA;        // Grade point average
};

// Function prototypes
void readStudentData ( apvector<Student> &stuList, int count ); // Lab 12
void calculateGPAs ( apvector<Student> &stuList, int count );    // Lab 12
int IDSearch ( const apvector<Student> &stuList, int count, int IDNumber );

int main()
{
    _____ ;    // apvector of students
    int numStudents,           // User input number of students
        IDRequest,             // Student ID to search for
        listIndex;             // Array index of student with matching ID
```

```
    cout << endl << "Enter the number of students: ";
    cin >> numStudents;
    _____.resize(numStudents);

    readStudentData(_____);
    calculateGPAs(_____);

    // Prompt the user for a student ID number.
    cout << endl << "Enter a student ID number: ";
    cin >> IDRequest;

    // If a student with this ID number is in the list, output
    // her or his GPA.
    listIndex = IDSearch(_____);
    if ( listIndex != -1 )
       cout << "The student's GPA is "
            << _____ << endl;
    else
       cout << "The student is not in the list." << endl;

    return 0;
}

// Add your function implementations from stulist.cpp (Lab 12:Core 2) here.


//------------------------------------------------------------------

int IDSearch ( const apvector<Student> &stuList, int count, int IDNumber )
// Linear search. Returns the array index of the entry for the
// student whose ID number matches IDNumber. Returns -1 if there is
// no such student.
{
    int index = 0;   // Array index returned

    // Continue searching while there are more students left in the
    // list and an ID matching IDNumber has not been found.
    while ( _____ )
        _____;

    // If index equals count, then the search failed.
    if ( index == count )
       index = -1;

    return index;
}
```

If you know that the data in an array is sorted in ascending order, you can improve the efficiency of the linear search algorithm somewhat by stopping the search whenever you encounter a value that is larger than the value you are searching for. After all, there is no point in searching the remainder of the array because all these values must be greater than the value you are searching for.

Add this modification to the IDSearch() function you just completed. Assume that the array of students is sorted in ascending order, based on student ID. Note that you need to change both the `while` condition that controls the search and the `if` condition that determines whether the search terminated unsuccessfully.

```
int IDSearch ( const apvector<Student> &stuList, int count, int IDNumber )
// Linear search of an array of students that is sorted in ascending
// order based on student ID number. Returns the array index of the
// entry for the student whose ID number matches IDNumber.
// Returns -1 if there is no such student.
{
    int index = 0;  // Array index returned

    // Continue searching while there are more students left in the
    // list and an ID that is greater than or equal to IDNumber has
    // not been found.
    while ( _____ )
          _____;

    // Check if the search failed.
    if ( _____ )
        index = -1;

    return index;
}
```

APPLICATION EXERCISE: Everyday's a Holiday

Sometimes when searching for a particular item in an array, instead of returning the index of where the item was found in the array (if found), you can return the item itself in a function parameter that was passed by reference. Then the function itself returns a `bool true` if the item was found; it returns `bool false` if the item wasn't found.

In this exercise you create a function that searches a list of holidays for a specified date (month and day pair) and returns the name (by reference parameter) of the holiday (if any) associated with that date.

```
bool findHoliday ( const apvector<DayData> &holidayList,
                   int month, int day, apstring &holiday,
                   int count )
```

Input parameters
`holidayList:` apvector list of holidays
`month, day:` month and day to search for
`count:` number of holidays in apvector list of holidays
Output parameter
`holiday:` apstring containing the name of the holiday associated with the specified month/day (if found).
Returns
`true` if the month and day pair is found, else return `false`.

Each entry in the `holidayList` array is a `DayData` structure containing a month (`month`), day (`day`), and holiday name (`holiday`).

```
struct DayData
{
   int month,
       day;
   apstring holiday;
};
```

The following is a sample list of holidays.

holidayList[0]	1 11 Hostas Day (Puerto Rico)
holidayList[1]	1 15 Martin Luther King Jr. Day
holidayList[2]	1 23 Handwriting Day
holidayList[3]	2 3 Setsubun bean-throwing festival (Japan)
holidayList[4]	2 5 Cham Cha Mapinduzi Day (Tanzania)
holidayList[5]	2 6 Babe Ruth's Birthday
holidayList[6]	2 9 Feast of Saint Appolonia (patron saint of dentists)
holidayList[7]	2 10 Feast of St. Paul's Shipwreck (Malta)

Step 1: Create the specified function `findHoliday()`. Assume that the list of holidays is sorted in ascending order according to date. Further assume that no date appears more than once in the list and that some dates may be missing from the list. Recall that three conditions are crucial when you are performing a linear search on an already sorted array: (1) Are there more items to search in the array? (2) Has the item been found in the array? (3) Has the item been passed in the array?

Step 2: Add your `findHoliday()` function to the program shell in the file *holidays.shl*. This shell includes all the code needed to read in a list of holidays from the file *holidays.dat*. Save your program as *holidays.cpp*.

Step 3: Complete the following test plan. A second input file *everyday.dat* is also supplied for additional testing.

Test Plan for *findHoliday( )*

Test case	Sample data	Expected result	Checked
Date appears in the list.	3 31	Bunsen Burner Day	
Date doesn't appear in the list.	10 11	No holiday listed	
Your birthday			

Step 4: Execute your program in the file *holidays.cpp*

Step 5: Check each case in your *holidays* test plan and verify the expected result. If you discover mistakes in your program, correct them and execute the test plan again.

LABORATORY 13: Core Exercise 2—Selection Sort

Background

As you saw in Core Exercise 1, finding a number in a sorted list is much easier than finding a number in an unsorted list, especially if the lists are long. There are many ways to sort a list. In this exercise, you use an intuitive—sorting algorithm called a **selection sort**.

Suppose that you have the following unsorted array of integers (`apvector<int>`).

Array index	0	1	2	3	4	5	6	7	8	9
Array entry	24	57	71	89	23	46	35	15	42	63

You are asked to sort the integers into ascending order (from smallest to largest). You begin a selection sort by locating the smallest integer value in the array. You do so by using a loop in which you examine each array entry while keeping track of the location where the smallest value found thus far is located (`minPos`).

```
minPos = 0;
for ( k = 1 ; k < count ; k++ )
    if ( list[k] < list[minPos] )
        minPos = k;
```

After checking the entire array, `minPos` is 7, indicating the array entry at index 7 contains the smallest value in the array.

Array index	0	1	2	3	4	5	6	7	8	9
Array entry	24	57	71	89	23	46	35	15	42	63

↑
minPos

Once you have located the smallest value, you exchange this value with the first element in the array (the element with index 0).

Array index	0	1	2	3	4	5	6	7	8	9
Array entry	15	57	71	89	23	46	35	24	42	63

Having positioned the smallest value in its correct location in the sorted array (shaded), you continue sorting by locating the next-to-smallest value. Note that you need only search the remaining (unshaded) array entries stored at index positions 1-9.

Array index	0	1	2	3	4	5	6	7	8	9
Array entry	15	57	71	89	23	46	35	24	42	63

minPos

You then exchange the next-to-smallest value with the second element in the array (the element with index 1).

Array index	0	1	2	3	4	5	6	7	8	9
Array entry	15	23	71	89	57	46	35	24	42	63

Repeating this process seven more times (with increasingly smaller subsets of the array) yields a sorted array.

Array index	0	1	2	3	4	5	6	7	8	9
Array entry	15	23	24	35	42	46	57	63	71	89

The following is an implementation of the selection sort algorithm.

```
void selectionSort (apvector<int> &list, int count )

// Selection sort routine. Sorts the list into ascending order.

{
    int temp,      // Temporary storage used in swapping
        minPos,    // Index of smallest value among remaining entries
        j,         // Outer loop counter
        k;         // Inner loop (min search) counter

    for ( j = 0 ; j < count-1 ; j++ )
    {
        // Initial smallest value is first value in remainder of array
        minPos = j;

        // Find smallest value in remainder of array.
        for ( k = j+1 ; k < count ; k++ )
           if ( list[k] < list[minPos] )
              minPos = k;
```

```
        temp = list[j];              // Exchange
        list[j] = list[minPos];
        list[minPos] = temp;
    }
}
```

 See the "Engaged Learning for Programming in C++" link on **http://www.jbpub.com/cs** for more information on sorting algorithms.

Warmup Exercise

Sorts are commonly performed on arrays of structures. Usually, the sort process focuses on a data member that identifies the entries in the array. The following program, for instance, uses a selection sort to order the students in ascending order based on student ID number. Complete this program by filling in the missing C++ code. A shell for this program is given in the file *stusort.shl*.

```cpp
#include <iostream.h>
#include <iomanip.h>
#include <apvector.h>

// Sorts student data.

// Definition of the Student data type
struct Student
{
    int IDNum,        // Student ID
        creditPts,    // Credit points
        creditHrs;    // Credit hours
    double GPA;       // Grade point average
};

// Function prototypes
void readStudentData ( apvector<Student> &stuList, int count );   // Lab 12
void calculateGPAs ( apvector<Student> &stuList, int count );     // Lab 12
void displayGPAs ( const apvector<Student> &stuList, int count ); // Lab 12
void IDSort ( apvector<Student> &stuList );

int main()
{
    _____;   // apvector of students
    int numStudents;            // User input number of students

    cout << endl << "Enter the number of students: ";
    cin >> numStudents;
    _____.resize(numStudents);
```

```
        readStudentData(_____);
        calculateGPAs(_____);

        // Sort the student list by ID number.
        IDSort(_____);

        displayGPAs(_____);
        cout << endl;
        return 0;
}


// Add your function implementations from stulist.cpp (Lab 12: Core 2) here
//------------------------------------------------------------------
void IDSort (apvector<Student> &stuList, int count )
// Selection sort routine. Sorts the list into ascending order.
{
        _____ temp; // Temporary storage used in swapping
        int minPos,    // Index of smallest value among remaining entries
            j,         // Outer loop counter
            k;         // Inner loop (min search) counter

        for ( j = 0 ; j < _____ ; j++ )
        {
            // Initial smallest value is first value in remainder of array.
            _____;

            // Find smallest value in remainder of array.
            for ( k = _____ ; k < _____ ; k++ )
                if ( _____ )
                    minPos = k;

            temp = stuList[j];                   // Exchange
            stuList[j] = stuList[minPos];
            stuList[minPos] = temp;
        }
}
```

APPLICATION EXERCISE: Behind Bars

When sorting an array, you may want to sort the items in **descending order,** based on a data member that identifies the entries in the array.

Universal Product Codes (UPCs) appear on almost everything you buy. If you look closely at a UPC bar code, you will see a sequence of numbers. These numbers are included so that supermarket checkout scanners can identify a product. Many—but not all—products carry a six-digit number designating the product manufacturer, followed by a five-digit number, designating the product item, followed by a single check digit. The check digit lets the scanner determine with a mathematical formula whether it scanned the number correctly.

 See the "Engaged Learning for Programming in C++" link on **http://www.jbpub.com/cs** for more information on UPC codes.

The codes from a box of Tide Free Detergent are

```
     037000        92297           1
  Manufacturer    Product    Check Digit
```

In this exercise, you create a program that reads information on a series of products from an input file, sorts the information in descending order, based on the six-digit product manufacturer's code, and outputs the information in sorted order to another file. The input file (*grocery.dat*) consists of the product data

manufacturer product check description

where *manufacturer*, *product*, and *check* are the UPC numbers identifying a product and *description* is a product description. Because the product manufacturer codes and product item codes may have leading zeros, you must read them as apstrings to preserve the leading zeros. The product description is read with getline() because it may contain embedded spaces (see Laboratory 12, Core Exercise 2 for how to use both the extraction operator >> and getline() when reading input).

Now, create the following functions. Note how to pass, by reference, an input or output file stream object name to a function.

```
void readData ( apvector<UPC> &productList, int &count, ifstream &inFile )
// Reads data from user specified input file into apvector
// productList. Resizes productList larger if necessary when
// reading from input file.
```
Input parameter
inFile: input file stream object
Input/Output parameter
productList: input—empty apvector of product information; output—unsorted apvector of product information
count: number of entries in apvector of product information

```
void selectionDescendingSort ( apvector<UPC> &productList, int count )
// Selection sort routine. Sorts the list into descending
// order by manufacturer code.
```
Input parameter
count: number of entries in apvector of product information

Input/Output parameter

`productList`: input—unsorted `apvector` of product information; output—sorted in descending order based on manufacturer code

```
void writeData ( const apvector<UPC> &productList, int count
                ofstream &outFile )
// Writes data from sorted apvector productList to user
// specified output file. Skips a line when the manufacturer
// code changes.
```

Input parameters

`productList`: sorted `apvector` of product information

`count`: number of entries in `apvector` of product information

`outFile`: output file stream object

Each entry in the `productList` array is a `UPC` structure containing a manufacturer code (`apstring`), product code (`apstring`), check digit (`int`), and product name (`apstring`).

Step 1: Your program should begin by asking the user for the name of the input file to process and the name of the output file to create (see Laboratory 10, Core Exercise 2). After opening both files, the program should read through the input file line by line (product by product) into an `apvector` product list, sort the product list by manufacturer code in descending order and output the product information (UPC numbers and description) to the output file.

Input: The name of the input file to process (user input)

The name of the output file to create (user input)

Output: Product information sorted by manufacturer's code in descending order with one blank line separating each different manufacturer's code

Step 2: Save your program as *upc.cpp*.

Step 3: Test your program by using the following test plan.

Test Plan for *upc*

Test case	Sample data	Expected result	Checked
	grocery.dat	upc.out	

Step 4: Execute your program in the file *upc.cpp*

Step 5: Check each case in your *upc* test plan and verify the expected result. If you discover mistakes in your program, correct them and execute the test plan again.

LABORATORY 13: Core Exercise 3—Binary Search

Background

In Core Exercise 1 you used a linear search to locate a value in an array. If the array is sorted, however, you can use a much more efficient method, called a **binary search**, to locate values. Unlike the linear search algorithm, the binary search algorithm doesn't simply iterate through the array from beginning to end. Instead, it rapidly narrows the range of entries in which the value might lie until it either locates the value or recognizes that there are no entries that might contain the value.

Suppose that you have the following sorted array of integers.

Array index	0	1	2	3	4	5	6	7	8	9	10	11	12	13	14	15
Array entry	4	7	11	15	23	29	35	37	42	46	51	54	67	72	78	86

You are asked to locate the value 46. At this point, the value 46 could lie anywhere within the array, so the initial search range is all 16 entries. We mark the beginning index of this range with the variable `low` and the end index of this range with the variable `high`.

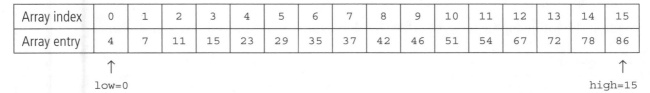

How do you narrow the search range? You begin by locating the entry in the middle of the search range. The index of this entry is the average of the indices `low` and `high`, or

```
middle = ( low + high ) / 2;
```

If `low` is 0 and `high` is 15, `middle` equals (0+15)/2 or 7.

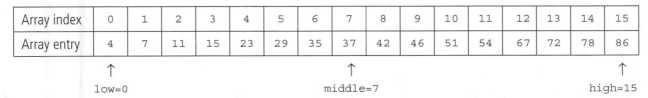

The entry with index 7 is 37. You narrow the search range by comparing the value you are searching for in this example, 46—with 37. The fact that 46 is greater than 37 indicates that you don't need to search through array entries at index positions 0–7 because these entries are less than or equal to 37 (the array is sorted) and therefore are less than 46. You reflect this narrowing of the search range by changing `low` to

```
low = middle + 1;
```

yielding the following result. Note that you have halved the size of the search range with just one comparison.

Array index	0	1	2	3	4	5	6	7	8	9	10	11	12	13	14	15
Array entry	4	7	11	15	23	29	35	37	42	46	51	54	67	72	78	86

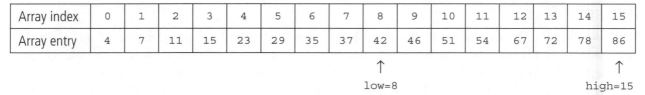

low=8   high=15

You continue the search by repeating the process. The average of low and high is (8+15)/2 or 11.

Array index	0	1	2	3	4	5	6	7	8	9	10	11	12	13	14	15
Array entry	4	7	11	15	23	29	35	37	42	46	51	54	67	72	78	86

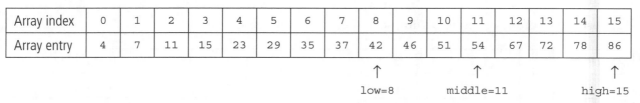

low=8   middle=11   high=15

The array entry with index 11 is 54. The fact that 46 is less than 54 indicates that you don't need to search entries 11-15, for these entries are greater than or equal to 54 and thus are greater than 46. You therefore change high to

    high = middle - 1;

yielding the following result. Note that you have once again halved the search range.

Array index	0	1	2	3	4	5	6	7	8	9	10	11	12	13	14	15
Array entry	4	7	11	15	23	29	35	37	42	46	51	54	67	72	78	86

low=8   high=10

In this case, the average of low and high is (8+10)/2 or 9.

Array index	0	1	2	3	4	5	6	7	8	9	10	11	12	13	14	15
Array entry	4	7	11	15	23	29	35	37	42	46	51	54	67	72	78	86

low middle high

The array entry with index 9 is 46—the value that you are searching for—so your search ends with success. More important, it only took three comparisons to locate 46.

APPLICATION EXERCISE: Splitting the Difference

In this exercise, you further explore the functioning of the binary search algorithm by using the following implementation from the file *binsrch.cpp*.

```
int binarySearch ( const apvector<int> &list, int searchKey )

// Binary search of an array that is sorted in ascending order.
// Returns the array index of the entry that matches searchKey.
// Returns -1 if searchKey is not in the array.

{
    int low  = 0,                      // Low index of current search range
        high = list.length() - 1,      // High index of current search range
        middle;                        // Middle of the current search range
    bool found = false;                // Flag indicating searchKey was found

    while ( low <= high  &&  !found )
    {
        middle = ( low + high ) / 2;         // Compute midpoint
        if ( searchKey < list[middle] )
            high = middle - 1;               // Search lower half
        else if ( searchKey > list[middle] )
            low = middle + 1;                // Search upper half
        else
            found = true;                    // searchKey found
    }

    if ( !found )
        middle = -1;    // searchKey not found, adjust index returned

    return middle;
}
```

Step 1:   The program in *binsrch.cpp* begins by generating an array containing the odd integers from 1 through 99. Use this program to complete the following table by filling in the intermediate values of variables low, middle, and high, as well as the result of the search.

Note that you must either use a debugger to trace through the program, noting changes in the values of variables low, middle, and high as the program executes, or you must add code that outputs the intermediate values of these variables.

Tracing the execution of *binarySearch()* function

Test case	Search value	Intermediate results	Result returned
Quick search	75	Low 0 25 Middle 24 37 High 49 49	37
Search goes longer	41	Low Middle High	
Search goes full depth	53	Low Middle High	
Search goes full depth	9	Low Middle High	
Search fails	62	Low Middle High	
Search fails	22	Low Middle High	

Step 2: A sorted array of any length has an upper limit to the number of comparisons that the `binarySearch()` function will make when searching for a value. Complete the following table by determining this limit for arrays containing 8, 16, 32, 64, and 128 entries. Note that you can change the length of the array in the program *binsrch.cpp* by changing the value of the constant `ARRAY_LENGTH`.

Sorted array length	Maximum number of comparisons required to locate a value
8	3
16	
32	
64	
128	

LABORATORY 13: Reinforcement Exercise—More Selection Sort

Sorting Things Out

In the application exercise for Core Exercise 1, you searched an array for a particular holiday based on two fields in the DayData structure, month and day. You can also sort an array based on two fields of a user-defined structure. For example, you could sort in descending order the UPC data from Core Exercise 2 on manufacturer's code and on product item code and the result would be:

```
051000 05977 2 Campbell's Healthy Cream of Chicken
051000 02548 7 Prego Spaghetti Sauce
051000 01251 7 Campbell's Chicken Noodle Soup

038000 13800 3 Kellogg's Low Fat Granola
038000 10401 5 Kellogg's Nutri-Grain Whole Wheat


 . . .


028000 31650 1 Taster's Choice French Vanilla
028000 24170 4 Nestle's Quik
```

Note that the entries have been sorted in descending order by manufacturer's code and, within every duplicate manufacturer's code, that the product item codes also have been sorted in descending order.

Step 1: Start with your program *upc.cpp* from Core Exercise 2. Change the condition in your selectionDescendingSort() function that you are using to find the array index of the largest manufacturer's code to instead find the array index of the largest manufacturer's code and product code pair.

Step 2: Save your program in the file *upc1.cpp*.

Step 3: Test your program by using the following test plan. If you discover mistakes in your program, correct them and execute the test plan again.

Test Plan for *upc1*

Test case	Sample data	Expected result	Checked
	grocery.dat	See preceding list of grocery items sorted by the manufacturer's code and the product item code.	

LABORATORY 13: Analysis Exercise

Searching Efficiently

Name _____

Hour/Period/Section _____

Date _____

Part A

What is the maximum number of IDs you would need to check in order to find a student ID in an *unsorted* array of 100 student IDs? Justify your answer.

Part B

What is the maximum number of IDs you would need to check in order to find a student ID in a *sorted* array of 100 student IDs? Justify your answer.

Creating Classes

OVERVIEW

In Laboratory 12, you used a structure to represent an aggregate data type containing a set of data members. In this lab, you expand the concept of an aggregate data type by bundling data members and the functions that manipulate them into a single entity by using the C++ class construct. Classes provide the foundation for object-oriented programming and help distinguish C++ from traditional structured programming languages such as C, Pascal, and FORTRAN. You have already used classes (`apstring`, `apvector`, and `apmatrix`) in earlier labs—in this lab you create your own `Calendar` class.

In Core Exercise 1 you learn how to declare a class, how to write class member functions, and how to construct class variables (objects). You also learn how to create, compile, link, and execute a multifile program. In Core Exercise 2 you implement modifier member functions that change an object's data members. In Core Exercise 3 you create a function that outputs a calendar as an HTML file.

LABORATORY 14: Cover Sheet

Name _____

Hour/Period/Section _____

Date _____

Place a check mark (✔) in the Assigned column next to the exercises that your instructor has assigned to you. Have this sheet ready when your lab instructor checks your work. If your exercises are being checked outside the laboratory session, attach this sheet to the front of the packet of materials that you submit.

Exercise		Assigned	Completed
Core 1	What Is a C++ Class? *Thirty Days Has September? (calendar.cpp)*		
Core 2	Default Constructors, `set()` Functions, and `get()` Functions *A Change for the Better (calendar.cpp)*		
Core 3	Displaying a Calendar Object Using HTML *Day After Day (calendar.cpp)*		
Analysis	Designing classes		
Total			

LABORATORY 14: Core Exercise 1—What Is a C++ Class?

Background

The following user-defined `Point` data type consists of a pair of real numbers that specify the x and y coordinates of a two-dimensional point.

```
struct Point
{
    double x;       // x-coordinate
    double y;       // y-coordinate
};
```

In order to use values of type `Point`, you need functions that perform basic actions such as initializing a point's coordinates, moving a point, displaying a point, and the like. You could create functions called `movePoint()`, `displayPoint()`, and so on. However, a more effective approach is to incorporate these functions into the `Point` data type. The result is a **class** consisting of a set of **data members** and a set of functions—called **member functions**—that manipulate these data members. The following class declaration from the file *point.h* includes several member functions that operate on two-dimensional points, or (x, y) ordered pairs.

```
// Declaration for a two-dimensional Point class.

class Point
{
  public:         // Member functions

    // Constructors
    Point ( double newX, double newY );      // Define a point
    Point ();                                // Default constructor

    // Return point attributes (accessor functions)
    double getX() const;                     // Get x coordinate
    double getY() const;                     // Get y coordinate
    double distance () const;                // Distance from (0,0)

    // Change point attributes (modifier functions)
    void move ( double deltaX, double deltaY ); // Move point
    void setX ( double newX );               // Set x coordinate
    void setY ( double newY );               // Set y coordinate

    // Outputs the data members -- used in testing and debugging
    void showDataMembers () const;

  private:

    // Data members
    double x,     // x coordinate
           y;     // y coordinate
};
```

You declare a variable—or **object**—of type `Point` as follows:

```
Point pt(2,5);
```

This declaration creates an object with an *x* coordinate of 2 and a *y* coordinate of 5. In Laboratory 12 you used the dot operator (.) to access a structure's data members. In the case of classes, you use the dot operator both to call its member functions (as you've seen with the AP classes) and, in selected cases, to access an object's data members. For example, to find the distance of a point from the origin, you use the name of the object followed by the dot operator and the name of the member function to be invoked.

```
cout << pt.distance();
```

Several points (no pun intended) need to be made about the `Point` class declaration. The declaration includes a **public** section containing the prototypes for the class's member functions and a **private** section containing its data members. By making the data members private, you prevent functions that are not members of the `Point` class from directly accessing and manipulating a `Point` object's data members. The code fragment

```
int main ()
{
    Point pt(1,2);
    pt.x = 5;        // Error -- attempts to access private data member

    return 0;
}
```

produces a compilation error because `x` is a private data member and therefore can only be accessed by one of `Point`'s member functions. Indirect access to the data members is provided by `Point`'s member functions. These functions are public and thus can be called by any function—either member or nonmember. Collectively, the member functions provide a **public interface** to the `Point` class.

The `Point` class declaration lists the class's member functions and data members. In order to use the `Point` class, you must first implement its member functions. Let's start by looking at how we specify member functions. For each function, we give the **precondition** that must exist before the function is called and the **postcondition** of the function—that is, what the function returns or what action the function performs. This style is used in the following member function specifications.

```
Point ( double newX, double newY )
```
Precondition
None
Postcondition
Constructor. Creates a point with coordinates `newX` and `newY`.

```
double distance () const
```
Precondition
None
Postcondition
Returns the distance from a point to the origin (0, 0).

The first of these functions is a special member function called a **constructor**. A constructor allocates memory for an object and initializes its data members. The constructor for a class is automatically called whenever an object of that class is declared in a program. The declaration

```
Point nextPt(2,4);
```

for example, invokes the `Point` class constructor, which initializes `nextPt`'s data members `x` and `y` to `2` and `4`, respectively. Note that a constructor has the same name as the class to which it belongs—`Point`, in this case—and does not have a return type. An implementation of the `Point` class constructor follows. The **scope resolution operator** (`::`) is used to signal the compiler that this function is a member function of the `Point` class.

```
Point:: Point ( double newX, double newY )
{
    x = newX;
    y = newY;
}
```

An alternative way to initialize values in a constructor is to use **member initialization:**

```
Point:: Point (double newX, double newY )
// Explicit constructor. Sets point to (newX,newY).
    : x(newX),
      y(newY)
{}
```

Note that a colon appears at the start of the initialization list, the items in the list are separated by commas, and there is no semicolon at the end. We discuss the use of initialization lists in more detail in Laboratory 15.

The second function in the `Point` class, `distance()`, returns the distance from a point to the origin (0, 0).

```
double Point:: distance () const
// Returns the distance from a point to the origin (0,0).
{
    return ( sqrt( pow(x,2) + pow (y,2) ) );
}
```

Once again, the scope resolution operator is used to indicate that this function is part of the `Point` class. Because `distance()` is a `Point` member function, it can reference the data members `x` and `y` directly.

The `Point` class `distance()` function is an example of an **accessor function**—a member function that does not change any data members of the class. Note the **const** specification in both the function declaration (prototype) and implementation of `distance()`. Any class member function that does not modify an object's data members should be declared a `const` **function**. If a `const` function attempts to modify an object's data members or to call a non-`const` function, the compiler will return a syntax error.

The following code fragment contains a pair of calls to the `distance()` function.

```
int main ()
{
    Point alpha(1,2),
          beta(3,5);

    cout << alpha.distance() << endl;
    cout << beta.distance() << endl;
    return 0;
}
```

When the call `alpha.distance()` is made, the `distance()` function automatically uses `alpha`'s `x` and `y` data members (e.g., `x=1` and `y=2`) but for the call `beta.distance()`, `distance()` uses `beta`'s data members.

Functions that change (modify) an object's data members are referred to as **modifier functions.** The following `Point` member function modifies a point's *x* and *y* coordinates.

void move (double deltaX, double deltaY)
Precondition
None
Postcondition
Moves a point by `deltaX` in the *x* direction and `deltaY` in the *y* direction.

Note that modifier functions are not `const` because they change an object data members.

Creating Multifile Programs

The declaration for a class and the implementation of its member functions are usually stored in separate files. The class declaration is stored in an appropriately named **header file**—*point.h* in the case of the `Point` class—and the **implementation** is stored in a similarly named source file. The class declaration in *point.h* and the member function implementations in *point.cpp* combine to form the `Point` class. The following is a portion of a copy of the file *point.cpp* containing the implementation of some of `Point`'s member functions.

```
#include <math.h>
#include "point.h"

//-------------------------------------------------------------

Point:: Point (double newX, double newY )
// Explicit constructor. Sets point to (newX,newY).
    : x(newX),
      y(newY)
{}
```

```
//---------------------------------------------------------------

double Point:: distance () const
// Returns the distance of a point from the origin (0,0).
{
    return ( sqrt( pow(x,2) + pow (y,2) ) );
}

//---------------------------------------------------------------

void Point:: move ( double deltaX, double deltaY )
// Moves a point by (deltaX, deltaY)
{
    x = x + deltaX;
    y = y + deltaY;
}

//---------------------------------------------------------------

void Point:: showDataMembers () const
// Displays a point's data members. Use for testing/debugging only.
{
    cout << "(" << x << "," << y << ")";
}
```

Note that any file that contains references to the `Point` class must include the header file *point.h* so that the compiler can resolve these references. Note also that *point.h* is included using `""` instead of `<>`. When `""` are used to include header files, the compiler looks for your *.h* file in the same directory as your implementation file.

Warmup Exercise

The following `main()` function from the file *testpt.cpp* uses the `Point` class to compute the distance from a pair of points to the origin.

```
#include <iostream.h>
#include "point.h"

int main()
{
    int testCase;

    cout << "Enter test case: "; cin >> testCase;

    switch ( testCase )
    {
        case 1  :    // Tests constructor, distance, move, showDataMembers
        {
            // Construct the points (10,5) and (7,8).
            Point pt1(10,5),
                  pt2(7,8);
```

```
        // Display both points' data members.
        cout << "Point 1: " ; pt1.showDataMembers();
        cout << "Point 2: " ; pt2.showDataMembers();

        // Display the distance from each point to (0,0).
        cout << "Distance from Point 1 to the origin: "
             << pt1.distance() << endl;
        cout << "Distance from Point 2 to the origin: "
             << pt2.distance() << endl;

        // Move Point 1 by (2,4)
        pt1.move(2,4);
        cout << "Point 1 after moving by (2,4) : ";
        pt1.showDataMembers();

        break;
        }
        . . .
    }
    return 0;
}
```

The resulting program is formed from the contents of three files: *testpt.cpp* (the `main()` function), *point.h* (the `Point` class declaration), and *point.cpp* (the implementations of `Point`'s member functions). Both *testpt.cpp* and *point.cpp* need to include *point.h* because both files contain references to the `Point` class. If you try to compile *testpt.cpp*, you will get a link error because *testpt.cpp* also needs to access the implementations of `Point`'s member functions. The standard way to handle this requirement is to create a multifile program that will contain both *testpt.cpp* and *point.cpp* so that they will be compiled together.

Check your compiler's documentation to determine how to construct a multifile program using *point.h*, *point.cpp*, and *testpt.cpp*. Compile, link, and run your multifile program.

 Various tutorials for creating multifile programs are available at http://www.jbpub.com/cs.

APPLICATION EXERCISE: Thirty Days Has September . . .

In this exercise, you begin to implement a class that you can use to generate HTML calendars to include in various Web-based projects. Each `Calendar` object is defined by a (*month, year*) pair and has an image (a *.gif* or *.jpg* file) associated with it. In order to display a calendar for a particular month you need to know other information about the (*month, year*) pair, such as the number of days in the month and on what day of the week the first day of the month occurs.

The declaration for the `Calendar` class from the file *calendar.h* is

```
#include <fstream.h>
#include <apstring.h>
class Calendar
{
  public:

    // Constructors
    Calendar ( int calMonth, int calYear, const apstring &calImage );
    Calendar();                  // Default constructor

    // Accessors
    int getMonth() const;             // Get the month
    int getYear() const;              // Get the year
    bool leapYear() const;            // Leap year?
    int daysInMonth () const;         // Number of days in month
    int dayNumber ( int day ) const;  // Days from Jan 1. to day in month
    int dayOfWeek ( int day ) const;  // Day of the week for day in month

    // Modifiers
    void setMonth ( int newMonth );   // Change the month to newMonth
    void setYear ( int newYear );     // Change the year to newYear
    void setImage ( const apstring &newImage );  // Change the image
                                      // to newImage
    // Output calendar in HTML form
    void outputHTML ( ofstream &HTMLFile ) const;

    // Outputs the data members -- used in testing and debugging
    void showDataMembers () const;


  private:    // Data members

    int month, year;            // Calendar month and year
    apstring imageFilename;      // Calendar image filename
};
```

When you first started using the AP string class, you didn't know how to work with multifile programs. In an effort to keep things simple, we told you to include the implementation of the AP string class (*apstring.cpp*) in your programs whenever you needed to use that class. In general, it's a bad idea to include code in this manner for at least a couple of reasons. First, it's inefficient. Every time you recompile your program, you would recompile the implementation of the AP string class. Second, it makes the code harder for you to find. In order to find all the functions in your program, you would need to look through all the `#include` statements to find the places where you included code (.*cpp* files) directly.

Now that you understand how multifile programs work, you should stop including *apstring.cpp*. Instead you should include *apstring.h* (i.e., `#include <apstring.h>`) in each file that references `apstring` and to add *apstring.cpp* to your multifile program.

Step 1: Implement the following `Calendar` class member functions. Prototypes for these functions are included in the declaration of the `Calendar` class in the file *calendar.h*.

```
Calendar ( int calMonth, int calYear,
           const apstring &calImage )
```
Precondition
Parameter `calMonth` is in the range 1–12 and parameter `calYear` is in the range 1901–2099.
Postcondition
Constructor. Creates a calendar for the month (`calMonth`, `calYear`) and associates it with image file `calImage`.

```
bool leapYear () const
```
Precondition
None
Postcondition
Returns `true(1)` if the calendar year is a leap year. Otherwise, returns `false(0)`.

```
int daysInMonth () const
```
Precondition
None
Postcondition
Returns the number of days in the calendar month.

The following example shows how one member function calls another member function within the same class. In this case, member function `daysInMonth()` calls member function `leapYear()` to determine whether the calendar year is a leap year. Note that `leapYear()` will operate on the same data members as the `daysInMonth ()` function.

```
int Calendar:: daysInMonth ()
{
    int result;

    ...

    if ( leapYear() )
       result=29;
    else
       result=28;

    ...

    return result;
}
```

Step 2: Save your implementation of these functions as the file *calendar.cpp*. Note that all the `Calendar` class's member functions do not need to be implemented for you to be able to use the header file *calendar.h* in your project.

Step 3: Add the implementation of the member function `showDataMembers()` given in the file *showdata.cpp* to the file *calendar.cpp*.

Step 4: Complete the following test plan for the constructor, `leapYear()` and the `daysInMonth()` functions.

Test Plan for *Test1* Test Program *testcal.cpp*

Test case	Sample data	Expected result	Checked

July 2000	7 2000
	july.jpg
		`month      : 7`
		`year       : 2000`
		`image      : july.jpg`
		`leapYear   : 1 (true)`
		`daysInMonth : 31`	

February 2001	2 2001
	february.jpg
		`month      : 2`
		`year       : 2001`
		`image      : february.jpg`
		`leapYear   :`
		`daysInMonth :`	

September 2004	9 2004
	september.jpg
		`month      : 9`
		`year       : 2004`
		`image      : september.jpg`
		`leapYear   :`
		`daysInMonth :`	

Step 5: Construct a multifile program by using your implementation of the `Calendar` class and the test program in the file *testcal.cpp* (remember also to add *apstring.cpp* to your multifile program). Compile, link, and run your multifile program.

Step 6: Check each case in the test plan for *Test 1* and verify the expected result. If you discover mistakes in your implementation, correct them and execute the test plan again.

Step 7: Implement the following `Calendar` class member functions. Prototypes for these functions are included in the declaration of the `Calendar` class in the file *calendar.h*.

```
int dayNumber ( int day ) const
```
Precondition
Parameter `day` is between 1 and `daysInMonth()` (inclusive).
Postcondition
Returns the number of days from the start of the calendar year to the specified `day` of the calendar month. For example, if the calendar month is July 2000, then the call `dayNumber(4)` returns `186`, the number of days from January 1, 2000 to July 4, 2000.

```
int dayOfWeek ( int day ) const
```
Precondition
Parameter `day` is between 1 and `daysInMonth()` (inclusive).

Returns the day of the week for the specified `day` of the calendar month, where the days are numbered from 0 (Sunday) to 6 (Saturday). For example, if the calendar month is July 2000, the call `dayOfWeek(4)` returns 2, indicating that July 4, 2000 is a Tuesday.

You can compute the day of the week corresponding to the date *month/day/year* by using the formula

$$\text{dayOfWeek}(day) = (\ 1 + nYears + nLeapYears + \text{dayNumber}(day)\ )\ \%\ 7$$

where *nYears* is the number of years since 1901 (not counting 1901) and *nLeapYears* is the number of leap years since 1901. This formula yields a value between 0 (Sunday) and 6 (Saturday) and is accurate for any date from January 1, 1901 through December 31, 2099. For example, the date July 4, 2000 yields the computation

nYears = 99

nLeapYears = 99 / 4 = 24

`dayNumber`(4) = 186

`dayOfWeek`(4) = (1 + 99 + 24 + 186) % 7 = 2

Step 8: Add these functions to your `Calendar` class implementation in the file *calendar.cpp*.

Step 9: Complete the following test plan for the `dayNumber()` and `dayOfWeek()` functions.

Test Plan for *Test2* Test Program *testcal.cpp*

Test case	Sample data	Expected result		Checked

July 4, 2000	7 2000
	july.jpg
	4
		`month`
		`year`
		`image`
		`dayNumber`
		`dayOfWeek`
			`: 7`
			`: 2000`
			`: july.jpg`
			`: 186`
			`: 2`	

First day of month
September 1, 2001
	9 2001
	september.jpg
	1
		`month`
		`year`
		`image`
		`dayNumber`
		`dayOfWeek`
			`: 9`
			`: 2001`
			`: september.jpg`
			`:`
			`:`	

Last day of leap year
December 31, 2004
	12 2004
	december.jpg
	31
		`month`
		`year`
		`image`
		`dayNumber`
		`dayOfWeek`
			`: 12`
			`: 2004`
			`: december.jpg`
			`:`
			`:`	

Step 10: Uncomment the sections of *testcal.cpp* that are used in *Test 2*.

Step 11: Construct a multifile program using your implementation of the `Calendar` class and the test program in the file *testcal.cpp*. Compile, link, and run your multifile program.

Step 12: Check each case in the test plan for *Test 2* and verify the expected result. If you discover mistakes in your implementation, correct them and execute the test plan again.

LABORATORY 14: Core Exercise 2—Default Constructors, `set()` Functions, and `get()` Functions

In some cases you may want a constructor that simply initializes an object's data members to some predetermined (default) values. For example, you might not know the values of an object's data members when you first declare the object. Rather than leaving the data members in an undefined state, you can assign them known default values when the object is constructed and then later assign them new values when you finally know what values you want to use.

A constructor with no arguments is referred to as a **default constructor.** For example, a default `Point` constructor might initialize a point's coordinates to (0,0), as in

```
Point:: Point ()
// Default constructor. Sets point to (0,0).
   : x(0),
     y(0)
{}
```

The declaration

```
Point pt1;
```

invokes the `Point` default constructor to create a point `pt1` and initialize it to (0,0).

Classes that have default constructors usually also have `set()` functions that assign values to an object's data members. Although the user of an object doesn't have direct access to the object's private data members, you can create public member functions that provide indirect access so that the user can retrieve or modify private data members. The following function sets a point's *x* coordinate to `newX`.

```
void Point:: setX ( double newX )
// Sets a point's x coordinate to the specified value.
{
    x = newX;
}
```

You might use this function to set point `pt1`'s *x* value to 2 as follows.

```
pt1.setX(2);
```

Just as you will sometimes want to set a data member indirectly, you may also want to access (get) a data member. You can do so by using `get()` functions. For example, the following function returns a point's *x* coordinate.

```
double Point:: getX ()
// Returns a point's x coordinate.
{
    return x;
}
```

You might be asking yourself, Why have set() and get() functions? Why not just access an object's data members directly? The answer is that you want to be able to change how you represent an object (i.e., change the object's data members) without breaking into every program that uses that object. Suppose that you have written a set of large programs that use your Point class. In doing so, you decide that your programs would work faster if the points were represented in polar coordinates (radius, angle) rather than Cartesian coordinates (x, y).

```
class Point
{
   ...

   private:

   // Data members
   double radius,      // Distance from (0,0)
          angle;       // Angle from the x-axis
};
```

Clearly, this change means reimplementing all the Point class member functions (nothing is free). However, because your large programs do not access the Point data members directly—but only through set() and get() functions—they will not need to be changed to work with the new implementation of the Point class.

Warmup Exercise

The following member functions set and get a point's *y* coordinate.

> **void setY (double newY)**
> **Precondition**
> None
> **Postcondition**
> Sets a point's *y* coordinate to newY.

> **double getY ()**
> **Precondition**
> None
> **Postcondition**
> Returns a point's *y* coordinate.

Complete the following functions by filling in the missing C++ code. A shell for these functions is given in the file *point.cpp*.

```
void Point:: setY ( double newY )
{


}

double Point:: getY ()
{



}
```

Compile, link, and run your updated Point class multifile program. Remember to uncomment the code for *Test 2* in *testpt.cpp*.

APPLICATION EXERCISE: A Change for the Better

Step 1: Implement the following Calendar class member functions. Prototypes for these functions are included in the declaration of the Calendar class in the file *calendar.h*.

Calendar ()
Precondition
None
Postcondition
Default constructor. Creates a calendar for the current month and year with an empty image string.

 See the "Engaged Learning for Programming in C++" link on **http://www.jbpub.com/cs** for information on how you can derive the month and year from your computer's system clock.

void setMonth (int newMonth)
Precondition
Parameter newMonth is in the range 1–12.
Postcondition
Changes the calendar month to newMonth (the calendar year remains unchanged).

```
void setYear ( int newYear )
```
Precondition
Parameter `newYear` is in the range 1901–2099.
Postcondition
Changes the calendar year to `newYear` (the calendar month remains unchanged)

```
void setImage ( const apstring &newImage )
```
Precondition
None
Postcondition
Changes the calendar image to `newImage` (the calendar month and year remain unchanged).

```
int getMonth () const
```
Precondition
None
Postcondition
Returns the calendar month as an integer value in the range 1–12.

```
int getYear () const
```
Precondition
None
Postcondition
Returns the calendar year as an integer value in the range 1901–2099.

Step 2: Add these functions to your implementation of the `Calendar` class in the file *calendar.cpp*.

Step 3: Complete the following test plan for the default constructor and the set and get functions.

Test Plan for *Test 3* **Test Program** *testcal.cpp*

Test case	Sample data	Expected result	Checked
| Current month with no image (default) changed to July 2000 | 7 2000<br>july.jpg | ```
DEFAULT
month :
year  :
image :

SET
month :  7
year   :  2000
image  :  july.jpg

getmonth()  :  7
getyear()   :  2000
``` | |
| Current month with no image (default) changed to April 2001 | 4 2001<br>april.jpg | ```
DEFAULT
month :
year  :
image :

SET
month :
year  :
image :

getmonth()  :
getyear()   :
``` | |

Step 4: Uncomment the code for *Test 3* in the file *testcal.cpp*.

Step 5: Construct a multifile program using your implementation of the Calendar class and the test program in the file *testcal.cpp*. Compile, link, and run your multifile program.

Step 6: Check each case in the test plan for *Test 3* and verify the expected result. If you discover mistakes in your implementation, correct them and execute the test plan again.

LABORATORY 14: Core Exercise 3—Displaying a Calendar Object Using HTML

APPLICATION EXERCISE: Day After Day

The following `Calendar` member function outputs a calendar. The output calendar is formatted in HTML so that it can be included as part of a Web page.

```
void outputHTML ( ofstream &HTMLFile ) const
```
Precondition
None
Postcondition
Outputs an HTML version of a calendar to the output file stream `HTMLFile`. The calendar image (if any) is placed to the left of the calendar body. The calendar body includes the following elements: the month name, the year number, a set of labels for the days of the week (S M T W T F S), and the days of the month oriented within a standard weekly grid.

You include the image by outputting the HTML tag

```
<img src=imageFilename align=left hspace=20>
```

where `imageFilename` is the name of the calendar image file. This tag indicates to a web browser that the image displayed should be aligned with the left margin with 20 pixels of blank space to the left and right of the image. Note that your `outputHTML()` function should omit this tag if the calendar image string is empty.

The calendar body (month name, year, and day labels, and day grid) should be enclosed within `<pre>` and `</pre>` HTML tags. These tags indicate to a browser that the text between them should be displayed in a "what you see is what you get" (WYSIWYG) form. Use the `setw()` output manipulator you learned in Laboratory 5 to align the days into columns.

Let's look at an example that shows these HTML tags in action. When a browser processes the HTML code

```
<img src=july.jpg align=left hspace=20>
<pre>
July          2000
 S  M  T  W  T  F  S
                   1
 2  3  4  5  6  7  8
 9 10 11 12 13 14 15
16 17 18 19 20 21 22
23 24 25 26 27 28 29
30 31
</pre>
```

it displays the image `july.jpg` to the left of the calendar for July 2000. The calendar itself is displayed with the layout shown preserved (because of the `<pre>` and `</pre>` tags).

 See the "Engaged Learning for Programming in C++" link on **http://www.jbpub.com/cs** for more information on these HTML tags.

```
July                          2000
   S    M    T    W    T    F    S
                                  1
   2    3    4    5    6    7    8
   9   10   11   12   13   14   15
  16   17   18   19   20   21   22
  23   24   25   26   27   28   29
  30   31
```

Step 1: Implement the `outputHTML()` member function specified. A prototype for this function is included in the declaration of the `Calendar` class in the file *calendar.h*.

Step 2: Add this function to your `Calendar` class implementation in the file *calendar.cpp*.

Step 3: Complete the following test plan for the `outputHTML()` function.

Test Plan for *Test 4* **Test Program** *testcal.cpp*

Test case	Sample data	Expected result	Checked

July 2000	7 2000
	july.jpg
		``
		<img src=july.jpg align=left hspace=20>
		<pre>
		July 2000
		 S M T W T F S
		                   1
		 2 3 4 5 6 7 8
		 9 10 11 12 13 14 15
		16 17 18 19 20 21 22
		23 24 25 26 27 28 29
		30 31
		</pre>
		``	

September 2001	9 2001 september.jpg		
Leap year	12 2000 december.jpg		

No Image	7 2000	```
		<pre>
		July 2000
		 S M T W T F S
		                   1
		 2 3 4 5 6 7 8
		 9 10 11 12 13 14 15
		16 17 18 19 20 21 22
		23 24 25 26 27 28 29
		30 31
		</pre>
		``	

Step 4: Uncomment the code for *Test 4* in the file *testcal.cpp*.

Step 5: Construct a multifile program using your implementation of the `Calendar` class and the test program in the file *testcal.cpp*. Compile, link, and run your multifile program.

Step 6: Check each case in the test plan for *Test 4* and verify the expected result. If you discover mistakes in your implementation, correct them and execute the test plan again.

LABORATORY 14: Analysis Exercise

Designing Classes

Name _____

Hour/Period/Section _____

Date _____

In this lab you were provided with class declarations and function specifications for the
Point and Calendar classes that you were asked to implement. In this exercise you specify
the member functions and data members for a new StopWatch class that can be used to
measure time intervals up to 60 min long.

Part A

Give function specifications for the member functions that form the public interface for
your StopWatch class. Use the function specification style presented in the Core Exercises.

Part B

List the private data members that you would include in your StopWatch class. Briefly describe the information stored in each data member.

Using Objects

OVERVIEW

In Laboratory 14 you studied the basics of designing and creating a C++ class. In this lab you use your `Calendar` class to create various Web-based applications. You should not need to change your `Calendar` class implementation, other than to fix any bugs you missed during your testing in Laboratory 14. Instead, reuse your previous work to complete the exercises in this laboratory.

In Core Exercise 1 you create a Web-page generator that creates simple seasonal calendars. In Core Exercise 2 you learn how to create client functions that use your `Calendar` class. In Core Exercise 3 you write a program that uses an `apvector` of `Calendar` objects to generate a yearly calendar. In Core Exercise 4 you create a `CalYear` class that contains an `apvector` of `Calendar` objects as a private data member.

LABORATORY 15: Cover Sheet

Name _____

Hour/Period/Section _____

Date _____

Place a check mark (✔) in the Assigned column next to the exercises that your instructor has assigned to you. Have this sheet ready when your lab instructor checks your work. If your exercises are being checked outside the laboratory session, attach this sheet to the front of the packet of materials that you submit.

Exercise		Assigned	Completed
Core 1	Using an Object in a Program *There Is a Season (season.cpp)*		
Core 2	Client Functions *Day by Day (matchcal.cpp)*		
Core 3	apvector of Objects *Block Party (blockcal.cpp)*		
Core 4	Objects as Data Members *Year In, Year Out (yearcal.cpp)*		
Analysis	Class Composition		
Total			

LABORATORY 15: Core Exercise 1—Using an Object in a Program

APPLICATION EXERCISE: There Is a Season

You are probably ready for an application that uses the `Calendar` class you developed in Laboratory 14. In this exercise, you create a program that generates a Web page consisting of a calendar with a seasonal theme.

Input: Calendar month and year

Output: Web page (*calendar.html*) that includes a calendar for the specified month, as well a background color and seasonal picture that are appropriate for that month. The following are suggested background colors and pictures.

Season	Months	Color	Picture
Spring	March April May	green	*spring.jpg*
Summer	June July August	aqua	*summer.jpg*
Fall	September October November	orange	*fall.jpg*
Winter	December January February	white	*winter.jpg*

A simple calendar Web page can be constructed as follows:

```
<html>
<body bgcolor=color>

... calendar ...

</body>
</html>
```

where `color` specifies the page's background color and `calendar` is the HTML calendar produced by your `Calendar` class `outputHTML()` function. For example, the HTML

```
<html>
<body bgcolor=orange>
<img src=fall.jpg align=left hspace=20>
<pre>
September      2000
  S  M  T  W  T  F  S
                 1  2
  3  4  5  6  7  8  9
 10 11 12 13 14 15 16
 17 18 19 20 21 22 23
 24 25 26 27 28 29 30
</pre>
</body>
</html>
```

produces a calendar for September 2000 on an orange background.

Step 1: Implement the program specified by using your implementation of the `Calendar` class from Laboratory 14. Do *not* change your `Calendar` class implementation—other than to fix any bugs you missed during your testing in Laboratory 14.

Step 2: Save your program as *season.cpp*.

Step 3: Complete the following test plan and use it to test your program.

Test Plan for *season.cpp*

Test case	Sample data	Expected result	Checked
Fall	10 2000	`Orange background and fall.jpg`	
Winter	1 2001	`White background and winter.jpg`	
Spring	4 2001	`Green background and spring.jpg`	
Summer	7 2001	`Aqua background and summer.jpg`	

Step 4: Construct a multifile program using your implementation of the `Calendar` class and save your program in the file *season.cpp* (remember to also add *apstring.cpp* to your multifile program). Compile, link, and run your multifile program.

Step 5: Check each case in the test plan for *season.cpp* and verify the expected result. If you discover mistakes in your program, correct them and execute the test plan again.

LABORATORY 15: Core Exercise 2—Client Functions

Background

You declare an object as a function parameter in the same way you declare any other function parameter—you specify the type of object (its class) and the name of the parameter. For example, the following function determines whether two points are the same distance from the origin.

```
bool equidistant ( Point pt1, Point pt2 )
// Returns true if pt1 and pt2 are the same distance from (0,0).
// Otherwise, returns false.
{
    return ( pt1.distance() == pt2.distance() );
}
```

Note that the `equidistant()` function is *not* a member function of the `Point` class. It does, however, use `Point` objects and member functions. Functions such as this are referred to as **client functions** of the `Point` class. Although this term may be unfamiliar, the concept is not. Many of the functions you have written in prior labs have been clients of the `apstring` and `apvector` classes.

As with other functions, if a client function does not make a change to an object (or if it makes changes that should not be returned), you pass the object to the function by using pass-by-value (as you did with the `equidistant()` function). But, if a client function makes changes to an object and returns the modified object, you pass the object to the function by using pass-by-reference. Finally, if a client function does not modify an object and if the object is large (in terms of the amount of memory it occupies), you pass the object to the function by using a pass-by-`const` reference.

Warmup Exercise

Complete the following program by filling in the missing C++ code. A shell for this program is given in the file *ptclient.shl*.

```
#include <iostream.h>
#include "point.h"
#include <math.h>

//Client functions using the Point class

bool equidistant ( Point pt1, Point pt2 )
// Returns true if pt1 and pt2 are the same distance from (0,0).
// Otherwise, returns false.
{
    return (pt1.distance() == pt2.distance());
}
```

```
int main()
{
    // Declare a point named point1 and initialize
    // its coordinates to (3,4).
    _____

    // Declare a point named point2 using the default constructor.
    _____

    // Assign coordinates to point2.
    point2.setX(-3); point2.setY(-4);

    // Distance from point1 to the origin.
    cout << "Distance from point1 to the origin: "
        << _____<< endl;

    // Test if the two points are equidistant from the origin.
    if ( _____ )
        cout << "The points are equidistant from (0,0)" << endl;
    else
        cout << "The points are not equidistant from (0,0)" << endl;

    return 0;
}
```

Construct a multifile program using your implementation of the Point class and your program in the file *ptclient.cpp*. Compile, link, and run your multifile program.

APPLICATION EXERCISE: Day by Day

In this exercise you create a **client function** for the Calendar class—that is, a function that is not a member of the Calendar class but that acts on Calendar objects using Calendar class member functions. By now you have probably output many different Calendar objects with your outputHTML() member function. You may have started to notice that different months can have the same layout—that is, they have the same days in the some position in the calendar grid. The following function compares the layouts of two Calendar objects to determine whether they are identical.

> **bool layoutsMatch (Calendar calA, Calendar calB)**
> **Input parameters**
> calA, calB: Calendars to compare
> **Returns**
> Returns true if calA and calB have the same calendar grid layouts. Otherwise, returns false.

Step 1: Implement the layoutsMatch() function specified by using your implementation of the Calendar class. You should not need to change your Calendar class implementation, other than to fix any bugs you missed during your testing in Laboratory 14.

Step 2: Add your `layoutsMatch()` function to the shell program in the file *matchcal.shl*. Save your program in the file *matchcal.cpp*.

Step 3: Complete the following test plan and use it to test your program.

Test Plan for *matchcal.cpp*

Test case	Sample data	Expected result	Checked
Identical month and year	2 2000 2 2000	`Layouts match`	
Match within same year	1 2000 7 2000		
No match within same year	1 2000 6 2000		
Match within different years	1 2000 12 2001		

Step 4: Construct a multifile program using your implementation of the `Calendar` class and your program in the file *matchcal.cpp* (remember also to add *apstring.cpp* to your multifile program). Compile, link, and run your multifile program.

Step 5: Check each case in the test plan for *matchcal.cpp* and verify the expected result. If you discover mistakes in your program, correct them and execute the test plan again.

Step 6: If you determine that the calendar layout for February in one year matches the calendar layout for February in another year, you can conclude that the calendar layouts for both years (all 12 mo) must match. Complete the following test plan and use it to test your program.

Test Plan for *matchcal.cpp*

Test case	Sample data	Expected result	Checked
Not matching years	2 2000 2 2001		
Matching years	2 2001 2 2007		

Step 7: Rerun your multifile program.

Step 8: Check each case in the test plan for *matchcal.cpp* and verify the expected result. If you discover mistakes in your program, correct them and execute the test plan again.

LABORATORY 15: Core Exercise 3—apvector **of Objects**

Background

You can create an apvector of objects in much the same way you create apvectors of integers, characters, and the like. You declare an apvector of objects by giving the type of object and its size. The declaration

```
apvector <Point> pt(5);          // apvector of points
```

creates an apvector of points named pt containing five points. Note that the default Point class constructor is automatically called for all five Point objects in apvector pts.

The following program from the file *ptarray.cpp* reads in an apvector of points. These points might represent the vertices of a polygon or the outline of a curve.

```
#include <iostream.h>
#include <apvector.h>
#include "point.h"

int main ()
{
    const int NUMBER_OF_POINTS=5;
    apvector <Point> pt(NUMBER_OF_POINTS);   // apvector of points
    int inputX, inputY,              // Input x and y coordinates
       j;                            // Loop counter

    // Read in the coordinate pairs.
    for ( j = 0 ; j < NUMBER_OF_POINTS ; j++ )
    {
       cout << "Enter the coordinates for pt[" << j << "]: ";
       cin >> inputX >> inputY;
       pt[j].setX(inputX);
       pt[j].setY(inputY);
       cout << "pt[" << j << "]: ";
       pt[j].showDataMembers();
    }
    return 0;
}
```

The program begins by asking the user to input a set of *x* and *y* coordinates. After each coordinate pair is entered, the program uses the Point class setX() and setY() functions to assign the input coordinate pair to an element in apvector pt.

```
pt[j].setX(inputX);
pt[j].setY(inputY);
```

If, for example, the user enters the coordinate pairs

```
6  3
8  4
10  5
12  6
14  7
```

apvector pt would contain the following data.

pt[0]	6 3
pt[1]	8 4
pt[2]	10 5
pt[3]	12 6
pt[4]	14 7

APPLICATION EXERCISE: Block Party

In this exercise you use your Calendar class to create a program that constructs an apvector of Calendar objects for a user-specified year and generates a web page containing a block calendar for that year.

Input: Year

Number of rows in the yearly block calendar (must be a factor of 12)

Output: Web page (*blockcal.html*) that contains a block calendar for the specified year. The block calendar should contain the specified number of rows and the individual calendars in the block calendar should *not* have images—that is, the block calendar contains only the calendar grids.

Number of rows = 6

January	February
calendar grid	calendar grid
March	April
calendar grid	calendar grid
May	June
calendar grid	calendar grid
July	August
calendar grid	calendar grid
September	October
calendar grid	calendar grid
November	December
calendar grid	calendar grid

Number of rows = 4

January	February	March
calendar grid	calendar grid	calendar grid
April	May	June
calendar grid	calendar grid	calendar grid
July	August	September
calendar grid	calendar grid	calendar grid
October	November	December
calendar grid	calendar grid	calendar grid

See the "Engaged Learning for Programming in C++" link on **http://www.jbpub.com/cs** for more information on HTML tables.

Step 1: Implement the program specified using your implementation of the Calendar class (*calendar.cpp*).

Step 2: Save your program as *blockcal.cpp*.

Step 3: Complete the following test plan and use it to test your program.

Test Plan for *blockcal.cpp*

Test case	Sample data	Expected result	Checked
Current year, 1 row		`Calendar for each month in the current year`	
Current year, 4 rows		`Calendar for each month in the current year`	
Next year, 6 rows		`Calendar for each month for next year`	

Step 4: Construct a multifile program using your implementation of the Calendar class and your program in the file *blockcal.cpp* (remember also to add *apstring.cpp* to your multifile program). Compile, link, and run your multifile program.

Step 5: Check each case in the test plan for *blockcal.cpp* and verify the expected result. If you discover mistakes in your program, correct them and execute the test plan again.

LABORATORY 15: Core Exercise 4—Objects as Data Members

Background

A class's data members are not limited to the built-in C++ data types (`int`, `double`, `char`, etc.). You can also use structures or objects as data members. The following declared `PointSet` class (and *pointset.h*) contains an `apvector` of `Point` objects.

```
// Declaration for a set of two-dimensional points.
#include <apvector.h>
#include "point.h"

class PointSet
{
  public:          // Member functions

    // Constructors
    PointSet ( int maxSize );          // Define a set of points

    // Modifier
    void addPoint ( Point newPoint );   // Add a Point

    // Outputs the data members -- used in testing and debugging
    void showDataMembers () const;

  private:

    // Data members
    apvector<Point> pt;
    int count;              // Number of points in the pt vector
};
```

Let's look at the declaration of the `pt` data member,

```
apvector<Point> pt;
```

This declaration says nothing about the length of the `pt` `apvector`. That seems easy enough to fix—simply include the length of the `apvector` in the declaration.

```
apvector<Point> pt(100);     // Invalid! Will produce a compilation error
```

Note the attempt to use one of the `apvector` class constructors to construct a vector of 100 points. Unfortunately, you can't make this call to the `apvector` constructor within a class declaration. Instead, you must call the `apvector` constructor within the initialization list of `PointSet` constructor.

```
PointSet:: PointSet ( int maxSize )
// Constructor.
  : pt(maxSize),
    count(0)
{}
```

The initialization

```
pt(maxSize)
```

calls the `apvector` constructor for the `pt` object and specifies the size of the vector to construct—in other words, this initialization constructs the `pt` vector. The initialization

```
count(0)
```

initializes the `count` data member to `0`, indicating that there are no points in the point set. You add points to the point set by using the `addPoint()` member function.

```
void PointSet:: addPoint ( Point newPoint )
// Add a point to the end of a point set.
{
    if ( count > pt.length() )
        pt.resize(pt.length()*2);     // apvector is too small, resize it

    pt[count] = newPoint;
    count++;                          // Increment the number of points
}
```

The following is a sample program that uses the `PointSet` class.

```
int main()
{
    const int NUMBER_OF_POINTS=5;
    PointSet ptSet(NUMBER_OF_POINTS);
    Point inputPt;
    int inputX, inputY, j;

    cout << "Enter " << NUMBER_OF_POINTS << " points: " << endl;
    for ( j=0; j<NUMBER_OF_POINTS; j++ )
    {
        cin >> inputX >> inputY;
        inputPt.setX(inputX);
        inputPt.setY(inputY);
        ptSet.addPoint(inputPt);
    }

    ptSet.showDataMembers();

    return 0;
}
```

This example is contained in the Laboratory 15 files *pointset.h*, *pointset.cpp*, *testset.cpp* and the Laboratory 14 files *point.h, point.cpp.*

APPLICATION EXERCISE: Year In, Year Out

In this exercise you create a new class, YearCal, which contains an apvector of 12 Calendar objects as a data member. The member functions allow the client program to specify the year for all the Calendar objects in the apvector and to output a yearly block HTML calendar (in a manner similar to that shown in Core Exercise 3).

```
// Declaration for a Calendar year class.
#include <apvector.h>
#include "calendar.h"

class YearCal
{
  public:          // Member functions

    // Constructors
    YearCal ();

    // Modifiers
    void setYear ( int newYear );     // Set the year in each calendar

    // Outputs a block HTML calendar year w/ the specified number of rows
    void outputHTML ( ofstream &HTMLFile, int numRows ) const;

  private:         // Data members

    apvector<Calendar> cal;
};
```

The member functions for this class are defined as follows.

YearCal()
Precondition
None
Postcondition
Constructor. Creates a set of 12 calendars, one for each month (for the current year).

setYear (int newYear)
Precondition
None
Postcondition
Sets the year in each calendar to newYear.

outputHTML (ofstream &HTMLFile, int numRows)
Precondition
None
Postcondition
Outputs a yearly block calendar containing numRows rows in HTML form to HTMLFile.

Step 1: Implement the YearCal class member functions specified. Prototypes for these functions are included in the declaration of the YearCal class in the file *yearcal.h*. You should not need to change your Calendar class implementation, other than to fix any bugs you missed during your testing in Laboratory 14.

Step 2: Save your implementation of these functions as the file *yearcal.cpp*.

Step 3: Complete the following test plan.

Test Plan for *testyear.cpp*

Test case	Sample data	Expected result	Checked
Current year, 1 row		`Calendar for each month in the current year`	
Current year, 4 rows		`Calendar for each month in the current year`	
2004, 6 rows		`Calendar for each month for 2004`	

Step 4: Construct a multifile program using your implementations of the Calendar and Calyear classes and the test program in the file *testyear.cpp* (remember also to add *apstring.cpp* to your multifile program). Compile, link, and run your multifile program.

Step 5: Check each case in the test plan for *testyear.cpp* and verify the expected result. If you discover mistakes in your program, correct them and execute the test plan again.

LABORATORY 15: Analysis Exercise

Class Composition

Name

Hour/Period/Section

Date

Three points can describe a triangle. Specify the member functions and data members for a new Triangle class based on your Point class.

Part A

a) Give function specifications for the member functions that form the public interface for your Triangle class (be sure to include a constructor).

b) List the private data members that you would include in your Triangle class. Briefly describe the information stored in each data member.

Part B

A polygon can be described as an *n*-sided closed planar figure bounded by intersecting straight lines. Specify the member functions and data members for a new Polygon class based on your Point class.

a) Give function specifications for the member functions that form the public interface for your Polygon class (be sure to include a constructor).

b) List the private data members that you would include in your Polygon class. Briefly describe the information stored in each data member.

Object-Oriented Programming Project

OVERVIEW

The programs you developed in previous labs solved very specific problems. These programs tended to be relatively short, and you were able to create them directly from the problem descriptions. As problems become more complex, however, breaking them into parts, creating formal program designs, and developing detailed test plans become necessary components of the program development process.

In this laboratory, we first introduce you to object-oriented programming via a child's calculator project. We then help you design and implement a programming project—Calendar Noteboard—using object-oriented design and programming techniques. The intent of the lab is for you to learn how to solve a complex problem by decomposing it into a set of interrelated objects and to give you a feel for how to create and test a multifile, multiobject program.

LABORATORY 16: Cover Sheet

Name _____

Hour/Period/Section _____

Date _____

Place a check mark (✔) in the Assigned column next to the exercises that your instructor has assigned to you. Have this sheet ready when your lab instructor checks your work. If your exercises are being checked outside the laboratory session, attach this sheet to the front of the packet of materials that you submit.

Exercise	Assigned	Completed
Object-Oriented Design Project—Child's Calculator		
Programming Project—Calendar Noteboard		
Phase 1 : Project Design		
Phase 2 : Project Test Plan		
Phase 3 : Project Implementation and Testing		
Phase 4 : Project Analysis		
Total		

LABORATORY 16: Object-Oriented Design Project—Child's Calculator

If you are given a complex problem, how do you begin to develop a program to solve it? Unfortunately, there is no simple answer to this question. How you look at the problem, what form you imagine the solution will take, and which programming language and techniques you intend to use all shape not only the solution but the process of finding a solution. You may also need to look at how code that you have already developed can be incorporated into your solution.

In this laboratory, you use a program development style called object-oriented programming in which you analyze a problem in terms of the objects in the problem. An **object** is something with a well-defined set of **attributes** and **behaviors**. A statue, a car, a fish, a movie, a party, and a trip—all are examples of objects from the real world. Human beings are expert at thinking about the world around them in terms of objects. **Object-oriented design** (OOD) and **object-oriented programming** (OOP) attempt to apply this ability to the design and creation of programs.

Rather than discussing object-oriented design in the abstract, let's identify the objects in the following problem.

Part of a children's math education program is a calculator that displays a sad face whenever the number displayed by the calculator is negative and a happy face when the number displayed is greater than or equal to 0. The calculator responds to the following commands (where *num* is a floating-point number): +*num*, -*num*, **num, /*num*, and c (clear). In addition, the child can use the Q (quit) command to end the program.

One object is obvious: the calculator. What attributes and behaviors are associated with the calculator? This depends on who is doing the associating—different people will produce different results. The following is one possible set of attributes and behaviors.

Object:	Calculator
Attributes:	Number displayed (the accumulator)
Behaviors:	Performs arithmetic operations
	Displays number

What other objects are there? The problem refers to a display that shows a happy face or a sad face, depending on the number stored in the calculator's accumulator. This face display is another object.

Object:	Face
Attributes:	State (happy or sad)
Behaviors:	Changes face to happy
	Changes face to sad
	Displays face

Can the Calculator and Face objects be combined into one object? Yes. The process of finding and using objects does not have a rigid set of rules. We chose a definition of calculators that fits a broad range of calculators, not just the one discussed in this problem, because other choices may be equally valid.

Finding the final object requires a little effort. Something must be coordinating the actions of the Calculator and Face objects based on the commands input by the child. This object is commonly called the interface.

Object:	Interface
Attributes:	Calculator
	Face
	Command
Behaviors:	Coordinates the calculator and face displays
	Reads a command
	Executes the command

Having identified a set of objects, we need to develop a C++ class for each object. As a general rule, an object's attributes become data members of the corresponding class, and its behaviors become member functions. Keep in mind, however, that in program design there are no inflexible rules, only guidelines.

Let's start with the Face object. This object has an attribute that indicates whether the face is a happy face or a sad face. It has behaviors that display the face and change it to happy or to sad. We represent the Face object by using a C++ class called Face in which the happy/sad attribute is represented by a Boolean data member state and the behaviors are represented by the member functions display(), makeHappy(), and makeSad(). The following is a declaration for the Face class and the specifications for its member functions. Included is a constructor that initializes a face to happy when it is created (constructed).

```
class Face
{
  public:

    Face ();                    // Constructor
    void makeHappy ();          // Set face to happy
    void makeSad ();            // Set face to sad
    void display () const;      // Display face

  private:

    // Data member
    bool state;                 // Face state (true=happy, false=sad)
};
```

```
Face ()
```
Precondition
None
Postcondition
Constructor. Creates a face and initializes it to happy.

```
void makeHappy ()
```
Precondition
None
Postcondition
Changes a face to happy.

```
void makeSad ()
```
Precondition
None
Postcondition
Changes a face to sad.

```
void display () const
```
Precondition
None
Postcondition
Displays a face.

Continuing with the Calculator object, we represent this object's accumulator attribute by a double-precision floating-point data member accum and its behaviors by the member functions add(), subtract(), multiply(), divide(), and display(). Adding a constructor and an accessor function, value(), completes the set of member functions. The constructor initializes the accumulator to 0, and the value() function communicates accumulator's value to other classes.

```
class Calculator
{
  public:

    Calculator ();                  // Construct calculator
    void add ( double num );        // Add to accumulator
    void subtract ( double num );   // Subtract from accumulator
    void multiply ( double num );   // Multiply accumulator
    void divide ( double num );     // Divide accumulator
    void clear ();                  // Clear accumulator
    double value () const;          // Return accumulator
    void display () const;          // Display calculator
```

```
   private:

      // Data member
      double accum;                    // Accumulator
};
```

Calculator ()
Precondition
None
Postcondition
Constructor. Creates a calculator and initializes the accumulator to zero.

void add (double num)
Precondition
None
Postcondition
Adds num to the accumulator.

void subtract (double num)
Precondition
None
Postcondition
Subtracts num from the accumulator.

void multiply (double num)
Precondition
None
Postcondition
Multiplies the accumulator by num.

void divide (double num)
Precondition
The value of num is not 0
Postcondition
Divides the accumulator by num.

void clear ()
Precondition
None
Postcondition
Clears the accumulator (sets it to 0).

```
double value () const
```
Precondition
None
Postcondition
Returns the value stored in the accumulator.

```
void display () const
```
Precondition
None
Postcondition
Displays a calculator.

We create the `Interface` class in much the same way we did the `Calculator` and `Face` classes. In this case, three data members, `calc`, `smiley`, and `userCmd`, represent the calculator, face, and command attributes.

```
class Interface
{
    ...
    // Data members
    Calculator calc;      // Calculator object
    Face smiley;          // Face object
    Command userCmd;      // User command
};
```

The first two data members are objects in other classes rather than one of C++'s predefined data types. One of the virtues of C++ is that this difference has little or no impact on how we declare (or later use) the `Interface` class. We simply treat the classes we develop as though they are built into C++. The `userCmd` data members store the last command the user entered along with the command's argument (if any).

```
struct Command
{
    char cmd;       // Command name (letter)
    double arg;     // Command argument
};
```

The member functions `generateDisplay()`, `getCommand()`, and `executeCommand()` represent the Interface object's behaviors. To these we add a constructor that initializes the data members and a `done()` function that indicates to the `main()` function that the child has entered the Q (quit) command and that the program should stop getting and executing commands. The following code shows the declaration for the `Interface` class and the specifications for its member functions.

```
class Interface
{
  public:

     Interface ();                        // Constructor
     void generateDisplay () const;       // Generate interface display
     void getCommand () ;                 // Get user command
     void executeCommand ();              // Process user command
     bool done () const;                  // Exit interface

  private:

     // Data members
     Calculator calc;     // Calculator object
     Face smiley;         // Face object
     Command userCmd;     // User command
};
```

Interface ()
Precondition
None
Postcondition
Constructor. Creates an interface and initializes its data members.

void generateDisplay () const
Precondition
None
Postcondition
Generates an interface display consisting of a calculator and a happy/sad face.

void getCommand ()
Precondition
None
Postcondition
Prompts the user for a command, reads in a command from the keyboard, and stores it in userCmd.

void executeCommand ()
Precondition
None
Postcondition
Executes the command in userCmd, using calls to the member functions for the Calculator and Face objects.

bool done () const
Precondition
None
Postcondition
Returns `true` if the child has entered the `Q` (quit) command. Otherwise, returns `false`.

We now have a set of well-defined classes for the children's calculator problem. Taken together, these object descriptions, class declarations, and function specifications provide a **design** for one solution to this problem. With a good design, developing an implementation is an easy task. With a bad design, the job is difficult, if not impossible. That's why the design process is so important—in many ways, it is the art that defines computer science. Creativity and insight in the design phase lead to programs that are easy to implement and maintain. More important, they result in programs that are enjoyable to use. Mistakes made in the design phase are costly to fix and often yield a poor product.

Having completed the design of the children's calculator program, our next task is to implement the member functions in the `Calculator`, `Face`, and `Interface` classes—as well as the calculator program's `main()` function. Before beginning these implementations, we save the class declarations for the `Calculator`, `Face`, and `Interface` classes in the header files *calc.h*, *face.h*, and *interf.h*, respectively (the declaration for the `Command` structure is also placed in *interf.h*). Later on, we store our implementations of these classes in the files *calc.cpp*, *face.cpp*, and *interf.cpp*. Note that *face.h* and *face.cpp* combine to form the `Face` class, *calc.h* and *calc.cpp* combine to form the `Calculator` class, and *interf.h* and *interf.cpp* combine to form the `Interface` class.

Let's start the implementation process with the `Calculator` class. This class's member functions are quite simple—no surprises here. The `display()` function forms the calculator from standard ASCII characters. This approach allows for generality of use—every environment supports ASCII text output—at the price of exciting visuals.

```
// Implementation of the Calculator class.

#include <iostream.h>
#include <iomanip.h>
#include "calc.h"

//------------------------------------------------------------------

Calculator:: Calculator ()

// Constructor. Creates a calculator and initializes its accumulator
// to zero.

{
    accum = 0;
}
```

```
//-------------------------------------------------------------------

void Calculator:: add ( double num )

// Adds num to the accumulator.

{
    accum = accum + num;
}
//-------------------------------------------------------------------

void Calculator:: subtract ( double num )

// Subtracts num from the accumulator.

{
    accum = accum - num;
}


//-------------------------------------------------------------------

void Calculator:: multiply ( double num )

// Multiplies the accumulator by num.

{
    accum = accum * num;
}
//-------------------------------------------------------------------

void Calculator:: divide ( double num )

// Divides the accumulator by num.

{
    accum = accum / num;
}


//-------------------------------------------------------------------

void Calculator:: clear ()

// Clears the accumulator (sets it to zero).

{
    accum = 0;
}
```

```
//-------------------------------------------------------------------

double Calculator:: value () const

// Returns the value stored in the accumulator.

{
    return accum;
}

//-------------------------------------------------------------------

void Calculator:: display () const

// Displays a calculator.

{
    cout << "----------------" << endl;
    cout << setiosflags (ios::fixed);
    cout << "|" << setw(12) << accum << "  |" << endl;
    cout << "|                |" << endl;
    cout << "|  1  2  3  +  |" << endl;
    cout << "|  4  5  6  -  |" << endl;
    cout << "|  7  8  9  *  |" << endl;
    cout << "|     0  C  /  |" << endl;
    cout << "----------------" << endl;
}
```

Implementing the `Face` class is an equally straightforward task. In this case, the `display()` function outputs the smiley face discussed in the design phase, using both its happy and sad versions.

```
// Implementation of the Face class.

#include <iostream.h>
#include "face.h"

//-------------------------------------------------------------------

Face:: Face()

// Constructor. Creates a face and initializes it to happy.

{
    makeHappy();
}

//-------------------------------------------------------------------
```

```
void Face:: makeHappy ()

// Changes a face to happy.

{
    state = true;
}

//-----------------------------------------------------------------

void Face:: makeSad ()

// Changes a face to sad.

{
    state = false;
}

//-----------------------------------------------------------------

void Face:: display () const

// Displays a face.

{
    if ( state )
       cout << ":-)";
    else
       cout << ":-(";
}
```

Implementing the Interface class is a bit trickier. Recall that this class has three data members—calc, smiley, and userCmd. Calc and smiley are Calculator and Face objects, and userCmd is a Command structure. The Interface class constructor initializes the command name (user-Cmd.cmd) to the null command.

```
Interface:: Interface ()

// Constructor. Creates an interface and initializes its data members

{
    userCmd.cmd = '\0';
}
```

The generateDisplay() member function uses the display() member functions in the Face and Calculator classes to display the smiley face followed by the calculator. Note that additional formatting is done to center the smiley face above the calculator.

```
void Interface:: generateDisplay () const

// Generates an interface display consisting of a happy/sad face and
// a calculator.

{
    cout << endl << "        ";
    smiley.display();
    cout << endl;
    calc.display();
}
```

User commands are read from the keyboard by the `getCommand()` member function. If a command has a numeric argument, this argument is read in as well. The input command and argument (if any) are stored in `userCmd`.

```
void Interface:: getCommand ()

// Prompts the user for a command, reads in a command from the
// keyboard, and stores it in userCmd and cmdArg.

{
    cout << "Enter command: ";
    cin >> userCmd;
    if ( userCmd.cmd == '+'  ||  userCmd.cmd == '-'  ||
         userCmd.cmd == '*'  ||  userCmd.cmd == '/'     )
        cin >> userCmd.arg;
}
```

The `executeCommand()` member function processes the user's last command. This function must rely on the member functions of the `Face` and `Calculator` classes to modify the `smiley` and `calc` objects.

```
void Interface:: executeCommand ()

// Executes the user's last command (in userCmd).

{
    switch ( userCmd.cmd )
    {
      case '+' :  calc.add(userCmd.arg);        break;
      case '-' :  calc.subtract(userCmd.arg);   break;
      case '*' :  calc.multiply(userCmd.arg);   break;
      case '/' :  if (userCmd.arg!= 0 )
                      calc.divide(userCmd.arg);
                  else
                      cout << "Cannot divide by 0" << endl;
                  break;
      case 'C' :
      case 'c' :  calc.clear();  break;
      case 'Q' :
      case 'q' :  break;
      default  :  cout << "Invalid command" << endl;
    }
```

```
        if ( calc.value() < 0 )    // Update the face
            smiley.makeSad();
        else
            smiley.makeHappy();
    }
```

Finally, the `done()` member function tests whether the user has input the `Q` (quit) command.

```
    bool Interface:: done () const

    // Returns true if the user has entered the Q (quit) command.
    // Otherwise, returns false.

    {
        return ( userCmd.cmd == 'Q'  ||  userCmd.cmd == 'q' );
    }
```

Having completed our implementation of the `Face`, `Calculator`, and `Interface` classes, all we need to do is create a `main()` function that moves the interface through repetitions of a three-step cycle: generate the display, get the command, and process the command (see the file *kid-calc.cpp*).

```
    // Main program for the children's calculator program.

    #include "interf.h"

    //-----------------------------------------------------------------

    int main ()
    {
        Interface cmdInterface;    // Interface object

        while ( !cmdInterface.done() )
        {
            cmdInterface.generateDisplay();
            cmdInterface.getCommand();
            cmdInterface.executeCommand();
        }

        return 0;
    }
```

We have completed development of the Children's Calculator Program. The question that now arises is How do we test and debug the program? One approach would be to throw everything together and test the program as a whole. The problem with this approach is that testing and debugging an even moderately large program can easily become overwhelming, with errors compounding errors and everything falling into chaos. A better approach is to test and debug the program using the same strategy that we used to develop it. First, we test each class. Once we've worked out the bugs in the individual classes, we combine them and test the complete program.

We start by testing the classes that do not depend on other classes and work our way up through the class hierarchy. Let's start with the Calculator class. We begin by developing a simple test program that gives us the ability to check each member function using various input values. The following is a simple interactive test program for the Calculator class (it is also given in the file *testcalc.cpp*).

```cpp
// Test program for the Calculator class.

#include <iostream.h>
#include "calc.h"

int main ()
{
    Calculator calc;    // Calculator object
    char oper;          // Input operator
    double num;         // Input number

    // Test the arithmetic functions and the value() function.

    cout << endl << "Start of testing" << endl;

    do
    {
        calc.display();

        cout << endl << "Enter operator (Q or q to end) and argument : ";
        cin >> oper;

        switch ( oper )
        {
          case '+' :  cin >> num; calc.add(num);        break;
          case '-' :  cin >> num; calc.subtract(num);   break;
          case '*' :  cin >> num; calc.multiply(num);   break;
          case '/' :  cin >> num; calc.divide(num);     break;
        }

        cout << "Calculator value : " << calc.value() << endl;
    }
    while ( oper != 'Q'  &&  oper != 'q' );

    // Test the clear() function.

    calc.clear();
    cout << endl << "Calculator cleared" << endl;
    calc.display();

    return 0;
}
```

Testing the Face class is equally straightforward (see the file *testface.cpp*).

Once the `Calculator` and `Face` classes have been thoroughly tested and debugged, we can begin testing the `Interface` class, which depends on the those two classes. Note that testing the `Interface` class before we are sure that the `Calculator` and `Face` classes work properly is asking for trouble. A simple modification to the `main()` function is all that is needed to check whether the `getCommand()` member function is reading in user commands correctly.

```
int main ()
{
    Interface cmdInterface;    // Interface object

    while ( !cmdInterface.done() )
    {
       cmdInterface.getCommand();
       cout << "Command:  " << userCmd.cmd;    // Echo the command
       cout << "Argument: " << userCmd.arg;    // Echo the argument
    }

    return 0;
}
```

Next, we test the `executeCommand()` function, using the calculator program's `main()` function. Finally, we run a systematic test of the entire program.

The following files contain the class declarations, implementations, and test programs for the classes that we developed.

Class	Header file	Implementation	Test program
Face	*face.h*	*face.cpp*	*testface.cpp*
Calculator	*calc.h*	*calc.cpp*	*testcalc.cpp*
Interface	*interf.h*	*interf.cpp*	*kidcalc.cpp* (with some modifications)

LABORATORY 16: Programming Project—Calendar Noteboard

Overview

Many people use a calendar to keep track of assignments, parties, appointments, and the like. In this project, you create a program that takes a set of dated notes and generates an HTML noteboard consisting of a set of monthly calendars and associated notes. The contents and appearance of the noteboard are specified by a noteboard file and a set of user-controlled content filters and appearance properties.

Noteboard File Format

The noteboard (data) file consists of three parts: the calendar year, the names of 12 image files (one for each month, in month order), and a set of notes of the form

   month day category text

where

- *month* and *day* identify the month and day to which the note applies,

- *category* identifies the category to which the note belongs (e.g., "personal", "school"), and

- *text* is the note's narrative text.

The following is a sample data file. Note that, although the image file names are listed in month order, the notes are unordered.

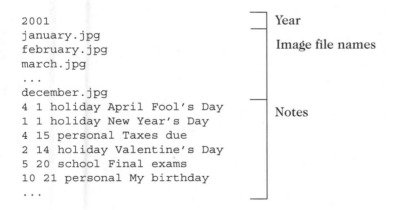

```
2001                              ⎤ Year
january.jpg                       ⎦
february.jpg                      ⎤ Image file names
march.jpg
...
december.jpg                      ⎦
4 1 holiday April Fool's Day      ⎤ Notes
1 1 holiday New Year's Day
4 15 personal Taxes due
2 14 holiday Valentine's Day
5 20 school Final exams
10 21 personal My birthday
...                               ⎦
```

Content Filters

Which months and which notes appear on the noteboard are determined by the following filters.

Content filter	Description
start *month*	The first month to display, where *month* is in the range 1–12. Default: 1
end *month*	The last month to display, where *month* is in the range 1–12. Default: 12
category *filter*	Only the notes in the specified category are included when the noteboard is generated. The category filter all indicates that all the notes should be included. Default: all

Appearance Properties

The appearance of the noteboard is determined by the following properties.

background *color*	Background color of the noteboard, where *color* is an HTML color constant (e.g., red, white, or blue). Default: white
text *color*	Text (foreground) color of the noteboard, where *color* is an HTML color constant. Default: black
layout *style*	The noteboard layout, where *style* is either horizontal or vertical. The corresponding layouts are as follows.

<table>
<tr><th colspan="2">horizontal</th><th>vertical</th></tr>
<tr><td>January calendar</td><td>January notes</td><td>January calendar
January notes</td></tr>
<tr><td>February calendar</td><td>February notes</td><td>February calendar
February notes</td></tr>
<tr><td>...</td><td>...</td><td></td></tr>
<tr><td>December calendar</td><td>December notes</td><td>December calendar
December notes</td></tr>
</table>

In either layout, each month's calendar consists of an image and a calendar day grid. In addition, the notes for each month are output in **ascending order based on day.**

Default: horizontal

User Interface

Your program begins by prompting the user for the name of a noteboard (data) file. It then reads in the calendar year, the calendar image file names, and the entire set of notes, grouping the notes by month as they are read in. You can assume that there are no more than 15 notes per month.

The user controls your program via a simple command-line interface. The current state of the content filters and appearance properties is displayed and the user is prompted to enter a command.

```
-----------------------------------------------------------
Filters
   start:         1
   end:           12
   category:      all
Appearance
   background:    white
   text:          black
   layout:        horizontal
-----------------------------------------------------------
Enter command:
```

The following is the set of user commands.

Command	Description
start *month*	Sets the first month to display, where *month* is in the range 1–12.
end *month*	Sets the last month to display, where *month* is in the range 1–12.
category *filter*	Sets the category filter, where *filter* is a text string (without white space).
background *color*	Sets the background color of the noteboard, where *color* is text string containing a valid HTML color constant.
text *color*	Sets the text (foreground) color of the noteboard, where *color* is the text string containing a valid HTML color constant.
layout *style*	Sets the noteboard layout, where *style* is either horizontal or vertical.
html *filename*	Generates an HTML calendar noteboard file named *filename* for the filtered months and notes, using the specified colors and layout.
help	Displays this list of commands along with a short description of each command.
quit	Terminates the program.

If the user enters a command other than one of these keyboard commands, your program should output the message "Invalid command."

Optional Feature (*Check with your instructor before including this feature in your project.*)

You can use the interactivity of Javascript to produce an interactive HTML noteboard consisting of

- a menu bar listing the months that can be displayed and
- the calendar and notes for the month the user selected from the menu bar.

The following is a sample interactive noteboard. If the user clicks "June," the calendar and notes for June are displayed. Similarly, if the user clicks "September," the calendar and notes for September are displayed.

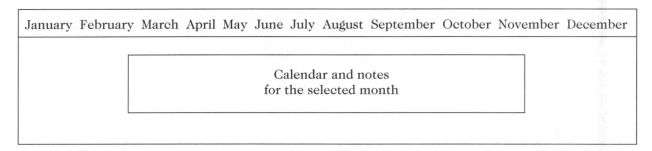

The `interactive` property is defined as follows.

Appearance property	Description
`interactive` *true/false*	Indicates whether the HTML file is interactive (`true`) or static (`false`).
	Default: `true`

Generating the interactive HTML noteboard is similar to generating the static noteboard that we discussed earlier. The HTML file still contains *all* the calendars and notes. The difference is that each month's calendar and note set are grouped into an identifiable `<div>` element. One `<div>` element is generated for each month, as in

```
<div id=month1
    style='position:absolute;left:0;top:60;visibility:hidden'>
 ... Calendar and notes for January ...
</div>
<div id=month2
    style='position:absolute;left:0;top:60;visibility:hidden'>
 ... Calendar and notes for February ...
</div>
 ...
```

Note that all the months have the same position (one on top of the other) and that all the months are initially marked as hidden (not visible).

The menu bar consists of a simple HTML table of the form

```
<table width=100%>
<tr>
<td><a style='color:black;text-decoration:none' href=#
      onclick=select('month1')>January</a></td>
<td><a style='color:black;text-decoration:none' href=#
      onclick=select('month2')>February</a></td>
...
</tr>
</table>
```

Clicking the name of a month on the menu bar activates the Javascript `select()` function for the corresponding month. This function, in turn, reveals the selected month's `<div>` element. The file *menu.js* contains the required Javascript code. You include this code in the HTML file as follows.

```
<head>
...
<script src=menu.js></script>
</head>
```

Putting all this together yields the following HTML framework for the interactive noteboard.

```
<html>
<head>
...
<script src=menu.js></script>
</head>

<table width=100%>
<tr>
<td><a style='color:black;text-decoration:none' href=#
      onclick=select('month1')>January</a></td>
<td><a style='color:black;text-decoration:none' href=#
      onclick=select('month2')>February</a></td>
...
</tr>
</table>

<div id=month1
     style='position:absolute;left:0;top:60;visibility:hidden'>
   ... Calendar and notes for January ...
</div>
<div id=month2
     style='position:absolute;left:0;top:60;visibility:hidden'>
   ... Calendar and notes for February ...
</div>
...
```

Note that the contents of the noteboard (months and notes) are still specified by the content filters and that the noteboard's appearance (colors and layout) is still specified by the appearance properties.

Phase 1: Project Design

Step 1: Identify the objects in the project. Be sure to look for objects that are not described explicitly in the problem statement but which are implicitly part of the problem. Examples of such "hidden" objects are

- objects that are collections (sets or lists) of other objects and

- objects that provide the means (information or actions) through which other objects interrelate—the role played by the Interface object in the Children's Calculator project, for instance.

List each object's attributes and behaviors.

Step 2: Design a C++ class for each object. Remember that, although there are no rigid rules for the design process, you must consider how the various classes (objects) in your design will interact with one another. Questions such as the following will help you do so.

- Does the class provide the functionality needed by the other classes?

- Is it clear what each member function does and how it is to be used?

- Is the class missing member functions or does it have extra (unused) member functions?

- Does the class maintain the information needed by other classes? If so, do these classes have a way of accessing this information?

- Do the classes in your design collectively provide the functionality required to solve the problem?

For each C++ class, provide

- a brief description of the class, focusing on what the class does and how it is used;

- a C++ class declaration, including data members and member functions; and

- a detailed function specification for each member function. Use the function specification format shown in the Children's Calculator project (and in Laboratories 14 and 15).

Phase 2: Project Test Plan

Step 1: Create a test plan and test program for each class in your design. A blank test plan form is given at the end of this laboratory.

Step 2: Create a test plan for the complete project. A blank test plan form is given at the end of this laboratory.

Phase 3: Project Implementation and Testing

Step 1: Implement each of the classes in your design, as well as the program's `main()` function. Be sure to document your code.

Step 2: Test the classes in your project using the class test plans and test programs you created in Step 1 of Phase 2. For each class, check each case in the class's test plan and verify the expected result. If you discover mistakes in a class implementation, correct them and execute the class's test plan again.

Step 3: Test your complete project. Check each case in your project test plan and verify the expected result. If you discover mistakes in your program, correct them and execute the project test plan again.

Phase 4: Project Analysis

What problems did you face in implementing your class designs? What caused these problems? How would you avoid these kinds of problems in future programming efforts?

Test Plan for the class

Test case	Sample data	Expected result	Checked

Functions II

OVERVIEW

You created different types of functions in Laboratory 8—those that return no value (void functions), those that return a single value, and those that return multiple values using pass-by-reference. In this laboratory, you expand your knowledge of the range of features supported by C++ functions. Core Exercise 1 is an exploration of recursive functions—that is, functions that call themselves. You learn how to create recursive functions and how to use them. In Core Exercise 2, you explore how function overloading allows you to give the same name to several functions that perform similar tasks, but which differ in the number of arguments or types of arguments they process.

LABORATORY 17: Cover Sheet

Name _____

Hour/Period/Section _____

Date _____

Place a check mark (✔) in the Assigned column next to the exercises that your instructor has assigned to you. Have this sheet ready when your lab instructor checks your work. If your exercises are being checked outside the laboratory session, attach this sheet to the front of the packet of materials that you submit.

Exercise	Assigned	Completed
Core 1 Recursion *Prestidigitation (testdig.cpp)*		
Core 2 Overloading *Boxed In (testbox.cpp)*		
Reinforcement Applying Recursion *Splitting the Difference, Again (rebinary.cpp)*		
Analysis Potential Pitfalls of Using Overloading and Recursion		
Total		

LABORATORY 17: Core Exercise 1—Recursion

Background

Recursive functions—that is, functions that call themselves—provide an elegant way of describing and implementing the solutions to a wide range of problems, including problems in mathematics, computer graphics, compiler design, and artificial intelligence. Let's begin by examining how to develop a recursive function definition, using the factorial function as an example.

You can express the factorial of a positive integer n by using the iterative formula

$$n! = n \cdot (n - 1) \cdot (n - 2) \cdot \cdots \cdot 1$$

Applying this formula to 4! yields the product $4 \cdot 3 \cdot 2 \cdot 1$. If you regroup the terms in this product as $4 \cdot (3 \cdot 2 \cdot 1)$ and note that $3! = 3 \cdot 2 \cdot 1$, you find that 4! can be written as $4 \cdot (3!)$. You can generalize this reasoning to form the recursive definition of factorial:

$$n! = n \cdot (n - 1)!,$$

where 0! is defined to be 1. Applying this definition to the evaluation of 4! yields the following sequence of computations:

$$4! = 4 \cdot (3!)$$
$$= 4 \cdot (3 \cdot (2!))$$
$$= 4 \cdot (3 \cdot (2 \cdot (1!)))$$
$$= 4 \cdot (3 \cdot (2 \cdot (1 \cdot (0!))))$$
$$= 4 \cdot (3 \cdot (2 \cdot (1 \cdot (1)))).$$

The first four steps in this computation are recursive, with $n!$ being evaluated in terms of $(n - 1)!$. The final step is not recursive, however. The following notation clearly distinguishes between the **recursive step** and the nonrecursive step (or **base case**) in the definition of $n!$.

$$n! = \begin{cases} 1 & \text{if } n = 0 \quad \text{(base case)} \\ n \cdot (n - 1) & \text{if } n > 0 \quad \text{(recursive step)}. \end{cases}$$

The following program from the file *refactrl.cpp* uses recursion to compute the factorial of a number.

```
// Computes n! using a recursive factorial function.

#include <iostream.h>

long factorial ( int n );  // Function prototype

int main()
{
    int num = 4;   // Number whose factorial is to be computed.
```

```
    // Display the factorial of the number.
    cout << num << "! is " << factorial(num) << endl;

    return 0;
}

long factorial ( int n )
// Recursive factorial function.
{
    long result;
    if ( n == 0 )
        result = 1;                        // Base case
    else
        result = n * factorial(n-1);   // Recursive step
    return result;
}
```

The program issues the call `factorial(4)`. Because 4 is not equal to 0 (the condition for the base case), the `factorial()` function issues the recursive call `factorial(3)`. The recursive calls continue until the base case is reached—that is, until n equals 0.

```
factorial(4)
        ↓ RECURSIVE STEP
    4*factorial(3)
            ↓ RECURSIVE STEP
        3*factorial(2)
                ↓ RECURSIVE STEP
            2*factorial(1)
                    ↓ RECURSIVE STEP
                1*factorial(0)
                        ↓ BASE CASE
                    1
```

The calls to `factorial()` are evaluated in reverse of the order they were made. The evaluation process continues until the value 24 is returned by the call `factorial(4)`.

```
factorial(4)
        ↑ RETURNS 24
    4*factorial(3)
            ↑ RETURNS 6
        3*factorial(2)
                ↑ RETURNS 2
            2*factorial(1)
                    ↑ RETURNS 1
                1*factorial(0)
                        ↑ RETURNS 1
                    1
```

See the "Engaged Learning for Programming in C++" link on **http://www.jbpub.com/cs** for more information on recursive algorithms.

Warmup Exercise

The greatest common divisor (GCD) of two positive integers x and y is the largest integer that evenly divides both x and y. A recursive definition expresses Euclid's algorithm for finding the GCD of two integers x and y.

$$GCD(x, y) = \begin{cases} x & \text{if } y = 0 \\ GCD(y, \text{the remainder of } x \text{ divided by } y) & \text{if } y \neq 0. \end{cases}$$

Using this algorithm to compute `GCD(30,12)` generates the following sequence of calls and returns the value `6`.

```
GCD(30,12)                          GCD(30,12)
     ↓ RECURSIVE STEP                    ↑ RETURNS 6
GCD(12,6)                           GCD(12,6)
     ↓ RECURSIVE STEP                    ↑ RETURNS 6
GCD(6,0)                            GCD(6,0)
     ↓ BASE CASE                         ↑ RETURNS 6
     6                                   6
```

In this exercise, you use Euclid's algorithm to compute the GCD of a pair of integers.

int gcd (int x, int y)
Input parameters
x, y: two integers
Returns
The greatest common divisor of x and y

Complete the following program by filling in the missing C++ code. A shell for this program is given in the file *gcd.shl*.

```
// Computes the greatest common divisor (GCD) of two numbers using
// recursion.

#include <iostream.h>

int gcd ( int x, int y );
```

```
int main()
{
    int num1, num2;
    cout << "Enter two integers: ";
    cin >> num1 >> num2;

    // Display the GCD of num1 and num2.
    cout << _____ << endl;

    return 0;
}

int gcd ( int x, int y )
{
    int result;
    if ( _____ )
        result = _____;              // Base case
    else
        result = _____;    // Recursive step
    return result;
}
```

APPLICATION EXERCISE: Prestidigitation

A recursive function need not return a value. The following recursive definition describes an algorithm for outputting the digits in a positive integer in reverse order.

$$
rightToLeft(n) \rightarrow \begin{cases} \text{Output } n & \textit{if } n < 10 \\[2ex] \text{Output the remainder of } n \text{ divided by } 10 & \textit{if } n \geq 10 \\ rightToLeft(\textit{the quotient of } n \textit{ divided by } 10) \end{cases}
$$

Note that in the second case (the recursive step) output is produced before the recursive call is made. Using this function to output the digits in the number 1384 generates the following sequence of calls and outputs the digits in reverse order (4831).

```
rightToLeft(1384)
        ↓        RECURSIVE STEP
   outputs 4   rightToLeft(138)
                     ↓          RECURSIVE STEP
             outputs 8   rightToLeft(13)
                              ↓          RECURSIVE STEP
                      outputs 3   rightToLeft(1)
                                       ↓         BASE CASE
                                  outputs 1
```

Step 1: Create a function `rightToLeft()` that outputs the digits in an integer in reverse order. Base your function on the following specification.

> `void rightToLeft ( int num )`
> **Input parameters**
> `num`: integer value
> **Outputs**
> Displays the digits in the number in reverse order, one per line.

Step 2: `Add your rightToLeft()` function to the shell program in the file *digit.shl*. Save your program in the file *digit.cpp*.

Step 3: Complete the following test plan and use it to test your program. If you discover mistakes in your program, correct them and execute the test plan again.

Test Plan for *rightToLeft()*

Test case	Sample data	Expected result	Checked
Three-digit number	123	3 2 1	
Four-digit number			

A slight modification to your `rightToLeft()` function will produce the function

> `void leftToRight ( int num )`
> **Input parameters**
> `num`: integer value
> **Outputs**
> Displays the digits in the number in order, one per line.

Step 4: Create the function `leftToRight()`.

Step 5: Add your `leftToRight()` function to the test program in the file *digit.cpp*.

Step 6: Complete the following test plan and use it to test your program. If you discover mistakes in your program, correct them and execute the test plan again.

Test Plan for *leftToRight( )*

Test case	Sample data	Expected result	Checked
Three-digit number	123	1 2 3	
Four-digit number			

LABORATORY 17: Core Exercise 2—Overloading

Background

As you begin to create a wider range of programs, you will often find yourself creating functions that perform essentially the same task, but which have different numbers of parameters or different types of parameters. You might, for example, need a function that returns the smaller of two characters (based on their ASCII codes) and another function that returns the smaller of two double-precision values. You could name the first function `minCharacter()` and the second function `minDouble()`, but giving both functions the same name would be more convenient. C++ allows you to assign the same name to several functions—provided the functions differ in the number or type of parameters—a feature called **function overloading**.

The following excerpt from the program in the file *minover.cpp* uses the overloaded function `min()` to determine the smaller of two characters and two double-precision numbers.

```
// Demonstrates function overloading

#include <iostream.h>

// Prototypes for two parameter functions
char min ( char x, char y );          // char parameters
double min ( double x, double y );    // double parameters
...

int main ()
{
    // Call min() with two character arguments.
    cout << endl << min('A','B') << " has the smaller ASCII value"
        << endl;

    // Call min() with two double-precision arguments.
    cout << min(10.5,20.0) << " is the smaller number" << endl;
    ...
}
//-------------------------------------------------------------
char min ( char x, char y )
// Returns the character with the smaller ASCII value.
{
    char result;    // Result returned
    if ( x < y )
        result = x;
    else
        result = y;
    return result;
}
//-------------------------------------------------------------
double min ( double x, double y )
// Returns the smaller of two double-precision values.
```

```
{
    double result;    // Result returned
    if ( x < y )
        result = x;
    else
        result = y;
    return result;
}
...
```

This excerpt produces the output

```
A has the smaller ASCII value
10.5 is the smaller of the two numbers
```

The compiler selects the appropriate `min()` function based on the data type of the arguments in the function call. When the call

```
min('A','B')
```

is executed in `main()`, for instance, the function

```
char min ( char x, char y )
```

is invoked because the call contains arguments of type `char`.

You can also overload functions based on the number of parameters they process. The following excerpt from *minover.cpp* uses the overloaded `min()` function to find the minimum of two or three double-precision values.

```
// Demonstrates function overloading

#include <iostream.h>

// Prototypes for two parameter functions
double min ( double x, double y );              // Double parameters
...
// Prototypes for three parameter functions
double min ( double x, double y, double z );   // Double parameters
...

int main ()
{
    ...
    // Call min() with two double-precision arguments.
    cout << min(10.5,20.0) << " is the smaller number" << endl;

    ...
    // Call min() with three double-precision arguments.
    cout << min(10.5,20.0,5.5) << " is the smallest number" << endl;
    return 0;
}
...

//----------------------------------------------------------------
double min ( double x, double y )
```

```
// Returns the smaller of two double-precision values.
{
    double result;    // Result returned
    if ( x < y )
        result = x;
    else
        result = y;
    return result;
}
...

//----------------------------------------------------------------
double min ( double x, double y, double z )
// Returns the smallest of two double-precision values.
{
    double result;    // Result returned
    if ( x < y )
        if ( x < z )
            result = x;
        else
            result = z;
    else
        if ( y < z )
            result = y;
        else
            result = z;
    return result;
}
```

In this case, the compiler invokes the appropriate `min()` function based on the number of arguments in the function call. For example, the call

```
min(10.5,20.0,5.5)
```

invokes the function

```
double min ( double x, double y, double z )
```

because the call contains three arguments of type `double`.

Warmup Exercise

In this exercise, you overload a `swap()` function so that you can use it to exchange either integers or characters.

void swap (int &x, int &y)
Input/output parameters
x, y: (input) two integers
          (output) the integers exchanged

```
void swap ( char &x, char &y )
```
Input/output parameters
x, y: (input) two characters
        (output) the characters exchanged

Complete the following program by filling in the missing C++ code. A shell for this program is given in the file *swapover.shl*.

```cpp
#include <iostream.h>

void swap ( _____ );   // Two char parameters
void swap ( _____ );   // Two integer parameters

void main ()
{
    char a, b;
    integer c, d;

    cout << endl << "Enter a two letter word: ";
    cin >> a >> b;

    // Exchange two characters.
    swap(a,b);
    cout << a << b << endl;

    cout << "Enter two numbers: ";
    cin >> c >> d;

    // Exchange two integers.
    swap(c,d);
    cout << c << ' ' << d;
    cout << endl;
}

//-----------------------------------------------------------------

void swap (                     )
// Exchanges two characters.
{



}
```

```
//-----------------------------------------------------------

void swap (                          )
// Exchanges two integers.
{



}
```

APPLICATION EXERCISE: Boxed In

In this exercise, you create an overloaded function `displayBox()` that displays a rectangular box. You overload `displayBox()` based on both the type and the number of parameters. The following are the specifications for the `displayBox()` functions.

void displayBox (int length)
Input parameter
`length`: length of the sides of the box
Outputs
Displays the specified box.

void displayBox (int length, char fillChar)
Input parameters
`length`: length of the sides of the box
`fillChar`: character to fill the box with
Outputs
Displays the specified box and fills it with repetitions of `fillChar`.

void displayBox (int width, int height)
Input parameters
`width`: width of the box
`height`: height of the box
Outputs
Displays the specified box.

void displayBox (int width, int height, char fillChar)
Input parameters
`width`: width of the box
`height`: height of the box
`fillChar`: character to fill the box with
Outputs
Displays the specified box and fills it with repetitions of `fillChar`.

Step 1: Create the overloaded function `displayBox()` specified. Form the top and bottom of the box using the character `'-'` and form the sides using `'|'`. The box displayed by the call `displayBox(15,5,'a')` is

```
 ---------------
|aaaaaaaaaaaaa|
|aaaaaaaaaaaaa|
|aaaaaaaaaaaaa|
 ---------------
```

If your system supports an extended character set, feel free to create continuous borders rather than the dashed borders shown above.

Step 2: Add your `displayBox()` functions to the shell program in the file *box.shl*. Save your program in the file *box.cpp*.

Step 3: Complete the following test plan.

Test Plan for *displayBox()*

Test case	Sample data	Expected result	Checked
Length of sides = 5	5	``` ----- | | | | | | ----- ```	
Fill box with '?'	?	``` ----- |???| |???| |???| ----- ```	
Width = 15, height = 4	15 4	``` --------------- | | | | --------------- ```	
Fill box with '$'	$		

Step 4: Execute your program in the file *box.cpp*.

Step 5: Check each case in your *displayBox* test plan and verify the expected result. If you discover mistakes in your program, correct them and execute the test plan again.

LABORATORY 17: Reinforcement Exercise—Applying Recursion

Splitting the Difference, Again

In Laboratory 13, Core Exercise 3, you learned about an efficient search, called a binary search, that locates values in a sorted array. The algorithm proceeds as follows (initially `low=0`, `high=arraySize-1`).

1. *Look for the search value at the middle index position in the array (between low to high).*

2. *If the search value is larger than the value at the middle index position, repeat Step 1 on the upper half (low=middleIndex+1 to high) of the array.*

3. *Else if the search value is smaller than the value at the middle index position, repeat Step 1 on the lower half (low to high=middleIndex-1) of the array.*

4. *Else you must have found the search value.*

The algorithm stops either on Step 4 if you find the search value or on Step 1 if `low` is greater than `high` (you did not find the search value). This algorithm can be implemented as a recursive function.

Step 1: Start with your program *binsrch.cpp* from Laboratory 13. Change the `binarySearch()` to a recursive function. The `low` and `high` variables will no longer be local to the function but will need to be arguments of the recursive function. The `while` loop is replaced with an `if` statement containing recursive calls to `binarySearch()` (repeat Step 1 in the algorithm). Pay close attention to the initial values of `low` and `high` for the first call to your recursive function from `main()` and how the recursive calls end (the base case).

Step 2: Save your program as *rebinary.cpp*.

Step 3: Use your program to complete the following table by filling in the intermediate values of the variables `low`, `middle`, and `high`, as well as the result of the search. If you discover mistakes in your program, correct them and execute the test plan again.

Note that you must either use a debugger to trace through the program, noting changes in the values of variables `low`, `middle`, and `high` as the program executes, or you must add code that outputs the intermediate values of these variables.

Tracing the execution of the *binarySearch()* function

Test case	Search value	Intermediate results			Result returned
Quick search	75	Low Middle High	0 24 49	25 37 49	37
Search goes longer	41	Low Middle High			
Search goes full depth	53	Low Middle High			
Search goes full depth	9	Low Middle High			
Search fails	62	Low Middle High			
Search fails	22	Low Middle High			

LABORATORY 17: Analysis Exercise

Potential Pitfalls of Using Overloading and Recursion

Name _____

Hour/Period/Section _____

Date _____

Part A

The following function prototypes generate a compiler error.

```
int cube ( double x );
double cube ( double x );
```

Briefly explain the source of this error.

Why isn't overloading functions in this way permitted?

Part B

What is wrong with the following flawed recursive factorial() function? Show how you would correct it.

```
long factorial ( int n )
// Flawed recursive factorial function.
{
    long result = 1;
    while ( n != 0 )
        result = n * factorial(n-1);
    return result;
}
```

Advanced Class Concepts

OVERVIEW

In this lab, you extend the object-oriented concepts from Laboratories 14, 15, and 16 by utilizing some advanced features of C++ classes.

In Laboratory 17 you learned about function overloading, the facility to assign the same name to several functions—provided the functions differ in the number or type of parameters. You can also overload member functions in user-defined classes. In Core Exercise 1 you overload the `Calendar outputHTML()` member function to add WWW hyperlinks to individual days in a month.

Overloading in user-defined C++ classes is not limited to member functions. C++ allows you to redefine the meaning of standard operators (arithmetic, relational, input/output, etc.) for user-defined classes. In Core Exercise 2 you overload the equality operator (`==`) to test whether two `Calendar` objects are the same.

A key feature of any object-oriented language is the ability to derive a new class from an existing class through **inheritance.** The derived class inherits the member functions and data members of the existing base class and can also have its own member functions and data members. In Core Exercise 3 you create a new `Ledger` class that is derived from your `Calendar` class.

LABORATORY 18: Cover Sheet

Name _____

Hour/Period/Section _____

Date _____

Place a check mark (✔) in the Assigned column next to the exercises that your instructor has assigned to you. Have this sheet ready when your lab instructor checks your work. If your exercises are being checked outside the laboratory session, attach this sheet to the front of the packet of materials that you submit.

Exercise		Assigned	Completed
Core 1	Member Function Overloading *Daily News (testover.cpp)*		
Core 2	Operator Overloading *Hello Operator (testopov.cpp)*		
Core 3	Inheritance *Deriver's Ed (ledger.cpp)*		
Analysis	Using Overloading and Inheritance		
Total			

LABORATORY 18: Core Exercise 1—Member Function Overloading

APPLICATION EXERCISE: Daily News

In Laboratory 17 you learned about function overloading, the facility to assign the same name to several functions—provided the functions differ in the number or type of parameters. You first saw the concept of function overloading applied to classes in Laboratory 10 when we discussed the apstring find() functions, which can take an argument of type char or an argument of type apstring. You can also overload member functions of user-defined classes in the same way. In fact, you already have done this when you created two constructors for your Calendar class in Laboratory 14.

The following Calendar member function overloads the function name outputHTML. This version differs from the original in that each day in the calendar can be linked to a Web page.

```
void outputHTML ( ofstream &HTMLFile,
                  const apvector<apstring> &link ) const
```

Precondition

None

Postcondition

Outputs an HTML version of a calendar to output stream HTMLFile. The calendar image (if any) is placed to the left of the calendar body. The calendar body includes the following elements: the month name, the year number, a set of labels for the days of the week (S M T W T F S), and the days of the month oriented within a standard weekly grid. Each day is linked to the Web page in the corresponding element in the link apvector (if any).

The links are represented as an apvector of apstring objects called link, where the string in element link[i] contains the link corresponding to day i+1. A set of sample links is shown below.

link[0]	"http://www.cs.iit.edu"	*Link for day 1*
link[1]	""	*Link for day 2*
link[2]	"http://www.earthday.net"	*Link for day 3*

...

Recall from Laboratory 6 that you can use the HTML <a href= > </a> tag to create links to web pages. The following links correspond to elements in the link apvector shown above.

```
<a href=http://www.cs.iit.edu>  1</a>
<a href=http://www.earthday.net>  3</a>
```

Note that your `outputHTML()` function should omit the `<a>` tag (but still output the day number) for any day if the corresponding `link[day-1]` element in the `link apvector` contains the empty string (`""`).

Step 1: Implement the `Calendar` class member function specified. Remember to add the member function prototype and `#include<apvector.h>` to the declaration of the `Calendar` class in the file *calendar.h*.

Step 2: Save your implementation of this function in the file *calendar.cpp*.

Step 3: Complete the following test plan for your overloaded `outputHTML()` function.

Test Plan for *testover.cpp*

Test case	Sample data	Expected result	Checked
January 2001 (one link)	1 2001 january.jpg january.dat		
April 2001 (more than one link)	4 2001 april.jpg april.dat		
October 2002 (no links)	10 2002 october.jpg october.dat		

Step 4: Construct a multifile program using your implementation of the `Calendar` class and the test program in the file *testover.cpp*. Compile, link, and run your multifile program.

Step 5: Check each case in the test plan for *testover.cpp*, and verify the expected result. If you discover mistakes in your implementation, correct them and execute the test plan again.

LABORATORY 18: Core Exercise 2—Operator Overloading

Background

C++ allows you to redefine the meaning of standard operators (arithmetic, relational, input/output, etc.) for user-defined classes. This technique, called **operator overloading,** enables you to redefine and use standard operators with user-defined class objects. In Laboratory 10 you used operators such as =, +, <, and >> that were overloaded for the apstring class. In this exercise you learn the basics of creating your own overloaded operators.

Because its syntax can be somewhat confusing, let's build on some things you already know before addressing operator overloading. In Laboratory 15, Core Exercise 2, you learned how to pass an object to a client function. You can also pass an object to a member function within the same class. The following Point member function determines whether two points are the same—that is, whether they have the same *x* and *y* coordinates.

```
bool Point ::sameAs ( Point rightPt ) const
// Returns true if rightPt has same coordinates as a point.
// Otherwise, returns false.
{
    return ( x == rightPt.x  &&  y == rightPt.y );
}
```

The following code fragment uses this function to compare two points.

```
if ( alpha.sameAs(beta) )
    cout << "Points are the same" << endl;
else
    cout << "Points are different" << endl;
```

When sameAs() is invoked, rightPt receives a copy of beta. The variables in the return statement are then resolved as follows.

```
return ( x == rightPt.x  &&  y == rightPt.y );
```
```
        alpha.x          alpha.y

     rightPt.x (copy of beta.x)      rightPt.y (copy of beta.y)
```

Both alpha and rightPt are Point objects (as is beta, for that matter). The sameAs() function is a member function of the Point class, so it can access any Point object's data members, including alpha's and rightPt's.

You may have noticed that the syntax for comparing two points using sameAs() is somewhat awkward and nondescriptive. You can express equality in a better way:

```
if ( alpha == beta )
    cout << "Points are the same" << endl;
else
    cout << "Points are different" << endl;
```

Fortunately, C++ allows you to create operators that share the symbol(s) of one of its pre-defined operators but that manipulate your objects rather than one of C++'s predefined types—the previously mentioned operator overloading mechanism. The following function, for example, overloads the equality operator (==) to compare two Point objects for equality.

```
bool Point:: operator == ( const Point &rightPt ) const
// Returns true if rightPt has same coordinates as a point.
// Otherwise, returns false.
{
    return ( x == rightPt.x  &&  y == rightPt.y );
}
```

You specify the operator to be overloaded by using the keyword operator followed by the operator symbol—in this case, ==. You also provide a return type—in this case, bool—just as you would for any other function. The compiler automatically uses this version of the == operator whenever it is asked to determine whether two Point objects are equal. Since we don't want our == operator to change the rightPt object, we pass this object using pass-by-const-reference.

Warmup Exercise

The following Point member overloads the assignment operator (=) to allow assignment of one Point object to another.

```
void operator = ( const Point &rightPt )
```
Precondition
None
Postcondition
Assigns (copies) the contents of rightPt to a point.

Complete the following function by filling in the missing C++ code.

```
void Point:: operator = ( const Point &rightPt )
// Assigns (copies) rightPt to a point.
{
    _____;  // Assign rightPt's x coordinate
    _____;  // Assign rightPt's y coordinate
}
```

Complete the following program by filling in the missing C++ code. A shell for this program is given in the file *testptov.shl*.

```
#include <iostream.h>
#include "point.h"
int main()
{
    // Declare a point named point1 and initialize its coordinates to
    // (20,10).
    _____;
```

```
    // Declare a point named point2 using the default constructor.
    _____;

    point1.showDataMembers();
    point2.showDataMembers();

    // Test if the two points are equal.
    if ( _____ )
        cout << "The points have the same coordinates" << endl;
    else
        cout << "The points have different coordinates" << endl;

    // Assign the coordinates of point1 to point2.
    _____;

    // Test if the two points are equal.
    cout << "After assignment -- " << endl;

    point1.showDataMembers();
    point2.showDataMembers();

    if ( _____ )
        cout << "the points have the same coordinates" << endl;
    else
        cout << "the points have different coordinates" << endl;

    return 0;
}
```

Add the overloaded equality operator (==) and assignment operator (=) functions to your *point.cpp* file from Laboratory 14. Remember to update your *point.h* file to include prototypes for each operator. Then construct a multifile program, using your updated implementation of the Point class and your program in the file *testptov.cpp*. Compile, link, and run your multifile program.

APPLICATION EXERCISE: Hello Operator

In this exercise you overload the equality operator (==) for your Calendar class.

```
bool operator == ( const Calendar &rightCalendar ) const
```
Precondition
None
Postcondition
Returns true if a calendar has the same month and year as rightCalendar (the calendar pictures are ignored). Otherwise, returns false.

Step 1: Implement the Calendar overloaded operator specified. Remember to add the overloaded operator prototype to the declaration of the Calendar class in the file *calendar.h*.

Step 2: Save your implementation of this function in the file *calendar.cpp*.

Step 3: Complete the following test plan for your equality operator function.

Test Plan for *testopov.cpp*

Test case	Sample data	Expected result	Checked
Same month, same year	1 2001 1 2001	`calA == calB : 1 (true)` `calB == calA : 1 (true)`	
Different months, same year	1 2001 2 2001	`calA == calB : 0 (false)` `calB == calA : 0 (false)`	
Same month, different years	1 2001 1 2002	`calA == calB : 0 (false)` `calB == calA : 0 (false)`	
Different months, different years	1 2001 2 2002	`calA == calB : 0 (false)` `calB == calA : 0 (false)`	

Step 4: Construct a multifile program using your implementation of the `Calendar` class and the test program in the file *testopov.cpp*. Compile, link, and run your multifile program.

Step 5: Check each case in the test plan for *testopov.cpp*, and verify the expected result. If you discover mistakes in your implementation, correct them and execute the test plan again.

LABORATORY 18: Core Exercise 3—Inheritance

A key feature of any object-oriented language is the ability to derive a new class from an existing class through **inheritance**. The **derived class** inherits the member functions and data members of the existing **base class** and can also have its own member functions and data members. In this exercise you utilize C++'s inheritance mechanism to create derived classes from your `Point` and `Calendar` classes.

Suppose that you want to create a `Pixel` class that you can use to position a pixel on a Web page (similar to your *animate.cpp* program in Laboratory 10). You could create an entirely new class with member functions for constructing and positioning a pixel. An alternative approach is to derive a `Pixel` class from your `Point` class, thereby inheriting the existing `Point` constructor and `set()` member functions (among others) from `Point`. This inheritance relationship is expressed in the following class declaration from the file *pixel.h*.

```
class Pixel : public Point
{
  public:

    Pixel ( int xCoord, int yCoord,              // Constructor
            const apstring &pixGIF );

    void setGIF (const apstring &pixGIF);        // Set pixel's GIF image

    void outputHTML (ofstream &HTMLFile) const;  // Output pixel

  private:

    // Data members
    apstring pixelGIF;
};
```

The `Pixel` class supplies its own constructor and member functions: `setGIF()` and `outputH-TML()`. It also has a private data member `pixelGIF` that specifies the name of the GIF image file to display for a pixel.

The declaration

```
class Pixel : public Point
```

indicates that the `Pixel` class is derived from the `Point` class. The keyword `public` specifies that this is a **public inheritance**—that is, the `Pixel` class inherits the `Point` class's public member functions, but *not* its private data members. For the `Pixel` class, you want the member functions in `Pixel` to be able to refer to the private data members in `Point`, so you must change the data members in the `Point` class declaration from `private` to `protected`, as follows.

```
class Point
{
  public:        // Member functions
    ...
```

```
protected:      // Data members

    int x;      // x coordinate
    int y;      // y coordinate
};
```

In a public inheritance, private `Point` data members can be accessed only by `Point` member functions. However, **protected** `Point` data members can be accessed by the member functions in any class derived from `Point`—in this case, the `Pixel` class.

A `Pixel` object can call any of the `Point` public member functions, as well as any of its own (`Pixel`) member functions. For example, the following code fragment repositions the object `dot` to (200,150) and changes its symbol to `"blackdot.gif"`.

```
Pixel dot(100,100,"reddot.gif");   // Red dot at (100,100) --
                                   // Pixel constructor

dot.setX(200);                     // Reposition to (200,150) --
dot.setY(150);                     // Point member functions

dot.setGIF("blackdot.gif");        // Change the pixel GIF image --
                                   // Pixel member function

dot.outputHTML(HTMLFile);          // Output pixel to a Web page --
                                   // Pixel member function
```

Before you can use the `Pixel` class, `Pixel`'s constructor, `setGIF()`, and `outputHTML()` member functions need to be implemented. The `Pixel` constructor from the file *pixel.cpp*

```
Pixel:: Pixel ( int xCoord, int yCoord,
                const apstring &pixGIF )
// Constructor.
    : Point(xCoord,yCoord),      // Initialize coordinates
      pixelGIF(pixGIF)           // Initialize pixel GIF data member
{}
```

uses member initialization to call the `Point` constructor (which sets the *x* and *y* coordinates) and to initialize the `pixelGIF` data member. The implementation of `outputHTML()`

```
void Pixel:: outputHTML (ofstream &HTMLFile) const
// Outputs pixel to HTML file.
{
    HTMLFile << "<div style=position:absolute;left:" << x
             << ";top:" << y << ">" << endl;
    HTMLFile << "<img src=" << pixelGIF << "></div>" << endl;
}
```

accesses the `Pixel` object's the *x* and *y* coordinates directly—even though these are part of the `Point` class. It can do this because we changed these data members to protected, rather than private.

Warmup Exercise

Complete the `Pixel` member functions `setGIF()` by filling in the missing C++ code. A shell for this function is given in the file *pixel.cpp*.

```
void Pixel:: setGIF ( const apstring &pixGIF )
// Sets the pixel's GIF image to the specified filename.
{


}
```

Complete the following program by filling in the missing C++ code. A shell for this program is given in the file *testpix.shl*.

```
#include <iostream.h>
#include "pixel.h"

int main ()
{
    int x=150, y=150;
    int radius, i;

    // Declare a Pixel named dot whose initial coordinates are at
    // (150,150) and whose image is "blackdot.gif".
    _____;

    cout << "Input radius for a circle (less than 100): ";
    cin >> radius;

    // Output the dot to an HTML file.
    ofstream HTMLFile;
    HTMLFile.open("pixel.html");

    // Output the HTML header.
    HTMLFile << "<html><head><title>Pixel Output</title></head>" << endl;
    HTMLFile << "<body>" << endl;

    for (i=-radius; i<radius; i++)
    {
        _____;             // Change the x coordinate to x+i

        // Bottom half of circle.
        _____;  // Change symbol to blackdot.gif
        dot.setY(y+sqrt(radius*radius-i*i));
        dot.outputHTML(HTMLFile);

        // Top half of circle.
        _____;  // Change symbol to bluedot.gif
        dot.setY(y-sqrt(radius*radius-i*i));
        dot.outputHTML(HTMLFile);
    }
```

```
      HTMLFile << "</body>" << endl;
      HTMLFile << "</html>" << endl;

      HTMLFile.close();

      cout << endl;
      cout << "Point your browser to the file pixel.html" << endl
           << endl;

   return 0;
}
```

Construct a multifile program using *point.h*, *point.cpp*, *pixel.h*, *pixel.cpp*, and *testpix.cpp*. Remember to change the data members in *point.h* from `private` to `protected` and also to add *apstring.cpp* to your multifile program. Compile, link, and run your multifile program.

APPLICATION EXERCISE: Deriver's Ed

A monthly ledger can be used to track daily activities (number of hours worked per day, daily expenses, and the like). The following class declaration from the file *ledger.h* derives a `Ledger` class from your `Calendar` class.

```
class Ledger : public Calendar
{
  public:

     Ledger ( int ledgerMonth, int ledgerYear );    // Constructor
     void setValue ( int day, double amount );       // Set the daily value
     double getValue ( int day );                    // Get daily value
     double sum ();                                   // Monthly sum

  private:

     // Data members
     apvector<double> value;                          // Monthly values
};
```

The `value` array is used to store the daily totals recorded in the ledger. The `setValue()` function is used to change a daily total and the `getValue()` function is used to retrieve a daily total. These `Ledger` class member functions are specified as

Ledger (int ledgerMonth, int ledgerYear)
Precondition
Parameter `ledgerMonth` is in the range 1–12 and parameter `ledgerYear` is in the range 1901–2099.
Postcondition
Constructor. Creates a ledger for the specified month and initializes all daily values to `0`.

```
void setValue ( int day, double amount )
```
Precondition
Parameter day is between 1 and the number of days in the ledger month.
Postcondition
Sets the value for the specified day to amount.

```
double getValue ( int day ) const
```
Precondition
Parameter day is between 1 and the number of days in the ledger month.
Postcondition
Returns the daily value for the specified day.

```
double sum () const
```
Precondition
None
Postcondition
Returns the sum of daily entries for the ledger month.

The following code fragment creates a ledger for April 2001, stores the values 8.5 and 2.5 as the daily values for April 1 and April 15 respectively, outputs the April 2001 calendar (in HTML), and outputs the monthly sum to the HTML file.

```
Ledger sample(4,2001);        // Sample ledger (April 2001)
sample.set(1,8.5);            // Sets the value to 8.5 for April 1
sample.set(15,2.5);           // Sets the value to 2.5 for April 15
sample.outputHTML(outFile);   // Output calendar for April ledger
outFile << sample.sum();      // Output monthly sum for April ledger
```

Step 1: Implement the Ledger class member functions specified. Prototypes for these functions are given in the Ledger class declaration in the file *ledger.h*.

Step 2: Save your implementation of these functions as the file *ledger.cpp*.

Step 3: Complete the following test plan for the `Ledger` class member functions.

Test Plan for *testldgr.cpp*

Test case	Sample data	Expected result	Checked
April 2001 Single daily entry	4 2001 15 6.75	15 : 6.75 HTML April 2001 calendar with monthly sum of 6.75	
January 2002 Multiple entries	1 2002 10 8.50 20 10 1 12.25	1 : 12.25 10 : 8.5 20 : 10 HTML January 2002 calendar with monthly sum of 30.75	

Step 4: Construct a multifile program using *calendar.h*, *calendar.cpp*, *ledger.h*, *ledger.cpp*, and *testldgr.cpp*. Remember to add *apstring.cpp* to your multifile program. Because the `Ledger` member functions do not need to access the `Calendar` data members, you can leave the data members in *calendar.h* as `private`. Compile, link, and run your multifile program.

Step 5: Check each case in the test plan for *testldgr.cpp* and verify the expected result. If you discover mistakes in your program, correct them and execute the test plan again.

LABORATORY 18: Analysis Exercise

Using Overloading and Inheritance

Name

Hour/Period/Section

Date

Part A

Overload another operator for either the `Point` or `Calendar` class. Give a function specification, the overloaded operator implementation, and a sample statement in which your overloaded operator is used.

Part B

Create a new class that inherits from either your `Point` class or your `Calendar` class. Give a class declaration (a *.h* file) and function specifications for your derived class.

APCS Marine Biology
Case Study

 See the "Engaged Learning for Programming in C++" link on **http://www.jbpub.com/cs** for the *APCS Marine Biology Case Study* resource page. The resource page links include the *APCS Marine Biology Case Study*, laboratory exercises, code samples, tutorials, and study questions.